What Your Colleagues Are Saying ...

"The list of generational math books to come along and truly synthesize what we know so far and what we need to know is a very short and exclusive list. Well, you can confidently add *Mathematize It!* to this collection. Written by three of the most respected math educators today, the book zeros in on that often poorly traveled journey between the question and answer in problem solving. *Mathematize It!* will be your go-to resource to install the mathematical play revolution in elementary classes everywhere!"

Sunil Singh
Author of *Pi of Life: The Hidden Happiness of Mathematics*
and *Math Recess: Playful Learning in an Age of Disruption*

"*Mathematize It!* is a must-read for anyone who has struggled to teach word problems and is ready to figure out what *really* works. The authors present a plethora of strategies that help students focus on the *thinking* part of the problem-solving process while gently helping the reader understand that so many of our 'tried-and-true' methods, such as key words, really don't work. They help us realize that the real work of solving word problems is in the sense-making phase—once students have made sense of a problem, calculating the solution is the simpler part of the process."

Kimberly Rimbey
National Board Certified Teacher
Co-Founder & CEO, KP Mathematics

"*Mathematize It!* addresses the complexity of problem solving more completely than any other individual resource. It is easy to say that we must teach students to 'mathematize situations' but this book helps us to actually help students learn to do it. The challenge and reflection pieces at the end of each chapter are a game changer for unveiling teaching opportunities, prompting discussion in your PLC, and moving this from a book on the professional shelf to a powerful tool to impact instruction."

Gina Kilday
Math Interventionist and MTSS Coordinator
Metcalf Elementary School, Exeter, RI
Presidential Award for Excellence in Mathematics and Science Teaching Awardee
Former member of the NCTM Board of Directors

"*Mathematize It!* is a book that should be on the shelf of every classroom teacher and division leader who supports mathematics teaching and leading. This valuable resource helps educators to think about the what, why, and the how to make sense of word problems. It gives a framework and visuals on how to support teachers' understanding around problem types and solving problems and excels in assisting teachers in how to make a commitment to teaching for greater understanding."

Spencer Jamieson
Past President, Virginia Council for Mathematics Supervision (VCMS)
Mathematics Specialist for Virginia Council of Teacher of Mathematics (VCTM)

"This is a game changer... even after 20 years of supporting students and their sensemaking of word problems, I am thrilled to learn even more from this trio of authors. They offer practical suggestions, opportunities for practice, and relevant research in order to increase awareness of best practices surrounding word problems. The only key word in this case is MATHEMATIZE! To have this resource in your hands is to have an invitation to the 'mathematizing sandbox'."

Beth Terry
Mathematics Coach
2004 Presidential Award for Excellence in Mathematics and Science Teaching Awardee
Riffa Views International School, Bahrain

"This dynamic author trio brings years of classroom experiences to one of the central problems of teaching and learning mathematics: making sense of word problems. Focusing on the construct of 'mathematizing'—drawing, constructing, describing, representing, and making sense of situations—this clear and practical guide needs to be required reading and discussion fodder for every elementary teacher of mathematics. It's just that clear, informative, and insightful!"

Steve Leinwand
Principal Researcher
American Institutes for Research, Washington, DC

"As our students begin to mathematize the world around them, it becomes extremely important that we listen to their thinking so that we can continue to move their understanding forward. What makes *Mathematize It!* such a useful tool for teachers is that it thoughtfully unpacks student strategies, which helps inform and guide our next move as a classroom teacher."

Graham Fletcher
Math Specialist
Atlanta, GA

"*Mathematize It!* engages readers deeply in the mathematics content through an easy-to-use visual analogy: playing in a sandbox. The authors have found a way to make problem-solving seem like a fun task—one that is akin to something we've all been doing forever: playing. Their clever and applicable problem-solving model of thinking provides a structure teachers can use to support students in tackling word problems and actually enjoying the process. It's time for you to play in the sandbox and more importantly, *Mathematize It!*"

Hilary Kreisberg
Director, Center for Mathematics Achievement
Lesley University, Cambridge, MA
Author of *Adding Parents to the Equation*

"The authors provide a detailed and practical guide on how to take a word problem, uncover the mathematics embedded in it, carefully consider representations, and use it all to solve the problem. The reader begins to realize that all models are not created equal. The authors' careful attention to the nuances within mathematical relationships illustrates how mathematizing differs from answer getting, yet shows us that ideas like operation sense and computation are related. The authors' plain-language explanations empower us to leverage those relationships in order to help students become better mathematicians."

Paul Gray
Chief Curriculum Officer, Cosenza & Associates, LLC
Past President, Texas Council of Teachers of Mathematics
NCTM Representative for NCSM: Leadership in Mathematics Education

"I can't wait to use *Mathematize It!* in my work with teachers and students! The excellent examples, including actual student work and teacher commentaries, highlight the complexity of the problem situations in a way that is clear and usable for classroom teachers and for those of us who support them. The focus on operation sense, understanding the role that each quantity plays, and connecting representations to problems makes this a must read for anyone helping students become successful problem solvers. I especially appreciate the inclusion of non-whole number examples!"

Julie McNamara
Associate Professor
Author of *Beyond Pizzas & Pies* (with Meghan Shaughnessy) and *Beyond Invert & Multiply*
California State University, East Bay, Hayward, CA

Mathematize It!
The Book at a Glance

Every chapter allows you to play and practice in the **mathematizing sandbox** and do some problem solving yourself!

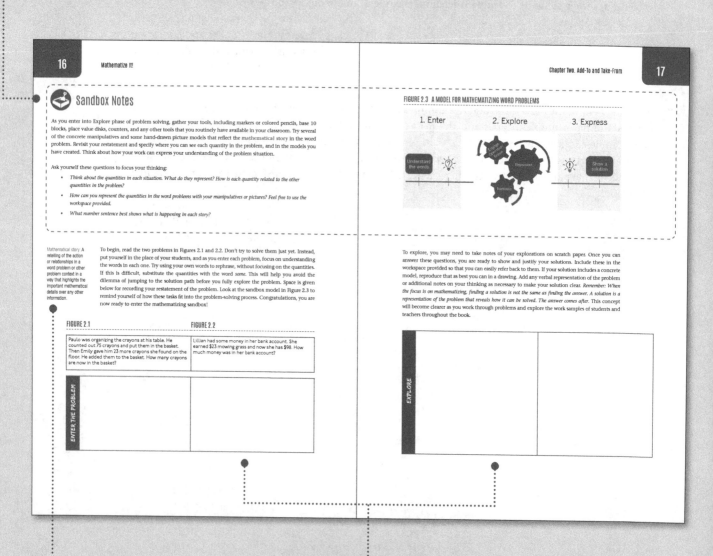

Sandbox Notes

As you enter into Explore phase of problem solving, gather your tools, including markers or colored pencils, base 10 blocks, place value disks, counters, and any other tools that you routinely have available in your classroom. Try several of the concrete manipulatives and some hand-drawn picture models that reflect the mathematical story in the word problem. Revisit your restatement and specify where you can see each quantity in the problem, and in the models you have created. Think about how your work can express your understanding of the problem situation.

Ask yourself these questions to focus your thinking:

- *Think about the quantities in each situation. What do they represent? How is each quantity related to the other quantities in the problem?*

- *How can you represent the quantities in the word problems with your manipulatives or pictures? Feel free to use the workspace provided.*

- *What number sentence best shows what is happening in each story?*

Mathematical story: A retelling of the action or relationships in a word problem or other problem context in a way that highlights the important mathematical details over any other information.

To begin, read the two problems in Figures 2.1 and 2.2. Don't try to solve them just yet. Instead, put yourself in the place of your students, and as you enter each problem, focus on understanding the words in each one. Try using your own words to rephrase, without focusing on the quantities. If this is difficult, substitute the quantities with the word *some*. This will help you avoid the dilemma of jumping to the solution path before you fully explore the problem. Space is given below for recording your restatement of the problem. Look at the sandbox model in Figure 2.3 to remind yourself of how these tasks fit into the problem-solving process. Congratulations, you are now ready to enter the mathematizing sandbox!

FIGURE 2.1

Paulo was organizing the crayons at his table. He counted out 75 crayons and put them in the basket. Then Emily gave him 23 more crayons she found on the floor. He added them to the basket. How many crayons are now in the basket?

FIGURE 2.2

Lillian had some money in her bank account. She earned $23 mowing grass and now she has $98. How much money was in her bank account?

ENTER THE PROBLEM

FIGURE 2.3 A MODEL FOR MATHEMATIZING WORD PROBLEMS

1. Enter
Understand the words

2. Explore
Represent

3. Express
Show a solution

To explore, you may need to take notes of your explorations on scratch paper. Once you can answer these questions, you are ready to show and justify your solutions. Include these in the workspace provided so that you can easily refer back to them. If your solution includes a concrete model, reproduce that as best you can in a drawing. Add any verbal representation of the problem or additional notes on your thinking as necessary to make your solution clear. *Remember: When the focus is on mathematizing, finding a solution is not the same as finding the answer. A solution is a representation of the problem that reveals how it can be solved. The answer comes after.* This concept will become clearer as you work through problems and explore the work samples of students and teachers throughout the book.

EXPLORE

Marginal definitions throughout for easy reference.

Practice the same problem-solving process your students will in these spaces as you **enter** and **explore** the word problem.

Explore how students use various representations to mathematize and describe their problem-solving process

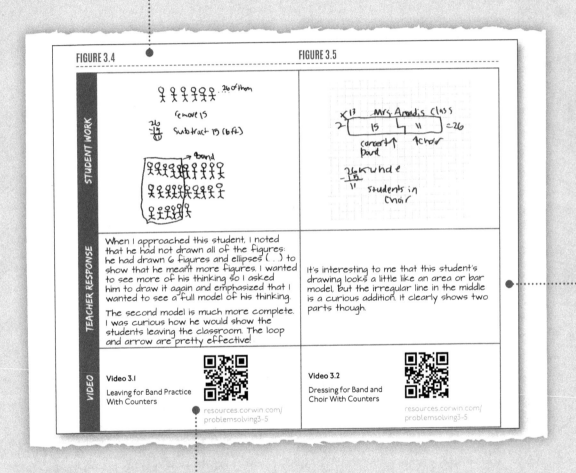

QR codes link to **videos** that actively demonstrate problem-solving thinking with manipulatives and drawings.

Learn from teachers' reflections on student work.

Addition and Subtraction Problem Situations

	Total Unknown	One Part Unknown	Both Parts Unknown
Part-Part-Whole	The 4th grade held a vote to decide where to go for the annual field trip. 32 students voted to go to the ice skating rink. 63 voted to go to the local park. How many students are in the 4th grade? $32 + 63 = x$ $x - 63 = 32$	The 4th grade held a vote to decide where the 95 students in the grade should go for their annual field trip. 32 students voted to go to the ice skating rink. The rest chose the local park. How many voted to go to the park? $32 + x = 95$ $x = 95 - 32$	The 4th grade held a vote to decide where the 95 students in the grade should go for their annual field trip. Some students voted to go to the ice skating rink and others voted to go to the local park. What are some possible combinations of votes? $x + y = 95$ $95 - x = y$

Note: These representations for the problem situations reflect our understanding based on a number of resources. These include the tables in the Common Core State Standards for mathematics (Common Core Standards Initiative, 2010), the problem situations as described in the Cognitively Guided Instruction research (Carpenter, Hiebert, & Moser, 1981), and other tools. See the Appendix and companion website for a more detailed summary of the documents that informed our development of this table.

KEY IDEAS

1. Addition and subtraction problems that reflect action are called Add-To and Take-From problem situations.

2. They follow a common structure in which there is a starting value (the beginning of the story), a change, and a result (the end of the story). Any one of the three parts of the problem may be the missing value.

3. The variations of Add-To and Take-From have a developmental sequence for proficiency in the Common Core State Standards learning progressions (McCallum et al., n.d.). Result Unknown problems are the most accessible, followed by Change Unknown. The Start Unknown variation is typically the most challenging for students.

4. Students should have experience with all problem situations at all grades, using the complexity of numbers determined by state standards for each grade.

5. An action problem situation can and should be retold in the student's own words. This "story" simplifies the details of the problem and focuses on the action.

6. When focusing on the meaning of word problems, students should focus on creating concrete or visual (often pictorial), verbal, and symbolic representations that closely match the action (or story) in the problem situation.

7. Students' understanding is also displayed through verbal and symbolic representations. To gauge, clarify, and extend student thinking, ask students to share the story in written or spoken form. Ask questions such as the following:

   - Tell me the story in your own words.

   - Try telling me the story without using any numbers.

   - Show me how you're representing the quantities in this situation with your manipulatives or pictures.

   - Is there action happening in this story? Where?

   - What number sentence best shows what is happening in this story?

8. When students are experiencing challenges, try one of these strategies:

   - Identify and pair up students who could assist each other or who have different approaches.

   - Ask students to justify their thinking, both when their approaches are correct as well as when they are incorrect.

Try It Out! to implement, practice, and
review the key ideas of the chapter.
Practice with a partner or group!

TRY IT OUT!

IDENTIFY THE PROBLEM SITUATION

Classify each of the following problems as an Add-To or Take-From situation. Which term is missing in each problem?

1. 20,136 fans arrived before the opening kickoff. Because of a traffic jam outside the stadium, another 5,433 arrived during the first half of the game. How many fans were in attendance at halftime? (You can assume that no one left the stadium.)

2. The farmer had 793 bales of hay stored for the winter. In December, the animals consumed 184 bales of hay. How many bales of hay remained for the rest of the winter?

3. The bakery earned $158.50 selling blueberry muffins. Their profit was $124.75 after they repaid the cost of the ingredients. How much did the ingredients cost?

4. Paulette was filling her car at the gas station. Before she filled the tank, the gas gauge read $\frac{3}{8}$ of a tank. After she filled the tank, the gauge read $\frac{7}{8}$ of a tank. How much gas did Paulette add to the gas tank?

WRITE THE PROBLEM

Write an Add-To or Take-From word problem represented by each of the following equations:

1. $2.5 + \alpha = 3.1$

2. $\alpha + 0.35 = 3.05$

3. $5\frac{8}{12} + \frac{11}{12} = \alpha$

4. $7\frac{5}{12} - \alpha = 4\frac{11}{12}$

Reflect sections give you an opportunity to bring some of your knowledge and resources to implementation. Share your answers with a partner or group.

REFLECT

1. We are using the "story" analogy to help students understand the elements of a word problem. What other tools for teaching stories do you have in your English/Language Arts curriculum that you can use to support this thinking?

2. Most teachers find that the Start Unknown situation is the most challenging. What are some other strategies you can use to help students become familiar with that structure?

3. Look at the word problems in the textbook you currently use and identify 8–10 Add-To and Take-From problems. Sort them based on which term is missing: start, change, or result. Rewrite the problems to move the missing term. For example, Result Unknown problems could be rewritten as Start Unknown or Change Unknown problems.

.... Opportunities to stop and think about and
create new problems within each problem type.

FIGURE 4.6 ADDITIVE COMPARISON SITUATIONS

CONTEXT	LESSER QUANTITY	DIFFERENCE	GREATER QUANTITY
Weight of pets	17 pounds	5 pounds	x
Baking temperature	325° F	x	350° F
Snowfall	x	3.1 inches	12.6 inches
Money saved			
Pounds of recycling collected			
Length of inchworm			

Mathematize It!
Grades 3-5

Mathematize It!

Going Beyond Key Words to Make Sense of Word Problems

Grades 3-5

Sara Delano Moore

Kimberly Morrow-Leong

Linda M. Gojak

CORWIN Mathematics

For information:

Corwin
A SAGE Company
2455 Teller Road
Thousand Oaks, California 91320
(800) 233-9936
www.corwin.com

SAGE Publications Ltd.
1 Oliver's Yard
55 City Road
London, EC1Y 1SP
United Kingdom

SAGE Publications India Pvt. Ltd.
B 1/I 1 Mohan Cooperative
    Industrial Area
Mathura Road, New Delhi 110 044
India

SAGE Publications Asia-Pacific Pte. Ltd.
18 Cross Street #10–10/11/12
China Square Central
Singapore 048423

Executive Editor, Mathematics: Erin Null
Developmental Editor: Paula Stacey
*Associate Content
  Development Editor:* Jessica Vidal
Production Editor: Tori Mirsadjadi
Copy Editor: Amy Marks
Typesetter: Integra
Proofreader: Susan Schon
Indexer: Maria Sosnowski
Cover and Interior Designer: Scott Van Atta
Marketing Manager: Margaret O'Connor

Library of Congress Cataloging-in-Publication Data

Names: Moore, Sara Delano, 1966- author. | Morrow-Leong, Kimberly, author. | Gojak, Linda, author.

Title: Mathematize it!: going beyond key words to make sense of word problems, grades 3–5 / Sara Delano Moore, Kimberly Morrow-Leong, and Linda M. Gojak.

Description: Thousand Oaks, California : Corwin, a Sage Company, [2020] | Includes bibliographical references and index.

Identifiers: LCCN 2019014842 | ISBN 9781506395272 (pbk.: alk. paper)

Subjects: LCSH: Word problems (Mathematics) | Mathematics–Study and teaching (Elementary)

Classification: LCC QA63 .M6475 2020 | DDC 372.7/049–dc23 LC record available at https://lccn.loc.gov/2019014842

19 20 21 22 23 10 9 8 7 6 5 4 3 2 1

Contents

Visit the companion website at
http://resources.corwin.com/problemsolving3-5
for online content.

List of Videos

Note From the Publisher: The authors have provided video and web content throughout the book that is available to you through QR (quick response) codes. To read a QR code, you must have a smartphone or tablet with a camera. We recommend that you download a QR code reader app that is made specifically for your phone or tablet brand.

Videos may also be accessed at **http://resources.corwin.com/problemsolving3-5**

Preface

The three of us (Sara, Kim, and Linda) spend a lot of time with teachers, talking about how students are successful and what challenges they face. Over and over, we hear that students struggle with problem solving, especially with word problems. We see challenge expressed on teacher comments on Twitter, on Facebook, on community sites like MyNCTM, in conference sessions, even in the news. We hear this frustration from parents, from principals, and from math coaches across the country and internationally. We've written this book for classroom teachers and coaches who want to help their students have a more successful and meaningful approach to problem solving. If the approaches you have tried, such as using key words, or even using reading strategies to help students comprehend the problem, have only yielded spotty or unsatisfying results, this book is for you. If your students compute naked numbers efficiently, but when faced with a word problem they seem to pull numbers at random from problems and end up successfully calculating the wrong equations, this book is for you. If your students have ever looked at an equation and wondered how it fits the problem, this book is for you. We've written this book for all of the teachers whose students look at a word problem and say, "I just don't get what they want me to do!"

How This Book Can Help You

Would you be surprised to know that every addition word problem you can think of can be classified into one of four categories? It's true! The same is true for every subtraction problem. Multiplication and division are a bit more complicated, but not as much as you might think. The hard part about a word problem isn't in using the operations (+ − × ÷) to compute an answer but, rather, it's in figuring out which operation to use in a problem and why. Once you understand the four kinds of addition problem types and can recognize them in a problem's story, the puzzle pieces can start to come together. We don't mean to oversimplify the learning that needs to take place, because it isn't simple, but we want you to know that there is something you can do to help students learn to tackle word problems productively. More important, we want students to tackle real problems that interest them and learn more mathematics as they do so.

> *Solving problems is not only a goal of learning mathematics but also a major means of doing so. Students should have frequent opportunities to formulate, grapple with and solve complex problems that require a significant amount of effort and should then be encouraged to reflect on their thinking.*

> —*Principles and Standards for School Mathematics*
> (National Council of Teachers of Mathematics, 2000, p. 52)

There is no magic elixir to solve the problem of word problems. This book shares our approach, which focuses on helping children mine the problem to uncover the underlying mathematics. Much needs to happen between the reading comprehension and computation stages of the problem-solving process. Yes, students need support to read and comprehend the words and language of the problem. Yes, they need to know how to compute the answer. But there is a whole middle ground of exploration and understanding that students often rush through, where they could instead turn what they read into a solvable mathematical story and apply their operation sense to solve the puzzle. This is where we so often see a gap. We've written this book to fill that gap. We want students to see their world mathematically and know that mathematics can help them solve real problems. This is bigger (and more important) than passing a test.

To that end, this book is about problem solving. It's about deciphering the kinds of word problems you see in normal, everyday lessons in classrooms like yours. It's about the kinds of problems that are placed at the end of the lessons in your textbooks, the ones that your kids skip because they don't know what to do. It's about word problems. Story problems. Make-sense-of the-math, practice-a-skill problems. Sometimes these problems can seem artificial or contrived, but their straightforward simplicity is also a strength because they target the mathematical thinking we want students to develop. Wrestling productively with word problems can lay a foundation for the more complex and open-ended problems students will also encounter. These problems also have the potential to *do* and *be* more in their own right.

> *Solutions to these (routine word) problems, particularly the solutions of younger children, do in fact involve real problem-solving behavior. ... Word problems can provide insights into the development of more complex problem-solving abilities.* (Carpenter, 1985, p. 17)

How to Use This Book

As a reader, you'll get the most out of this book if you dig in and do the mathematics along the way. We've given you space to restate problems and draw pictures of your thinking with a focus on the mathematics. You'll also find a collection of manipulatives helpful as you work through the book. Gather some counters, some base 10 blocks, and a fraction tool or two to use as aids while you solve problems. Think about how your students can use them too. Pictures and manipulatives can hold an idea in place right in front of you so that you can think about it more deeply. With manipulatives, you can do even more. You can make a change more quickly and easily: Manipulatives allow students to act out what happens in a problem, and to use attributes like color and size to highlight features of a problem. As you'll see, the best tool for the job depends on the problem. There will be plenty of examples for you to explore.

There are places in the book where we've suggested you stop and talk with your colleagues. If you're reading the book as part of a professional learning community, plan your discussions around these stopping points. You'll find that there are plenty of opportunities for conversations about student thinking and the operations. But you're never truly reading alone! Throughout each chapter you'll find work samples inspired by student work. Several times in each chapter you'll also find teacher commentary on the work samples. These comments are honest. Sometimes the teachers are bewildered, and sometimes the teachers are excited by what they see. Let these teacher voices be your companions as you tackle the new ideas. Use the teacher comments and the thinking breaks as reminders to take a pause and extend your own ideas a little further. The end of each chapter also has exercises and reflection questions that will help you and your colleagues connect what you've learned to your own classrooms.

After each chapter we also suggest that you look at the problems in your textbook and categorize them—not just for practice recognizing the structures you'll soon learn about, but also to evaluate how much exposure your students are getting to the full range of problem types. If you discover that your textbook does not present enough variety, this book will give you the tools needed to make adjustments.

We recognize that many of the problems shared in this book will be unfamiliar contexts for your students. If you find yourself thinking that your students will not understand a problem context, we invite you to change the problem! Make sense of the problem situation yourself so that you know what mathematical features are important and then change the details. Even better, invite your students to craft and pose their own meaningful word problems to solve. With your new understanding of the problem situations, you will have all the tools you need to guide your students.

We have to be honest. The ideas in this book may challenge your current understandings of some mathematical ideas. At times, we will ask you to look at something you have been doing since you were eight years old and revisit it with new eyes. This may cause some disequilibrium, and it may be uncomfortable at first. It's as if we are asking you to walk but by switching the foot you lead with. (Try it! It's not easy!) When the familiar becomes unfamiliar, we encourage you to take a deep breath, trust us, and lead with the other foot. We'll get you there. Here's to lifelong learning!

Acknowledgments

You can't write a book like this in a vacuum. We have met and worked with countless educators over the years and have discussed the ideas in this book with them. You know who you are and we hope you hear your voice in these pages. Thank you for your contribution to these thoughts and ideas. We credit you and appreciate you deeply.

We would also like to thank Erin Null, who started with one vision of this book, received a draft of another interpretation, and worked with us to land on the third—and we think best—vision. Your patience, support, and diligence pushed us continually forward. We also extend a profound debt of gratitude to Paula Stacey, who asked us the questions we needed to answer in a way that made the manuscript better. Thank you also to Kimberly Rimbey, Julie McNamara, and Jeff Shih, whose thoughtful comments challenged us to know better and do better. We are indebted to you for your positive feedback, but even more so for your constructive criticism. Any flaws that remain are ours alone.

Thanks to Kim and Linda for coming on this journey with me. I appreciate your knowledge, your experience, your care, and your friendship. Thanks to Margie Mason, who first brought me into the world of mathematics education, and to all my friends and colleagues in this community, including those at ETA hand2mind and ORIGO Education, who have encouraged and supported me along the way. Thank you to the teachers who came before me, particularly my mother and grandmother, for showing me that learning is important and good teaching is invaluable. And thanks to Bill, for loving and supporting me always.

—Sara

I would first like to thank Linda and Sara for trusting me enough to invite me to join this project. I appreciate your confidence, but more than anything, I appreciate your friendship. I also want to thank Dr. Megan Murray of the University of Hull, who introduced me to the idea that addition and subtraction problems weren't all the same. To the staff of GBW, Julie, Pat, and Michelle and her friend the second-grade teacher: Thank you for sharing your time and brilliant students who have helped us collect and interpret their thinking from many different angles. Finally, thank you to my husband, Greg, who watched me take the big leap of writing a book and never questioned my sanity.

—Kim

Writing a book is always a challenge! While it seems that writing on a topic you feel passionate about should be easier, it is actually a bigger challenge because you want to get it right. I thank Kim and Sara for their vision and our many long conversations. I learned so much from both of you. I want to thank the elementary teachers and coaches with whom I work who challenge my thinking and force me to make ideas clearer. I thank my colleagues Ruth Harbin Miles, Annemarie Newhouse, and Jerry Moreno, whose friendship I value and who make this career a joy.

—Linda

Publisher's Acknowledgments

Corwin gratefully acknowledges the contributions of the following reviewers:

Kevin Dykema
Middle School Math Teacher
Mattawan Middle School
Mattawan, MI

Julie McNamara
Assistant Professor of Mathematics Education
California State University, East Bay
Hayward, CA

Kimberly Rimbey
Executive Director of Curriculum, Instruction, and Assessment
Buckeye Elementary School District
Buckeye, AZ

About the Authors

Sara Delano Moore currently serves as director of professional learning at ORIGO Education. A fourth-generation educator, Sara's work emphasizes the power of deep understanding and multiple representations for learning mathematics. Her interests include building conceptual understanding to support procedural fluency and applications, incorporating engaging and high-quality literature into mathematics and science instruction, and connecting mathematics with engineering design in meaningful ways. Prior to joining ORIGO Education, Sara served as a classroom teacher of mathematics and science in the elementary and middle grades, a mathematics teacher educator at the University of Kentucky, director of the Kentucky Center for Middle School Academic Achievement, and director of mathematics and science at ETA hand2mind. She has authored numerous articles in professional journals and is a contributing author to *Visible Learning for Mathematics*. She has also coauthored the grades 3–5 and grades 6–8 volumes of the *Teaching Mathematics in the Visible Learning Classroom* series for Corwin Mathematics. Sara earned her BA in natural sciences from The Johns Hopkins University, her MSt in general linguistics and comparative philology from the University of Oxford, and her PhD in educational psychology from the University of Virginia. She lives in Kent, Ohio.

Kimberly Morrow-Leong is an adjunct instructor at George Mason University in Fairfax, Virginia, a part-time researcher at American Institutes for Research, and a consultant for Math Solutions. She is a former grade 5–9 classroom teacher, K–8 mathematics coach, and coordinator of elementary professional development for the National Council of Teachers of Mathematics (NCTM). She recently completed an elected term as vice president and 2018 program chair for NCSM, Leadership in Mathematics Education. She holds a BA in French language and a masters in linguistics (TESOL). She also holds an MEd and PhD in mathematics education leadership from George Mason University. Kim is the 2009 recipient of the Presidential Award for Excellence in Mathematics and Science Teaching (PAEMST) from Virginia. She is happiest when working with teachers and students, putting pencils down and getting messy with manipulatives!

Linda M. Gojak worked as an elementary mathematics specialist and classroom teacher for 28 years. She directed the Center for Mathematics and Science Education, Teaching, and Technology at John Carroll University for 16 years, providing support for districts and more than 10,000 teachers. Linda continues to work with K–8 mathematics teachers and coaches nationally and internationally. She is a recipient of the PAEMST from Ohio. She served as the president of NCTM, NCSM, and the Ohio Council of Teachers of Mathematics. Linda is the coauthor of three other books for Corwin Mathematics—*The Common Core Math Companion, K–2, The Common Core Math Companion, 6–8*, and *Visible Learning for Mathematics, Grades K–12*. Linda also wrote *Path to Problem Solving for Grades 3–6* (ETA Hand to Mind, 2008) and *What's Your Math Problem?* (Teacher Created Materials, 2011).

CHAPTER ONE

Introduction
Why You Need to Teach Students to Mathematize

Imagine you are a new teacher. You are teaching fifth grade at a new school and are eager to get to know your students—their interests, skills, and how prepared they are to meet the challenges of fifth grade. You have just emerged from your teacher education program knowing various approaches you have seen modeled in classrooms and described in the literature, some of which you have tried with varying degrees of success. You aren't sure what approaches you want to use but are excited about challenging your students, introducing the rigor you have read so much about. But first, you need to know what your students can and can't do.

You decide to start with a couple of word problems, ones that involve relatively simple mathematical operations:

> Mrs. King has 25 books to give to 8 students for summer reading after grade 4. If each student gets the same number of books, how many will she have left?

> Richard measured and packed enough flour to make brownies and a cake during the week at a cabin. He is baking the brownies first and the cake later. He has 5 cups of flour. The brownie recipe calls for $1\frac{1}{2}$ cups of flour, and whatever is left he will use for the cake. How much flour is left to use for the cake recipe?

You circulate around the room, noting who draws pictures, who writes equations, and who uses the manipulatives you have put at the center of the table groups. While some students take their time, quite a few move quickly. Their hands go up eagerly, indicating they have solved the problems. As you check their work, one by one, you notice most of them got the first problem wrong, writing the equation $25 - 8 = 17$. Some even include a sentence saying, "Mrs. King will have 17 books left." Only one student in this group draws a picture. It looks like this:

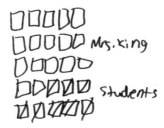

Even though the second problem demands an understanding of fractions, a potentially complicating feature, most of these same students solve the second problem correctly. They write the equation $5-1\frac{1}{2}$ and are generally able to find the correct solution of $3\frac{1}{2}$ cups of flour left for the cake. You notice a few students use the fraction tiles available at tables to help them solve this problem. A number of students draw pictures for this problem. They often look something like this:

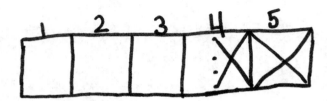

To learn more about how your students went wrong with the first problem, you call them to your desk one by one and ask about their thinking. A pattern emerges quickly. All of the students you talk to zeroed in on two key elements of the problem: (1) the total quantity of books the teacher started with and (2) how many were left. One student tells you, *"Left* always means to subtract. I learned that a long time ago." Clearly, she wasn't the only student who read the word *left* and assumed she had to subtract. This assumption, which led students astray in problem 1, luckily worked for these students in problem 2, where simple subtraction yielded a correct answer.

Problem-Solving Strategies Gone Wrong

In our work with teachers, we often see students being taught a list of "key words" that are linked to specific operations. Students are told, "Find the key word and you will know whether to add, subtract, multiply, or divide." Charts of key words often hang on classroom walls. Key words are a strategy that works often enough that teachers continue to rely on them. As we saw in the book-distribution problem, however, not only are key words not enough to solve a problem, but they also can easily lead students to an incorrect operation or to a single operation when multiple operations need to come into play. As the book problem reveals, different operations could successfully be called upon, depending on how the student approaches the problem—using division or even addition to distribute the books evenly, then determining how many remain. Subtraction could even be used, but it would not be the simple one-step subtraction operation we saw in the student's drawing, the one another student associated with the key word *left.*

Let's return to your imaginary classroom. Having seen firsthand the limitations of key words—a strategy you had considered using—where to begin? What approach to use? A new colleague has a suggestion. She agrees that relying on only key words can be too limiting. Instead, she is an enthusiastic proponent of a procedure called CUBES, which stands for teaching students these steps:

Circle the numbers

Underline important information

Box the question

Eliminate unnecessary information

Solve and check

She tells you that whenever she introduces a new kind of word problem, she walks students through the CUBES protocol using a "think-aloud," sharing how she is using the process to take apart the problem to find what to focus on. That evening, as you settle down to plan, you decide to walk through some problems like the book-distribution problem using CUBES. Circling the numbers is easy enough. You circle 25 (students), 8 (books), wondering briefly what students might do with the 4. Perhaps you will leave it out.

Then you tackle "important information." What is important here in this problem? Maybe the verb, that the teacher is *giving* students books. Certainly, it's important that all students get the same number of books. You box the question, but unfortunately the question contains that problematic word, *left*.

If you think this procedure has promise as a way to guide students through an initial reading of the problem, but leaves out how to help students develop a genuine understanding of the problem, you would be correct.

What is missing from procedural strategies such as CUBES and strategies such as key words, is—in a word—*mathematics* and the understanding of where it lives within the situation the problem is presenting. Rather than helping students learn and practice quick ways to enter a problem, we need to focus our instruction on helping them develop a deep understanding of the mathematical principles behind the operations and how they are expressed in the problem. They need to learn to *mathematize*.

What Is Mathematizing? Why Is It Important?

Mathematizing is the uniquely human process of constructing meaning in mathematics (from Freudenthal, as cited in Fosnot & Dolk, 2001). Meaning is constructed and expressed by a process of noticing, exploring, explaining, modeling, and convincing others of a mathematical argument. When we teach students to mathematize, we are essentially teaching them to take their initial focus off specific numbers and computations and put their focus squarely on the actions and relationships expressed in the problem, what we will refer to throughout this book as the **problem situation**. At the same time, we are helping students see how these various actions and relationships can be expressed and the different operations that can be used to express them. If students understand, for example, that equal-groups division problems, as in the book-distribution problem, involve fair sharing and that one way sharing can be expressed is by dividing, then they can learn where and how to apply the numbers in the problem, in order to develop an appropriate equation. If we look at problems this way, then finding a **solution** involves connecting the problem's context to its general kind of problem situation and to the operations that go with it. The rest is computation.

Making accurate and meaningful connections between different problem situations and the operations that can fully express them requires **operation sense**. Students with a strong operation sense

- Understand and use a wide variety of models of operations beyond the basic and

Mathematizing: The uniquely human act of modeling reality with the use of mathematical tools and representations.

Problem situation: The underlying mathematical action or relationship found in a variety of contexts. Often called "problem type" for short.

Solution: A description of the underlying problem situation along with an approach (or approaches) to finding an answer to the question.

Operation sense: Knowing and applying the full range of work for mathematical operations (for example, addition, subtraction, multiplication, and division).

Intuitive model of an operation: An intuitive model is "primitive," meaning that it is the earliest and strongest interpretation of what an operation, such as multiplication, can do. An intuitive model may not include all the ways that an operation can be used mathematically.

intuitive models of operations (Fischbein, Deri, Nello, & Marino, 1985)

- Use appropriate representations of actions or relationships strategically

- Apply their understanding of operations to any quantity, regardless of the class of number

- Can mathematize a situation, translating a contextual understanding into a variety of other mathematical representations

FOCUSING ON OPERATION SENSE

Many of us may assume that we have a strong operation sense. After all, the four operations are the backbone of the mathematics we were taught from day one in elementary school. We know how to add, subtract, multiply, and divide, don't we? Of course we do. But a closer look at current standards reveals nuances and relationships within these operations that many of us may not be aware of, may not fully understand, or may have internalized so well that we don't recognize we are applying an understanding of them every day when we ourselves mathematize problems both in real life and in the context of solving word problems. For example, current standards ask that students develop conceptual understanding and build procedural fluency in four kinds of addition/subtraction problems, including Add-To, Take-From, Compare, and what some call Put Together/Take Apart (we will refer to this category throughout the book as Part-Part-Whole). Multiplication and division have their own unique set of problem types as well. On the surface, the differences between such categories may not seem critical. But we argue that they are. Only by exploring these differences and the relationships they represent can students develop the solid operation sense that will allow them to understand and mathematize word problems and any other problems they are solving, whatever their grade level or the complexity of the problem. It does not mean that students should simply memorize the problem types. Instead they should have experience exploring all of the different problem types through word problems and other situations. Operation sense is not simply a means to an end. It has value in helping students naturally come to see the world through a mathematical lens.

USING MATHEMATICAL REPRESENTATIONS

Problem context: The specific setting for a word problem.

Mathematical representation: A depiction of a mathematical situation using one or more of these modes or tools: concrete objects, pictures, mathematical symbols, context, or language.

What would such instruction—instruction aimed at developing operation sense and learning how to mathematize word problems—look like? It would have a number of features. First it would require that we give students time to focus and explore by doing fewer problems, making the ones they do count. Next, it would facilitate students becoming familiar with various ways to represent actions and relationships presented in a problem context. We tend to think of solving word problems as beginning with words and moving toward number sentences and equations in a neat linear progression. But as most of us know, this isn't how problem solving works. It is an iterative and circular process, where students might try out different representations, including going back and rewording the problem, a process we call telling "the story" of the problem. The model that we offer in this book is based on this kind of active and expanded exploration using a full range of mathematical representations. Scholars who study mathematical modeling and problem solving identify five modes of representation: verbal, contextual, concrete, pictorial, and symbolic representations (Lesh, Post, & Behr, 1987).

VERBAL A problem may start with any mode of representation, but a word problem is first presented verbally, typically in written form. After that, verbal representations can serve many uses as students work to understand the actions and relationships in the problem situation. Some examples are restating the problem; thinking aloud; describing the math operations in words rather than symbols; and augmenting and explaining visual and physical representations including graphs, drawings, base 10 blocks, fraction bars, or other concrete items.

CONTEXTUAL The contextual representation is simply the real-life situation that the problem describes. Prepackaged word problems are based on real life, as is the earlier book-distribution problem, but alone they are not contextual. Asking students to create their own word problems based on real-life contexts will bring more meaning to the process and will reflect the purposes of mathematics in real life, such as when scientists, business analysts, and meteorologists mathematize contextual information in order to make predictions that benefit us all. This is a process called **mathematical modeling**, which Garfunkel and Montgomery (2019) define as the use of "mathematics to represent, analyze, make predictions or otherwise provide insight into real-world phenomena."

Mathematical modeling: A process that uses mathematics to represent, analyze, make predictions or otherwise provide insight into real-world phenomena.

CONCRETE Using physical representations such as blocks, concrete objects, and real-world items (for example, money, measuring tools, or items to be measured such as beans, sand, or water), or acting out the problem in various ways, is called **modeling**. Such models often offer the closest and truest representation of the actions and relationships in a problem situation.

Modeling: Creating a physical representation of a problem situation.

PICTORIAL Pictures and diagrams can illustrate and clarify the details of the actions and relationships in ways that words and even physical representations cannot. Using dots and sticks, bar models, arrows to show action, number lines, boxes to show regrouping, and various graphic organizers helps students see and conceptualize the nature of the actions and relationships.

SYMBOLIC Symbols can be operation signs ($+$, $-$, $\times$, $\div$), relational signs ($=$, $<$, $>$), variables (typically expressed as x, y, a, b, etc.), or a wide variety of symbols used in later mathematics (k, ∞, ϕ, π, etc.). Even though numerals are familiar, they are also symbols representing values (2, 0.9, $\frac{1}{2}$, $1,000$).

There are two things to know about representations that may be surprising. First, mathematics can be shared *only* through representations. As a matter of fact, it is impossible to share a mathematical idea with someone else without sharing it through a representation! If you write an equation, you have produced a *symbolic* representation. If you describe the idea, you have shared a *verbal* representation. Representations are not solely the manipulatives, pictures, and drawings of a mathematical idea: They are any mode that communicates a mathematical idea between people.

Second, the strength and value of learning to manipulate representations to explore and solve problems is rooted in their relationship to one another. In other words, the more students can learn to move deftly from one representation to another, translating and/or combining them to fully illustrate their understanding of a problem, the deeper will be their understanding of the operations. Figure 1.1 reveals this interdependence. The five modes of representation are all equally important and deeply interconnected, and they work synergistically. In the chapters that follow, you will see how bringing multiple and synergistic representations to the task of problem solving deepens understanding.

FIGURE 1.1 FIVE REPRESENTATIONS: A TRANSLATION MODEL

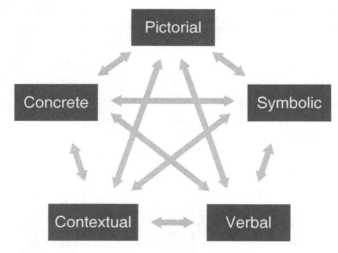

Source: Adapted from Lesh, Post, and Behr (1987).

Teaching Students to Mathematize

As we discussed earlier, learning to mathematize word problems to arrive at solutions requires time devoted to exploration of different representations with a focus on developing and drawing on a deep understanding of the operations. We recognize that this isn't always easy to achieve in a busy classroom, hence, the appeal of the strategies mentioned at the beginning of the chapter. But what we know from our work with teachers and our review of the research is that, although there are no shortcuts, structuring exploration to focus on actions and relationships is both essential and possible. Doing so requires three things:

1. Teachers draw on their own deep understanding of the operations and their relationship to different word problem situations to plan instruction.

2. Teachers use a model of problem solving that allows for deep exploration.

3. Teachers use a variety of word problems throughout their units and lessons, to introduce a topic and to give examples during instruction, not just as the "challenge" students complete at the end of the chapter.

In this book we address all three.

BUILDING YOUR UNDERSTANDING OF THE OPERATIONS AND RELATED PROBLEM SITUATIONS

The chapters that follow explore the different operations and the various kinds of word problems—or problem situations—that arise within each. To be sure that all of the problems and situational contexts your students encounter are addressed, we drew on a number of sources, including the Common Core State Standards for Mathematics (National Governors Association Center for Best Practices and Council of Chief State School Officers, 2010), the work done by the Cognitively Guided Instruction projects (Carpenter, Fennema, & Franke, 1996), earlier research, and our own work with teachers to create tables, one for addition and subtraction situations (Figure 1.2) and another for multiplication and division situations (Figure 1.3). Our versions of the problem situation tables represent the language we have found to resonate the most with teachers and students as they make sense of the various problem types, while still accommodating the most comprehensive list of categories. These tables also appear in the Appendix at the end of the book.

NOTES

_____

_____

_____

_____

_____

_____

_____

_____

_____

_____

_____

_____

_____

FIGURE 1.2 ADDITION AND SUBTRACTION PROBLEM SITUATIONS

ACTIVE SITUATIONS

	Result Unknown	Change Addend Unknown	Start Addend Unknown	
Add-To	Paulo counted out 75 crayons and put them in the basket. Then he found 23 more crayons under the table. He added them to the basket. How many crayons are now in the basket? $75 + 23 = x$ $23 = x - 73$	Paulo counted out 75 crayons and put them in the basket. Then he found some more crayons under the table. He added them to the basket and now there are 98 crayons in the basket. How many crayons were under the table? $75 + x = 98$ $75 = 98 - x$	Paulo was organizing the crayons at his table. He found 23 crayons under the table and added them to the basket. When he counted, there are now 98 crayons in the basket. How many crayons were in the basket before Paulo looked under the table for crayons? $x + 23 = 98$ $98 - 23 = x$	
Take-From	There are 26 students in Mrs. Amadi's class. 15 left to get ready to play in the band at the assembly. How many students are not in the band? $26 - 15 = x$ $15 + x = 26$	There are 26 students in Mrs. Amadi's class. After the band students left the class for the assembly, there were 11 students still in the classroom. How many students are in the band? $26 - x = 11$ $x + 11 = 26$	15 band students left Mrs. Amadi's class to get ready to play in the assembly. There were 11 students left in the classroom. How many students are in Mrs. Amadi's class? $x - 15 = 11$ $15 + 11 = x$	

RELATIONSHIP (NON-ACTIVE) SITUATIONS

	Total Unknown	One Part Unknown		Both Parts Unknown
Part-Part-Whole	The 4th grade held a vote to decide where to go for the annual field trip. 32 students voted to go to the ice skating rink. 63 voted to go to the local park. How many students are in the 4th grade? $32 + 63 = x$ $x - 63 = 32$	The 4th grade held a vote to decide where the 95 students should go for their annual field trip. 32 students voted to go to the ice skating rink. The rest chose the local park. How many voted to go to the park? $32 + x = 95$ $x = 95 - 32$		The 4th grade held a vote to decide where the 95 students should go for their annual field trip. Some students voted to go to the ice skating rink and others voted to go to the local park. What are some possible combinations of votes? $x + y = 95$ $95 - x = y$
	Difference Unknown	Greater Quantity Unknown	Lesser Quantity Unknown	
Additive Comparison	Jessie and Roberto both collect baseball cards. Roberto has 53 cards and Jessie has 71 cards. How many fewer cards does Roberto have than Jessie? $53 + x = 71$ $53 = 71 - x$	Jessie and Roberto both collect baseball cards. Roberto has 53 cards and Jessie has 18 more cards than Roberto. How many baseball cards does Jessie have? $53 + 18 = x$ $x - 18 = 53$	Jessie and Roberto both collect baseball cards. Jessie has 71 cards and Roberto has 18 fewer cards than Jessie. How many baseball cards does Roberto have? $71 - 18 = x$ $x + 18 = 71$	

FIGURE 1.3 MULTIPLICATION AND DIVISION PROBLEM SITUATIONS

ASYMMETRICAL (NON-MATCHING) FACTORS

	Product Unknown	Multiplier (Number of Groups) Unknown	Measure (Group Size) Unknown	
Equal Groups (Ratio/Rate)*	Mayim has 8 vases to decorate the tables at her party. She places 3 flowers in each vase. How many flowers does she need? $8 \times 3 = x$ $x \div 8 = 3$	Mayim has some vases to decorate the tables at her party. She places 3 flowers in each vase. If she uses 24 flowers, how many vases does she have? $x \times 3 = 24$ $x = 24 \div 3$	Mayim places 24 flowers in vases to decorate the tables at her party. If there are 8 vases, how many flowers will be in each vase? $8 \times x = 24$ $24 \div 8 = x$	

	Resulting Value Unknown	Scale Factor (Times as many) Unknown	Original Value Unknown	
Multiplicative Comparison	Amelia's dog is 5 times older than Wanda's 3 year-old dog. How old is Amelia's dog? $5 \times 3 = x$ $x \div 5 = 3$	Sydney has $15 to spend at the movies. Her sister has $5. How many times more money does Sydney have than her sister has? $x \times 5 = 15$ $5 = 15 \div x$	Mrs. Smith has 15 puzzles in her classroom. That is 3 times the number of puzzles in Mr. Jackson's room. How many puzzles are in Mr. Jackson's room? $3 \times x = 15$ $15 \div 3 = x$	

SYMMETRICAL (MATCHING) FACTORS

	Product Unknown	One Dimension Unknown	Both Dimensions Unknown
Area/Array	Bradley bought a new rug for the hallway in his house. One side measured 5 feet and the other side measured 8 feet. How many square feet does the rug cover? $5 \times 8 = x$ $x \div 8 = 5$	The 40 members of the student council lined up on the stage to take yearbook pictures. The first row started with 8 students and the rest of the rows did the same. How many rows were there? $8 \times x = 40$ $x = 40 \div 8$	Daniella was building a house foundation using her building blocks. She started with 40 blocks. How many blocks long and wide could the foundation be? $x \times y = 40$ $40 \div x = y$

	Sample Space (Total Outcomes) Unknown	One Factor Unknown	Both Factors Unknown
Combinations** (Fundamental Counting Principle)	Karen has 3 shirts and 7 pairs of pants. How many unique outfits can she make? $3 \times 7 = x$ $3 = x \div 7$	Evelyn says that she can make 21 unique and different ice cream sundaes using just ice cream flavors and toppings. If she has 3 flavors of ice cream, how many kinds of toppings does Evelyn have? $3 \times x = 21$ $21 \div 3 = x$	Audrey can make 21 different fruit sodas using the machine at the restaurant. How many different flavorings and sodas could there be? $x \times y = 21$ $x = 21 \div y$

*Equal Groups problems, in many cases, are special cases of a category that includes all ratio and rate problem situations. Distinguishing between the two categories is often a matter of interpretation. The Ratio and Rates category, however, becomes a critically important piece of the middle school curriculum and beyond so the category is referenced here. It will be developed more extensively in the grades 6–8 volume of this series.

**Combinations are a category addressed in middle school mathematics standards. They are introduced briefly in chapter 8 for illustration purposes only and will be developed more extensively in the grades 6–8 volume of this series.

In the chapters—each of which corresponds to a particular problem situation and a row on one of the tables—we walk you through a problem-solving process that enhances your understanding of the operation and its relationship to the problem situation while modeling the kinds of questions and explorations that can be adapted to your instruction and used with your students. Our goal is *not* to have students memorize each of these problem types or learn specific procedures for each one. Rather, our goal is to help you enhance your understanding of the structures and make sure your students are exposed to and become familiar with them. This will support their efforts to solve word problems with understanding—through mathematizing.

In each chapter, you will have opportunities to stop and engage in your own problem solving in the workspace provided. We end each chapter with a summary of the key ideas for that problem situation and some additional practice that can also be translated to your instruction.

PLAYING IN THE MATHEMATIZING SANDBOX: A PROBLEM-SOLVING MODEL

To guide your instruction and even enhance your own capacities for problem solving, we have developed a model for solving word problems that puts the emphasis squarely on learning to mathematize (Figure 1.4). The centerpiece of this model is what we call the "mathematizing sandbox," and we call it this for a reason. The sandbox is where children explore and learn through play. Exploring, experiencing, and experimenting by using different representations is vital not only to developing a strong operation sense but also to building comfort with the problem-solving process. Sometimes it is messy and slow, and we as teachers need to make room for it. We hope that this model will be your guide.

FIGURE 1.4 A MODEL FOR MATHEMATIZING WORD PROBLEMS

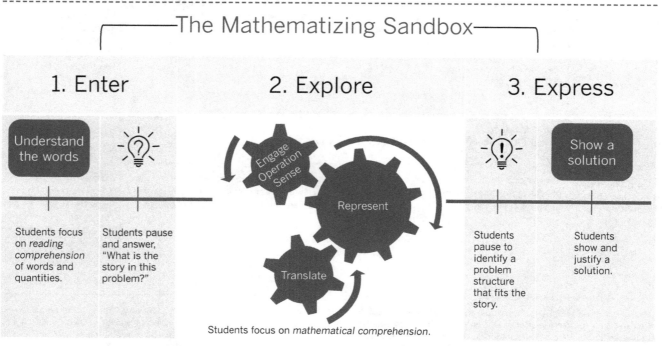

The Mathematizing Sandbox

1. Enter   2. Explore   3. Express

Understand the words

Engage Operation Sense

Represent

Translate

Show a solution

Students focus on *reading comprehension* of words and quantities.

Students pause and answer, "What is the story in this problem?"

Students pause to identify a problem structure that fits the story.

Students show and justify a solution.

Students focus on *mathematical comprehension*.

The mathematizing sandbox involves three steps and two pauses:

Step 1 (Enter): Students' first step is one of reading comprehension. Students must understand the words and context involved in the problem before they can really dive into mathematical understanding of the situation, context, quantities, or relationships between quantities in the problem.

 Pause 1: This is a crucial moment when rather than diving into an approach strategy, students make a conscious choice to look at the problem a different way, with a mind toward reasoning and sense making about the *mathematical story* told by the problem or context. You will notice that we often suggest putting the problem in your own words as a way of making sense. This stage is critical for moving away from the "plucking and plugging" of numbers with no attention to meaning that we so often see (SanGiovanni & Milou, 2018).

Step 2 (Explore): We call this phase of problem-solving stepping into the mathematizing sandbox. This is the space in which students engage their operation sense and play with some of the different representations mentioned earlier, making translations between them to truly understand what is going on in the problem situation. What story is being told? What are we comparing, or what action is happening? What information do we have, and what are we trying to find out? This step sometimes is reflected in mnemonics-based strategies such as STAR (stop, think, act, review) or KWS (What do you know? What do you want to know? Solve it.) or Pólya's (1945) four steps to problem solving (understand, devise a plan, carry out a plan, look back) or even CUBES. But it can't be rushed or treated superficially. Giving adequate space to the Explore phase is essential to the understanding part of any strategic approach. This is where the cognitive sweet spot can be found, and this step is what the bulk of this book is about.

 Pause 2: The exploration done in the mathematizing sandbox leads students to the "a-ha moment" when they can match what they see happening in the problem to a known problem situation (Figures 1.2 and 1.3). Understanding the most appropriate problem situation informs which operation(s) to use, but it also does so much more. It builds a solid foundation of operation sense.

Step 3 (Express): Here students leave the sandbox and are ready to express the story either symbolically or in words or pictures, having found a solution they are prepared to discuss and justify.

Final Words Before You Dive In

We understand that your real life in a school and in your classroom puts innumerable demands on your time and energy as you work to address ambitious mathematics standards. Who has time to use manipulatives, draw pictures, and spend time writing about mathematics? Your students do! This is what meeting the new ambitious standards actually requires. It may feel like pressure to speed up and do more, but paradoxically, the way to build the knowledge and concepts that are currently described in the standards is by slowing down. Evidence gathered over the past 30 years indicates that an integrated and connected understanding of a wide variety of representations of mathematical ideas is one of the best tools in a student's toolbox (or sandbox!) for a deep and lasting understanding of mathematics (Leinwand et al., 2014). We hope that this book will be a valuable tool as you make or renew your commitment to teaching for greater understanding.

PART ONE

Addition and Subtraction

	Result Unknown	Change Addend Unknown	Start Addend Unknown	
Add-To	Paulo counted out 75 crayons and put them in the basket. Then he found 23 more crayons under the table. He added them to the basket. How many crayons are now in the basket? $75 + 23 = x$ $23 = x - 75$	Paulo counted out 75 crayons and put them in the basket. Then he found some more crayons under the table. He added them to the basket and now there are 98 crayons in the basket. How many crayons were under the table? $75 + x = 98$ $x = 98 - 75$	Paulo was organizing the crayons at his table. He found 23 crayons under the table and added them to the basket. When he counted, there were 98 crayons in the basket. How many crayons were in the basket before Paulo looked under the table for crayons? $x + 23 = 98$ $98 - 23 = x$	
Take-From	There are 26 students in Mrs. Amadi's class. After lunch, 15 left to get ready to play in the band at the assembly. How many students are not in the band? $26 - 15 = x$ $26 = 15 + x$	There are 26 students in Mrs. Amadi's class. After the band students left the classroom for the assembly, there were 11 students still in the classroom. How many students are in the band? $26 - x = 11$ $x + 11 = 26$	After lunch, 15 band students left Mrs. Amadi's class to get ready to play in the assembly. There were 11 students still in the classroom. How many students are in Mrs. Amadi's class? $x - 15 = 11$ $15 + 11 = x$	

	Total Unknown	One Part Unknown		Both Parts Unknown
Part-Part-Whole	The 4th grade held a vote to decide where to go for the annual field trip. 32 students voted to go to the ice skating rink. 63 voted to go to the local park. How many students are in the 4th grade? $32 + 63 = x$ $x - 63 = 32$	The 4th grade held a vote to decide where the 95 students in the grade should go for their annual field trip. 32 students voted to go to the ice skating rink. The rest chose the local park. How many voted to go to the park? $32 + x = 95$ $x = 95 - 32$		The 4th grade held a vote to decide where the 95 students in the grade should go for their annual field trip. Some students voted to go to the ice skating rink and others voted to go to the local park. What are some possible combinations of votes? $x + y = 95$ $95 - x = y$
	Difference Unknown	Greater Quantity Unknown	Lesser Quantity Unknown	
Additive Comparison	Jessie and Roberto both collect baseball cards. Roberto has 53 cards and Jessie has 71 cards. How many fewer cards does Roberto have than Jessie? $53 + x = 71$ $71 - 53 = x$	Jessie and Roberto both collect baseball cards. Roberto has 53 cards and Jessie has 18 more cards than Roberto. How many baseball cards does Jessie have? $53 + 18 = x$ $x - 18 = 53$	Jessie and Roberto both collect baseball cards. Jessie has 71 cards and Roberto has 18 fewer cards than Jessie. How many baseball cards does Roberto have? $71 - 18 = x$ $x + 18 = 71$	

CHAPTER TWO

Add-To and Take-From
Locating the Change

Thinking About Active Addition and Subtraction Situations

In this chapter we introduce two addition and subtraction problem situations, Add-To and Take-From. These are what we call active situations, a designation that will become more meaningful as you work through this chapter and the next, explore the characteristics of these problem types, and make comparisons with other problem types that show relationships. You'll notice that these situations are labeled Result Unknown, Change Addend Unknown, and Start Addend Unknown. After we do some mathematics, we will return to a discussion of these variations. Let's get started.

Pretend you are walking into a workshop. This is the first of seven workshops exploring problem situations that all students will encounter in grades 3–5. In this workshop, as in the other six, you will be exploring in detail aspects of these problems and the operations associated with them that you may not have considered before. Doing so requires that you take on the role of student, see the problems with new eyes, and let yourself try out representations and models for yourself.

Addition and Subtraction Problem Situations

	Result Unknown	Change Addend Unknown	Start Addend Unknown	
Add-To	Paulo counted out 75 crayons and put them in the basket. Then he found 23 more crayons under the table. He added them to the basket. How many crayons are now in the basket? $75 + 23 = x$ $23 = x - 75$	Paulo counted out 75 crayons and put them in the basket. Then he found some more crayons under the table. He added them to the basket and now there are 98 crayons in the basket. How many crayons were under the table? $75 + x = 98$ $x = 98 - 75$	Paulo was organizing the crayons at his table. He found 23 crayons under the table and added them to the basket. When he counted, there were 98 crayons in the basket. How many crayons were in the basket before Paulo looked under the table for crayons? $x + 23 = 98$ $98 - 23 = x$	
Take-From	There are 26 students in Mrs. Amadi's class. After lunch, 15 left to get ready to play in the band at the assembly. How many students are not in the band? $26 - 15 = x$ $26 = 15 + x$	There are 26 students in Mrs. Amadi's class. After the band students left the classroom for the assembly, there were 11 students still in the classroom. How many students are in the band? $26 - x = 11$ $x + 11 = 26$	After lunch, 15 band students left Mrs. Amadi's class to get ready to play in the assembly. There were 11 students still in the classroom. How many students are in Mrs. Amadi's class? $x - 15 = 11$ $15 + 11 = x$	

Note: These representations for the problem situations reflect our understanding based on a number of resources. These include the tables in the Common Core State Standards for mathematics (Common Core Standards Initiative, 2010), the problem situations as described in the Cognitively Guided Instruction research (Carpenter, Hiebert, & Moser, 1981), and other tools. See the Appendix and companion website for a more detailed summary of the documents that informed our development of this table.

ACTIVE SITUATIONS

	Result Unknown	Change Addend Unknown	Start Addend Unknown	
Add-To	Paulo counted out 75 crayons and put them in the basket. Then he found 23 more crayons under the table. He added them to the basket. How many crayons are now in the basket? $75 + 23 = x$ $23 = x - 75$	Paulo counted out 75 crayons and put them in the basket. Then he found some more crayons under the table. He added them to the basket and now there are 98 crayons in the basket. How many crayons were under the table? $75 + x = 98$ $x = 98 - 75$	Paulo was organizing the crayons at his table. He found 23 crayons under the table and added them to the basket. When he counted, there were 98 crayons in the basket. How many crayons were in the basket before Paulo looked under the table for crayons? $x + 23 = 98$ $98 - 23 = x$	
Take-From	There are 26 students in Mrs. Amadi's class. After lunch, 15 left to get ready to play in the band at the assembly. How many students are not in the band? $26 - 15 = x$ $26 = 15 + x$	There are 26 students in Mrs. Amadi's class. After the band students left the classroom for the assembly, there were 11 students still in the classroom. How many students are in the band? $26 - x = 11$ $x + 11 = 26$	After lunch, 15 band students left Mrs. Amadi's class to get ready to play in the assembly. There were 11 students still in the classroom. How many students are in Mrs. Amadi's class? $x - 15 = 11$ $15 + 11 = x$	

RELATIONSHIP (NONACTIVE) SITUATIONS

	Total Unknown	One Part Unknown		Both Parts Unknown
Part-Part-Whole	The 4th grade held a vote to decide where to go for the annual field trip. 32 students voted to go to the ice skating rink. 63 voted to go to the local park. How many students are in the 4th grade? $32 + 63 = x$ $x - 63 = 32$	The 4th grade held a vote to decide where the 95 students in the grade should go for their annual field trip. 32 students voted to go to the ice skating rink. The rest chose the local park. How many voted to go to the park? $32 + x = 95$ $x = 95 - 32$		The 4th grade held a vote to decide where the 95 students in the grade should go for their annual field trip. Some students voted to go to the ice skating rink and others voted to go to the local park. What are some possible combinations of votes? $x + y = 95$ $95 - x = y$
	Difference Unknown	Greater Quantity Unknown	Lesser Quantity Unknown	
Additive Comparison	Jessie and Roberto both collect baseball cards. Roberto has 53 cards and Jessie has 71 cards. How many fewer cards does Roberto have than Jessie? $53 + x = 71$ $71 - 53 = x$	Jessie and Roberto both collect baseball cards. Roberto has 53 cards and Jessie has 18 more cards than Roberto. How many baseball cards does Jessie have? $53 + 18 = x$ $x - 18 = 53$	Jessie and Roberto both collect baseball cards. Jessie has 71 cards and Roberto has 18 fewer cards than Jessie. How many baseball cards does Roberto have? $71 - 18 = x$ $x + 18 = 71$	

Sandbox Notes

As you enter into Explore phase of problem solving, gather your tools, including markers or colored pencils, base 10 blocks, place value disks, counters, and any other tools that you routinely have available in your classroom. Try several of the concrete manipulatives and some hand-drawn picture models that reflect the **mathematical story** in the word problem. Revisit your restatement and specify where you can see each quantity in the problem, and in the models you have created. Think about how your work can express your understanding of the problem situation.

Ask yourself these questions to focus your thinking:

- *Think about the quantities in each situation. What do they represent? How is each quantity related to the other quantities in the problem?*

- *How can you represent the quantities in the word problems with your manipulatives or pictures? Feel free to use the workspace provided.*

- *What number sentence best shows what is happening in each story?*

Mathematical story: A retelling of the action or relationships in a word problem or other problem context in a way that highlights the important mathematical details over any other information.

To begin, read the two problems in Figures 2.1 and 2.2. Don't try to solve them just yet. Instead, put yourself in the place of your students, and as you enter each problem, focus on understanding the words in each one. Try using your own words to rephrase, without focusing on the quantities. If this is difficult, substitute the quantities with the word *some*. This will help you avoid the dilemma of jumping to the solution path before you fully explore the problem. Space is given below for recording your restatement of the problem. Look at the sandbox model in Figure 2.3 to remind yourself of how these tasks fit into the problem-solving process. Congratulations, you are now ready to enter the mathematizing sandbox!

FIGURE 2.1

Paulo was organizing the crayons at his table. He counted out 75 crayons and put them in the basket. Then Emily gave him 23 more crayons she found on the floor. He added them to the basket. How many crayons are now in the basket?

FIGURE 2.2

Lillian had some money in her bank account. She earned $23 mowing grass and now she has $98. How much money was in her bank account?

ENTER THE PROBLEM

FIGURE 2.3 A MODEL FOR MATHEMATIZING WORD PROBLEMS

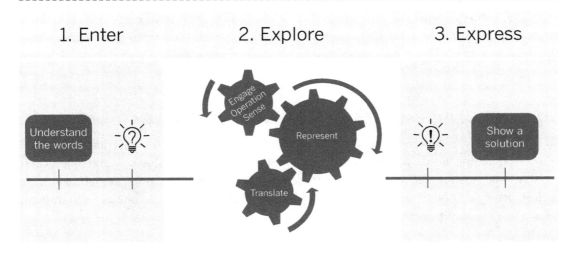

To explore, you may need to take notes of your explorations on scratch paper. Once you can answer these questions, you are ready to show and justify your solutions. Include these in the workspace provided so that you can easily refer back to them. If your solution includes a concrete model, reproduce that as best you can in a drawing. Add any verbal representation of the problem or additional notes on your thinking as necessary to make your solution clear. *Remember: When the focus is on mathematizing, finding a solution is not the same as finding the answer. A solution is a representation of the problem that reveals how it can be solved. The answer comes after.* This concept will become clearer as you work through problems and explore the work samples of students and teachers throughout the book.

You have taken your first trip to the mathematizing sandbox. You've translated the story of each problem into your own words and explored several different concrete, pictorial, and symbolic representations of the problem situations. You likely have translated your representations into a number sentence that you can then solve, or the answer may have come out of another representation. You have used your operation sense to approach these word problems in a way that reflects deep understanding rather than simply computational knowledge.

STUDENTS AND TEACHERS THINK ABOUT THE PROBLEMS

Look at the student work in Figures 2.4 and 2.5 and consider how these students describe or draw what is happening in the same word problems. Look at the teacher commentary that follows and consider what the teachers noticed in the student work. There is also a video available showing each student's solution to the problem, which you may want to watch once you have read through the student work and teacher comments.

What do you notice? Did you notice that there is action in both of these problems? Emily gives Paulo crayons while Lillian earns money. This action of *giving* crayons, or *earning* money and putting it into an account signals addition. These are both examples of an Add-To situation. We want to highlight an important feature of Add-To problem situations: They all require the action of adding something to occur in the story, but as the comment in Figure 2.5 suggests, they do not necessarily refer to the operation used to find the solution. In this case, the student's number line representation shows addition, but the teacher expected a subtraction equation. As we explore the nature of Add-To and Take-From problem situations, the distinction between the computation used to arrive at the answer and the operation associated with the problem situation will become increasingly clear.

> Add-To: A problem situation that includes action happening in the problem: Some quantity is being added to the original quantity.

FINDING THE UNKNOWN, THREE STORY STRUCTURES

These active mathematical stories have a narrative structure—a beginning, a middle, and an end. In the beginning there is a starting value. How many crayons does Paulo have to start with? How many cookies were on the plate? How much money was in Lillian's bank account? The middle of the story brings a change in quantity: More crayons are acquired. More cookies are baked. Lillian earns money. And the end of the story is the result of the change: the final number of crayons in the basket, cookies on the plate, dollars in the bank. In most word problems only one of these three quantities is unknown. Thus, as the table at the beginning of the chapter indicates, the unknown could be the start, the change, or the result, reflecting the arc of your storyline. Identifying the unknown—in other words, the information we need to know—is the first step in problem solving.

RESULT UNKNOWN In kindergarten, students first learn to solve the Result Unknown variation of the problem, where we know the starting value and the change (McCallum, Daro, & Zimba, n.d.). This is the most straightforward version for young learners to act out and to help them understand

FIGURE 2.4

FIGURE 2.5

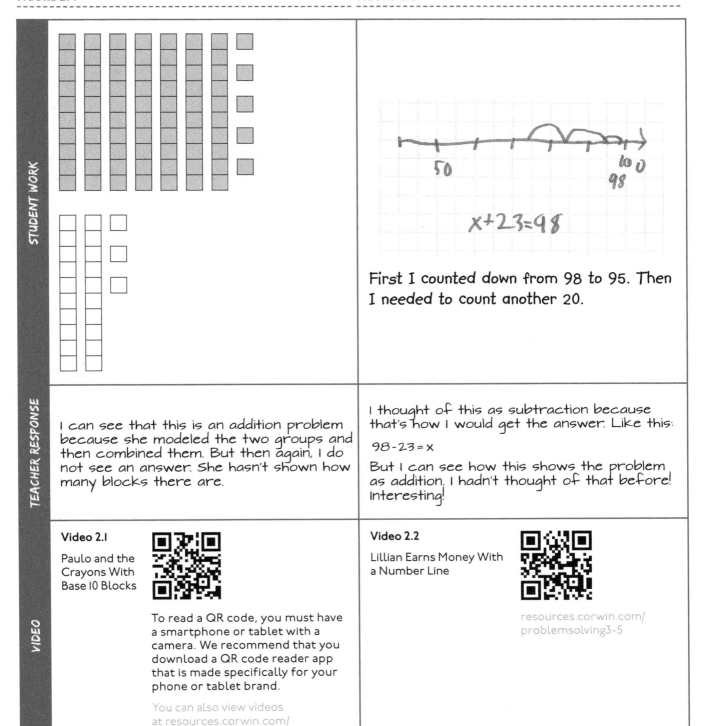

STUDENT WORK

First I counted down from 98 to 95. Then I needed to count another 20.

$$x + 23 = 98$$

TEACHER RESPONSE

I can see that this is an addition problem because she modeled the two groups and then combined them. But then again, I do not see an answer. She hasn't shown how many blocks there are.

I thought of this as subtraction because that's how I would get the answer. Like this:

$98 - 23 = x$

But I can see how this shows the problem as addition. I hadn't thought of that before! Interesting!

VIDEO

Video 2.1

Paulo and the Crayons With Base 10 Blocks

To read a QR code, you must have a smartphone or tablet with a camera. We recommend that you download a QR code reader app that is made specifically for your phone or tablet brand.

You can also view videos at resources.corwin.com/problemsolving3-5

Video 2.2

Lillian Earns Money With a Number Line

resources.corwin.com/problemsolving3-5

that addition is the operation we can use to describe the action of adding something. The crayon problem that opened this chapter is an example of an Add-To, Result Unknown problem situation (Figure 2.1). Note that the values in this problem are more appropriate for students in second grade.

> *Paulo was organizing the crayons at his table. He counted out 75 crayons and put them in the basket. Then Emily gave him 23 more crayons she found on the floor. He added them to the basket. How many crayons are now in the basket?*
>
> $75 + 23 = x$

CHANGE UNKNOWN The next variation students explore is Change Unknown. Students are often expected to be proficient with this variation in first grade. In this case, we know the beginning and the end of the story (the starting and resulting values) and have to figure out what happened in the middle—what change led from the start to the result. Here is a typical problem that we might expect first graders to be able to make sense of:

> *Thuy knew she had 8 friends to play on her team. More friends also joined. Now Thuy has 11 people on her team. How many friends joined Thuy's team?*
>
> $8 + x = 11$

START UNKNOWN The Start Unknown variation is the most challenging for students. In this case, we are working backward from the end of the story, through the change, to figure out the starting value (the beginning of the story). This requires more abstract reasoning, and students are often expected to have mastered this final variation (with grade-appropriate values) by the end of second grade. The second problem in the opening of the chapter (Figure 2.2) illustrates the Start Unknown variation of an Add-To problem situation.

> *Lillian had some money in her bank account. She earned $23 mowing grass and now she has $98. How much money was in her bank account?*
>
> $x + 23 = 98$

STORY STRUCTURES: IMPLICATIONS FOR TEACHING

When we ask teachers to compose Add-To word problems, we find that almost 75 percent are of the Result Unknown variation. No wonder problems that are Change Unknown or Start Unknown sometimes feel like trick questions to teachers and students! Without being aware of it, teachers may be ignoring these kinds of problems to their students' detriment. Skipping these variations not only limits students' ability to grasp the dynamics of these stories, but it also limits their ability to transfer their thinking to other problem situations. As you'll see in the examples that follow, it is easy to adjust a problem from one variation to another, and it is critically important to expose students to a broad range of problems. By making sure your students have experience with all three variations, you will better prepare them to recognize Add-To situations in any form.

Your students in grades 3–5 should be familiar with all three variations of Add-To problems, but they might not be. If this is the case, you can still provide them with opportunities to experience all varieties! You don't have to start from scratch, but introducing the problem situations with familiar fact families will free your class to focus more on the structure of the problem than on the numbers themselves. People who work with these problem types in many settings with children recommend that all students see examples of all of the variations of the problem types, even those that have proved to be more challenging (Franke, 2018).

As students in grades 3–5 develop their number sense about larger and larger whole number values, the underlying structure of the problem situations does not change. Their strategies for modeling and finding solutions, however, can change to be more practical for the numbers in the problem. They may move from marked number lines to open number lines or use place value chips instead of base 10 blocks to represent the problem situation. It will be helpful to build on this foundation as you work with your students on the more complex number categories of fractions and decimals (described later in this chapter).

Let's look again at the two problems we started with in this chapter, this time considering their different problem structures. The crayon problem (Figure 2.1) is an Add-To, Result Unknown variation, the one we are most familiar with, whereas Lillian's mowing problem (Figure 2.2) is an Add-To, Start Unknown problem situation. It can be difficult to model a Start Unknown story when the beginning quantity is unknown. The number line solution that the student used does an excellent job, helping the student represent the unknown at the beginning and coming up with a number sentence that reflects the action in the story (Figure 2.5). It's challenging to tell a story when you don't know the beginning of it! For this reason, this particular variation is introduced early, but proficiency is not expected until the end of second grade. As we saw in the teacher's response, a subtraction operation is often used to compute an answer to this problem type, even though the problem is still of an Add-To variety. In the next chapter we will explore more of what happens when the problem situation does not match the operation used to find a solution, including connecting to inverse operations.

To help with thinking about or planning your instruction, use the chart in Figure 2.6 to list some Add-To action situations that will be familiar to your students. As you read the list, visualize the story and focus less on the quantities and more on the setting and the action. Imagine yourself in that setting and consider what story you or your students could craft that matches each prompt in the table. The first few have been done for you.

FIGURE 2.6 ADD-TO ACTION SITUATIONS

CONTEXT	START (Beginning Value)	CHANGE (Action in the Story)	RESULT (Ending Value)
Soccer Game	Points on the board	Points are earned	Final score
Party Food	Cookies on the plate	More cookies are made	Cookies on the plate
Shopping	Books on the bookshelf	Books are bought	Books on the bookshelf
Winning a Contest	Pets in the house	Some goldfish are won	Pets in the house
Trading Cards			
		A baby is born	

(continued)

(continued)

CONTEXT	START (Beginning Value)	CHANGE (Action in the Story)	RESULT (Ending Value)
			Dirty pots in the sink
	Movies you've seen		

Asking students to come up with their own word problems while leaving the quantities blank can be an effective strategy for helping them consider the structure of the story within the problem without the added complication of coming up with an answer. It's important to help your students realize that mathematics isn't just about number and values. It is about solving problems, whether they are problems in textbooks, or on tests, or real-life problems that matter to them.

One way to start is by introducing students to a context or setting that interests them or, better yet, let the events in your classroom, school, or community serve as the setting for the story, but keep the emphasis on **quantities** they can count or measure (Kelemanik, Lucenta, & Creighton, 2016).

Quantity: A number, including its unit of measure.

Once students are comfortable with creating stories, you can move to developing stories that are built around quantities. Encourage your students to see the mathematics in the world around them as stories. One strategy for encouraging this is to ask students, for example, to add quantities to a story one at a time. Observe a starting quantity (a value and unit) in your classroom context and ask students to tell a number story beginning with that quantity in its context and then add another quantity. For example, start with "I see six children wearing snow boots today. What happens next?" Encourage students to include new quantities in the next line in the story. Your students are mathematizing here; they are seeing the world around them in mathematical terms. As students become more comfortable with this process, they will probably become more inventive. You may need to encourage them to think about how realistic their values are. Of course, students may choose to inject a different action into the story. When creating their own stories, this is acceptable, but as students' awareness of the mathematical story structure evolves, challenge them occasionally to limit their contributions to stories that focus on a single variation of a problem situation.

FOCUS ON TAKE-FROM SITUATIONS

Up to this point, we have focused only on Add-To problem situations. Now let's look at Take-From situations, keeping in mind that the three story structures we described earlier also apply to Take-From problems.

As you look at the problem in Figure 2.7, think about the many ways it could be represented. Translate it into your own words and think about the drawings or manipulatives you might use to represent the story in the problem. What equation would you use to describe the action? What tools might your students choose?

FIGURE 2.7

Manuel was playing a video game and he had 58 points on the board. His baby brother distracted him and he lost some points, leaving him with 16 points. How many points did Manuel lose because of his baby brother?

The representation in Figure 2.8 shows one student's initial work during the explore phase of the mathematizing sandbox. Note the comments and questions his teacher asked him as she monitored his work. Think about what other kinds of representations might also support his exploration.

FIGURE 2.8

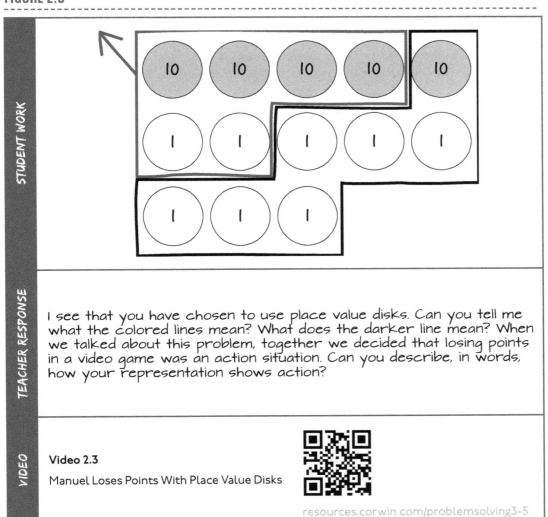

STUDENT WORK

TEACHER RESPONSE

I see that you have chosen to use place value disks. Can you tell me what the colored lines mean? What does the darker line mean? When we talked about this problem, together we decided that losing points in a video game was an action situation. Can you describe, in words, how your representation shows action?

VIDEO

Video 2.3

Manuel Loses Points With Place Value Disks

resources.corwin.com/problemsolving3-5

Take-From: A problem situation that includes an action and a quantity being removed from the original quantity.

Because this is an active problem situation and action involves the losing of points, it is a **Take-From** problem situation. The place value disks used in the student sample displayed in Video 2.3 show the quantity of 58 points represented using five 10-disks and eight 1-disks. The benefit of using place value disks in modeling the problem is that the student can show not only the starting quantity of points but also the change and the result. Place value disks are particularly useful with larger quantities.

The arrow helps us understand which of the circled groups was lost and which remains. The benefit for students in circling the disks rather than physically removing them is that they can see all of the values simultaneously, and repeatedly perform the action in the problem. Video 2.3 shows this student solution "in action." It may help you see the action the arrow represents. Even though the representation in Figure 2.8 seems clear, without a written explanation or an accompanying equation (verbal and symbolic representations), we are only making assumptions about this student's thinking. For this student, exploration in the mathematizing sandbox should continue. The teacher asked the student to go a step further and describe his thinking so that she could verify that his representation did what both of them think it does. This is the value of the mathematizing sandbox approach. Students are encouraged to fully elaborate on their initial thinking, checking and verifying it with numerous representations of the problem they are working on.

In most standards, Take-From situations are taught in a similar progression to Add-To situations: Result Unknown, then Change Unknown, and then Start Unknown variations. As with Add-To situations, if you are not sure if your students have had exposure to problem situations, start with easy-to-calculate numbers and maintain focus on the problem contexts initially.

MODELING THE ACTIVE PROBLEM SITUATION

One of the things we know about mathematics is that there is always more than one way to approach a problem. Students can benefit from using concrete and pictorial models where they can show the action unfold in an active problem situation. The model they use can involve **grouped** or **ungrouped counters** used to act out a problem situation or it can be a number line that uses arrows or other marks to show action.

Grouped counters: Objects that represent units that are grouped together, such as a base 10 rod.

Ungrouped counters: Objects that represent an individual or single unit with a quantity of one.

Before we look closely at how the students modeled the next two problems, read through each carefully, putting their stories in your own words (Figures 2.9 and 2.10). Note which quantity is missing: the start, the change, or the result?

FIGURE 2.9

FIGURE 2.10

At the end of the first half of the football game, the Tigers had 14 points. At the end of the game, they had scored a total of 35 points. How many did they score in the second half?	Hannah read 14 books in the first month of school. In the second month she checked out more books and read them all. The librarian said that she had read 35 books so far. How many did she check out the second month?

The student work in Figures 2.11 and 2.12, and the teacher comments that accompany the samples, explore a variety of models students might produce to reflect the action in an Add-To problem situation.

FIGURE 2.11   **FIGURE 2.12**

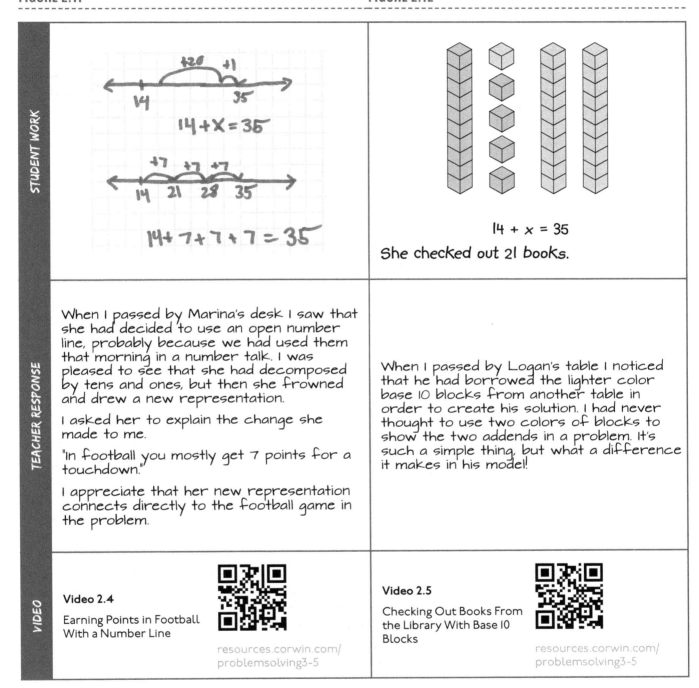

14 + x = 35

She checked out 21 books.

STUDENT WORK

TEACHER RESPONSE

When I passed by Marina's desk I saw that she had decided to use an open number line, probably because we had used them that morning in a number talk. I was pleased to see that she had decomposed by tens and ones, but then she frowned and drew a new representation.

I asked her to explain the change she made to me.

"In football you mostly get 7 points for a touchdown."

I appreciate that her new representation connects directly to the football game in the problem.

When I passed by Logan's table I noticed that he had borrowed the lighter color base 10 blocks from another table in order to create his solution. I had never thought to use two colors of blocks to show the two addends in a problem. It's such a simple thing, but what a difference it makes in his model!

VIDEO

Video 2.4

Earning Points in Football With a Number Line

resources.corwin.com/ problemsolving3-5

Video 2.5

Checking Out Books From the Library With Base 10 Blocks

resources.corwin.com/ problemsolving3-5

Counters or other manipulatives, like the base 10 blocks used in Figure 2.12, allow students to act out the action in the problem. Although the action can be more difficult to show on a number line, there are strategies for making action visible. In Video 2.4, the arrow shows the action or movement from the starting value to the ending value. The distance covered is the amount of change. The video narrates solving the problem using this open number line model and identifies the three elements of the story.

Notice that Marina's first number line was influenced by the value of the numbers and an efficient strategy for computation, relying initially on multiples of 10, while her second number line focused on multiples of 7 to reflect how a real football game is scored (Figure 2.11). It is interesting that both approaches contribute to her understanding of the problem situation: the first by making the computation easy, which allows her to focus on the problem situation itself, the second, once she has mastered this, allows her to take the problem into the real world.

In Video 2.5, we see Logan chose to use base 10 blocks in two colors to represent the checked-out books from the library. When looking at a static drawing, although we can clearly see the quantities in the change of color, we cannot see the change itself. The video for this problem shows how acting out a problem situation is far more effective for demonstrating an Add-To problem situation than a picture or equation alone can be. In the next chapter we will discuss strategies for adding details to pictures in order to distinguish actions in the pictorial representations.

Teaching Students to Use Concrete and Pictorial Models

Diagram: An abstract representation of a situation, rather than literal one.

In the previous section we shared two pictorial representations, one object based and the other a number line diagram. These are representations that one can reasonably expect students in grades 3–5 to be able to use meaningfully. But that's a large assumption that may not be true yet for your students. Moving from more literal pictures (sketches of base 10 blocks, for example) to using diagrams such as number lines is a process, and exposure and experience are the best strategies for building student competence using these models of problem situations (Gutstein & Romberg, 1995).

Why are diagrams necessary? First, diagrams help students record what they understand about the elements of a problem and the relationships between the quantities in it. They may already understand the relationship, but putting it down on paper or capturing it in a set of objects reflects their own thinking back at them. Think of such visuals as a placeholder for their thinking. Second, using a diagram may help students start to sort out the different relationships and actions inherent in the problem situations. Perhaps they might not otherwise recognize that an Add-To or Take-From problem situation implies that action takes place. Finally, deep mathematical understanding comes when students are comfortable using all five forms of representations we described in Chapter 1: concrete, pictorial, verbal, contextual, and symbolic. This is the thinking behind the problem-solving model we offer here and in particular the role of the mathematizing sandbox. Learning to create their own diagrams is an important component of generating visual representations of the elements and relationships in a problem. As a matter of fact, the capacity to translate among all five forms of representations defines deeper understanding.

How many forms of visual representation should students know how to create? Some may think that limiting the variety of models we ask students to learn is the best strategy. Others would prefer to offer students an open smorgasbord of models and allow students to make their own choices. Others believe that we should offer no guidance on selecting models but, instead, make materials available. The strongest evidence supports offering students a variety of tools and allowing them to make their own choices but with some guidance (Leinwand et al., 2014). In general, we recommend the approach outlined in Figure 2.13 when supporting students as they express their mathematical thinking using multiple representations, particularly concrete and pictorial representations.

FIGURE 2.13 ENCOURAGING MULTIPLE MODELS IN PROBLEM SOLVING

1. **Choose**: Encourage individual choice of physical and pictorial representations.

2. **Explain**: Ask students to explain what the parts of their pictorial representation mean and to explain the relationships between those parts.

3. **Justify**: Challenge students to defend their choices. Challenge students' correct representations just as much as you would ask them to justify incorrect representations.

4. **Model**: Explicitly model new forms of diagrams or manipulatives that you choose to use, explaining your decisions as you demonstrate how you are using the tool. We are *not* suggesting you explicitly teach students to use the tool. Simply model your own thinking process as you employ a visual, but reinforce to students that you are held to the same standard for justifying your decisions as they are.

5. **Connect**: Ask students to describe how two representations or models relate to each other. Encourage them to identify how each element of the problem appears in each model. Ask them to explain when they might prefer one model or representation over another.

6. **Share**: Ask students to explain a novel visual approach to their peers and discuss how they model their thinking process.

7. **Expect**: Communicate that you expect to see visual diagrams or manipulatives used to explain mathematical ideas.

8. **Crash**: No representation works in every context or situation. Expect any model to fail at some point, and encourage students to change their representation when the model crashes.

We recognize that students in grades 3–5 work with larger whole number values, but we recommend following our example in this chapter and using smaller, easier-to-manipulate numbers when introducing students to exploring the connectedness between mathematical representations. Ample evidence indicates that when faced with more challenging numbers, students resort to "number plucking and plugging," grabbing numbers and applying randomly chosen operations to them (SanGiovanni & Milou, 2018), even if they already have a firm grasp of the problem situations (Bell, Fischbein, & Greer, 1984; Bell, Greer, Grimison, & Mangan, 1989; Sowder, 2002). Expect this and start with more manageable numbers before working your way into the grade-appropriate quantities.

Moving Beyond Whole Numbers

In this part of the chapter we expand our set of numbers to include fractions and decimals, to align more closely with the grade-level content that students in grades 3–5 should learn. The numbers in the problems should not affect students' understanding of problem situations, which is our focus in this book. But in our experience, when the computation itself poses challenges, students cannot rely as much on good estimates to propose an answer. If they don't have experience modeling quantities

Warning: The next pages include student examples of the problem situations you will be practicing. If you find it difficult to resist looking forward while practicing in the sandbox on page 28, consider covering the facing page (page 29) with a sheet of paper.

or problem situations, or if they don't have experience modeling with fractions and decimals, they have little else to fall back on. That's when we are likely to hear, "I don't get what they want me to do!"

The two problems in Figures 2.14 and 2.15 are Take-From problem situations. When you solve them, pull out a set of manipulatives that you have available to you and think about other types of drawings, diagrams, and pictorial images you might use to capture the action in these problem situations. We will share different manipulative models, some of which you may not currently have access to. You may find that you have good substitutes, or you may find a "must-have" tool for next year's supply list!

As you pause before entering the mathematizing sandbox, think about how you can use the manipulatives to focus student attention on the actions taking place in the problem. Act out the problems. Anticipate challenges students might encounter. For example, it's tempting to worry right away about renaming 2 as $1\frac{8}{8}$, which is something we do when *computing* an answer to this problem. Instead, focus first on the *context* of the problems and how the manipulative model chosen supports students' understanding of what happens in the problem.

If you get stuck, revisit the Sandbox Notes earlier in the chapter for guiding questions and other suggestions.

FIGURE 2.14

FIGURE 2.15

The art teacher is helping the class make bows for decorations for the class party. They start with a 2-yard piece of ribbon. They cut off $1\frac{5}{8}$ yards to make one bow. How much ribbon is left after each bow is made?	The cook had 2 cups of flour. He used some flour to make gravy and now has $1\frac{5}{8}$ cups of flour. How much flour did he use to make the gravy?

ENTER THE PROBLEM

EXPLORE

STUDENTS AND TEACHERS THINK ABOUT THE PROBLEMS

The student work in Figures 2.16 and 2.17 shows some possible responses to these typical word problems. The teacher comments feature a view into a fellow teacher's practice, and they can help you consider how you might handle similar situations in your own classroom.

FIGURE 2.16   **FIGURE 2.17**

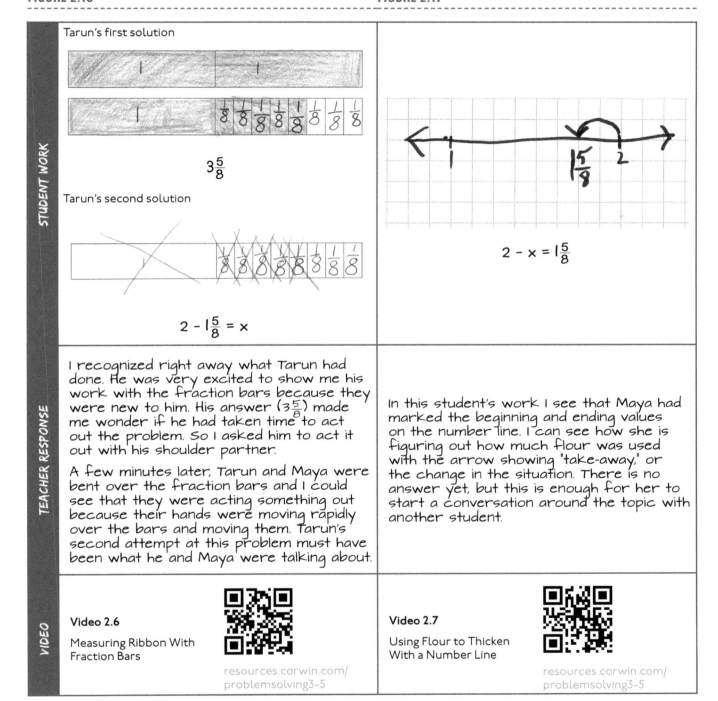

STUDENT WORK

Tarun's first solution

$3\frac{5}{8}$

Tarun's second solution

$2 - 1\frac{5}{8} = x$

$2 - x = 1\frac{5}{8}$

TEACHER RESPONSE

I recognized right away what Tarun had done. He was very excited to show me his work with the fraction bars because they were new to him. His answer ($3\frac{5}{8}$) made me wonder if he had taken time to act out the problem. So I asked him to act it out with his shoulder partner.

A few minutes later, Tarun and Maya were bent over the fraction bars and I could see that they were acting something out because their hands were moving rapidly over the bars and moving them. Tarun's second attempt at this problem must have been what he and Maya were talking about.

In this student's work I see that Maya had marked the beginning and ending values on the number line. I can see how she is figuring out how much flour was used with the arrow showing "take-away," or the change in the situation. There is no answer yet, but this is enough for her to start a conversation around the topic with another student.

VIDEO

Video 2.6

Measuring Ribbon With Fraction Bars

resources.corwin.com/
problemsolving3-5

Video 2.7

Using Flour to Thicken With a Number Line

resources.corwin.com/
problemsolving3-5

Before we consider the two students' work, let's take a moment to identify the problem situation and problem structures here. The word problems in Figures 2.14 and 2.15 are both active Take-From problems. Both problems even use the same values: 2, $1\frac{5}{8}$, and $\frac{3}{8}$. But only the ribbon problem uses a Result Unknown structure, while the flour problem uses a Change Unknown structure. The fact that we are now including fractions and decimals in our problems has no effect on the underlying pattern or structure. This is an important reminder for students especially if fractions throw them off. If that happens, encourage them to go back to building models and acting out the action.

TEACHING OPPORTUNITIES IN THE STUDENT WORK SAMPLES

Tarun's initial work on the ribbon problem is not an unusual response for a problem like this. We aren't sure exactly what Tarun was thinking, but the teacher suspected that he had added the two numbers in the problem together and did not recognize that this didn't solve the problem that was asked. To help Tarun, the teacher decided to engage the Share strategy (one of the strategies we outline for encouraging multiple models in problem solving; see Figure 2.13) by asking him to work with Maya, who had been trying to translate her thinking about the situation into an equation. Sometimes we put students who are doing similar thinking in groups to do work. This example shows that sometimes pairing students who are thinking differently about a mathematical idea can have beneficial results.

Tarun's second model in Figure 2.16 now represents a Take-From situation rather than an Add-To situation. You can watch Tarun's model of the second problem in Video 2.6. Earlier we noted that it's important not to enter the mathematizing sandbox by focusing on the fact that 2 can be renamed as $1\frac{8}{8}$. In the end, however, Tarun does do exactly that, using the fraction tiles, but only after he was challenged to model the problem situation. Waiting to address the subtraction computation allowed Tarun to reveal his fragile understanding of the problem situation and for the teacher to introduce an intervention to support his learning.

The work in Figure 2.17 to represent the action of the flour problem is more abstract, relying, as we have noted in other problems, on the arrow to show that the student likely understands that the quantity is being reduced. This is confirmed by the equation, which expresses a take-away action. As the teacher notes, no answer is given, yet there are some potential entry points for talking with this student. This is an ideal opportunity for the teacher to engage the Justify strategy (Figure 2.13), asking the student to explain her thinking. It is a good habit to ask students to justify their thinking when they have incorrect answers and even when they have correct answers. When an answer is incomplete, as we see in Maya's work, asking for justification is just as important. As you watch Video 2.7, think about the contribution Maya made in her conversation with Tarun. What could he learn from her approach to the problem? What does Maya learn from Tarun?

COMPLICATING THINGS: THE START UNKNOWN VARIATION

As we noted early on in this chapter, the Start Unknown variation of an active problem type (either as an Add-To or as a Take-From) is the last variation students are expected to become proficient with. As you read the two problems in Figures 2.18 and 2.19, think about the challenges that Start Unknown problems present. Also think about how retelling the stories, creating matching models, and acting out the problems can contribute to student sense making.

FIGURE 2.18

FIGURE 2.19

Andrea wants to save $29.50 to purchase a game. She figured out that if she earns $5.25 walking the neighbor's dog this weekend, it will get her exactly to her goal. How much does Andrea already have saved?	John wants to purchase a new book to read on his vacation. He spends $10.30 of his vacation money on the book. Now he has $31.75 left to spend on his trip. How much money did John originally save for the trip?

Before examining the work samples, note that Figure 2.18, the dog walking problem, is an Add-To version of a Start Unknown problem with Andrea adding money to her savings. By contrast, Figure 2.19 is a Take-From problem but also with the start unknown. Remember that what defines a Start Unknown problem is not where the unknown falls in the wording of the problem but, rather, where it falls in the story that the problem tells. In this story we don't know the total amount John starts out with. As you examine the student work samples in Figures 2.20 and 2.21, think about what operation is used to solve each of the problems.

MODELING In challenging problem structures like these, it is even more important to enter the mathematizing sandbox with tools in hand. Creating models helps students see the story in the problem. In Figure 2.20, the student's strategy of using money to model helped her identify the change in the quantity that yielded the result. But it is also important to ask her to try a verbal representation by telling the story in her own words. This will help build her awareness of all of the features of the problem situation—that is, an Add-To problem with the start unknown—that might lead her to identify an Add-To equation for the situation as $x + 5.25 = 29.50$.

TRYING A SIMPLER CASE Students who have good operation sense are able to see the structures and identify an appropriate operation no matter what kind of numbers are in the problem. If students struggle to see the situation because they have difficulty with the numbers, the time-tested problem-solving strategy of Trying a Simpler Case can be helpful. In John's book-purchasing problem (Figure 2.19), for example, the problem could be restated using only whole number values: "John spent $10 on a book and now has $31 left. How much money did he have to start out?" Intermediate students can estimate the solution as $41 and then use that estimation to model the situation or to say the problem in their own words.

By using only the whole dollar values (and not even rounding), it is easier to see which number in the problem goes where when the equation is revised to reflect the exact values in the problem: $x - \$10.30 = \$31.75$ or $x = 31.75 + 10.30$. Now the student can use the strategy of his choice to find the exact solution and check against the estimate of $41. The open number line in Figure 2.21 shows this same reasoning. This student began with the $31.75 that remained after purchasing the book. Then the arrow moving right "undoes" spending $10.30 and ends at the starting value of $42.05.

FIGURE 2.20

FIGURE 2.21

STUDENT WORK

???

+

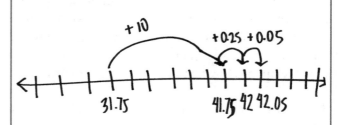

=

At first I was confused by this problem because I didn't know how much money Andrea had! Then I counted out what she earned. Then I saw how much her game was. Then I noticed something! I saw the $5.25 she earned in both piles of money. I circled it so you could see it. I think she had $24.25 because that's the rest of the money.

31.75 + 10 = 41.75
41.75 + 0.25 = 42.00
42 + 0.05 = 42.05

$42.05

TEACHER RESPONSE

When I saw this student pick up the play money from the manipulative table, I hoped that she wasn't taking the problem too literally, you know, by playing cashier. But as it turned out, that worked really well for her!

When I saw this student start with a number line, I wondered how he would use a number line when the starting quantity was unknown. I mean, where would you start? That didn't seem to trouble him at all. He started with what he had left and counted up the cost of the book.

VIDEO

Video 2.8

Andrea Earns Money With Play Money

resources.corwin.com/
problemsolving3-5

Video 2.9

John Spends Money With a Number Line

resources.corwin.com/
problemsolving3-5

DISTINGUISHING COMPUTATION, OPERATION, AND OPERATION SENSE The book-purchasing problem in Figure 2.19 is an Add-To problem situation that can be solved through subtraction or addition. So, let's look briefly again at a question we have discussed: How is it possible that the operation of the problem situation is not the same as the computational process students use to find a solution? We call those processes addition and subtraction, but for the purposes of discussion we need to distinguish between accurately modeling a problem situation and the process one would use to compute a solution. Remember our discussion in Chapter 1 about operation sense: Operation sense is not about getting an answer but, rather, about knowing what work the operation does in the problem. For this reason, we look at the situation to identify the work that is being done. In the case of Add-To problems, this means seeing the action of something coming into the situation. This is referred to more formally as "joining sets." That's addition, but it doesn't necessarily mean that students need to or even should compute the solution using addition. As we have seen throughout this chapter, whether subtraction or addition is used to compute the solution depends on how the equation is written. This is important and bears repeating. Determining the action or relationship between the quantities in the problem and deciding which problem situation best represents them is the first step of mathematizing the situation, another element of operation sense. *Identifying the problem situation type is separate and distinct from deciding which strategies to use to compute a final answer.*

The Power of Writing Stories

The story-writing strategy has been shown to be an effective strategy for students to make sense of the problem situations we are describing in this book. As a matter of fact, students who engaged in telling math stories much like the ones we describe here were far more successful at problem solving than students who learned a more general problem-solving approach. In one study, two groups of students were taught to "problem solve" in two different ways (Rudnitsky, Etheredge, Freeman, & Gilbert, 1995). One group learned something called *structure-plus-writing*, or writing math stories (in this case, *structure* refers to the problem situations we talk about in this book). The other group learned a problem-solving strategy that resembles the ones often introduced in mathematics textbooks, and included steps like "make a plan," "check your answer," and the like. Not only did students experience more problem-solving success after engaging in writing math stories than in following a problem-solving plan, but these results were also more enduring. Even months later, the story-writing students were more successful tackling word problems. Stories have meaning to students. They are valuable in the reading context, but they also have value in the mathematics classroom.

All of the problems in this chapter are about the action of a story with a beginning value (the start), a change in quantity (the change), and then an ending value (the result). In the next chapter we will explore problems that do not embody action but, instead, show a different kind of relationship.

KEY IDEAS

1. Addition and subtraction problems that reflect action are called Add-To and Take-From problem situations.

2. They follow a common structure in which there is a starting value (the beginning of the story), a change, and a result (the end of the story). Any one of the three parts of the problem may be the missing value.

3. The variations of Add-To and Take-From have a developmental sequence for proficiency in the Common Core State Standards learning progressions (McCallum et al., n.d.). Result Unknown problems are the most accessible, followed by Change Unknown. The Start Unknown variation is typically the most challenging for students.

4. Students should have experience with all problem situations at all grades, using the complexity of numbers determined by state standards for each grade.

5. An action problem situation can and should be retold in the student's own words. This "story" simplifies the details of the problem and focuses on the action.

6. When focusing on the meaning of word problems, students should focus on creating concrete or visual (often pictorial), verbal, and symbolic representations that closely match the action (or story) in the problem situation.

7. Students' understanding is also displayed through verbal and symbolic representations. To gauge, clarify, and extend student thinking, ask students to share the story in written or spoken form. Ask questions such as the following:

    *   Tell me the story in your own words.

    *   Try telling me the story without using any numbers.

    *   Show me how you're representing the quantities in this situation with your manipulatives or pictures.

    *   Is there action happening in this story? Where?

    *   What number sentence best shows what is happening in this story?

8. When students are experiencing challenges, try one of these strategies:

    *   Identify and pair up students who could assist each other or who have different approaches.

    *   Ask students to justify their thinking, both when their approaches are correct as well as when they are incorrect.

TRY IT OUT!

IDENTIFY THE PROBLEM SITUATION

Classify each of the following problems as an Add-To or Take-From situation. Which term is missing in each problem?

1. 20,136 fans arrived before the opening kickoff. Because of a traffic jam outside the stadium, another 5,433 arrived during the first half of the game. How many fans were in attendance at halftime? (You can assume that no one left the stadium.)

2. The farmer had 793 bales of hay stored for the winter. In December, the animals consumed 184 bales of hay. How many bales of hay remained for the rest of the winter?

3. The bakery earned $158.50 selling blueberry muffins. Their profit was $124.75 after they repaid the cost of the ingredients. How much did the ingredients cost?

4. Paulette was filling her car at the gas station. Before she filled the tank, the gas gauge read $\frac{3}{8}$ of a tank. After she filled the tank, the gauge read $\frac{7}{8}$ of a tank. How much gas did Paulette add to the gas tank?

WRITE THE PROBLEM

Write an Add-To or Take-From word problem represented by each of the following equations:

1. $2.5 + \alpha = 3.1$
2. $\alpha + 0.35 = 3.05$
3. $5\frac{8}{12} + \frac{11}{12} = \alpha$
4. $7\frac{5}{12} - \alpha = 4\frac{11}{12}$

BRANCH OUT

Numberless word problems are just as the name suggests: word problems without numbers getting in the way. This isn't a new idea, but Brian Bushart (n.d.) has updated the idea for today. Bushart's model starts with a typical word problem, strips the numbers from the problem, focuses on the relationships, and gradually adds numbers back in. Numberless word problems focus student attention on the story, the relationships, and the operations in the problem. Here is the basic process for creating and using numberless word problems:

1. Find any original problem. Without showing it to students, identify the number relationships and operations.

2. Show the problem to students with no numbers and with only one relationship.

(continued)

(continued)

3. Add one number to the problem.

4. Add a second number.

5. Reveal the original word problem.

Much of what Bushart is describing in this process is what we call mathematizing in the sandbox. The one suggestion we would add is to incorporate concrete or pictorial models into the process of the slow reveal of the problem. Select a problem from this chapter or from your textbook and try this approach with your students.

REFLECT

1. We are using the "story" analogy to help students understand the elements of a word problem. What other tools for teaching stories do you have in your English/Language Arts curriculum that you can use to support this thinking?

2. Most teachers find that the Start Unknown situation is the most challenging. What are some other strategies you can use to help students become familiar with that structure?

3. Look at the word problems in the textbook you currently use and identify 8–10 Add-To and Take-From problems. Sort them based on which term is missing: start, change, or result. Rewrite the problems to move the missing term. For example, Result Unknown problems could be rewritten as Start Unknown or Change Unknown problems.

NOTES

CHAPTER THREE

Part-Part-Whole
Understanding the Relationship

Thinking About Part-Part-Whole Situations

In Chapter 2 we explored active addition and subtraction problems and how finding the story, the placement of the unknown, and teaching students to model this using pictorial and physical representations is critical to developing strong operation sense. In this chapter we explore how students can use equations to represent what they see in a problem and how to model and understand a problem situation that is based not on action but on a relationship: the Part-Part-Whole problem situation. In the beginning of the chapter, we will pay special attention to the distinction between these two kinds of problem situations.

Addition and Subtraction Problem Situations

	Total Unknown	One Part Unknown	Both Parts Unknown
Part-Part-Whole	The 4th grade held a vote to decide where to go for the annual field trip. 32 students voted to go to the ice skating rink. 63 voted to go to the local park. How many students are in the 4th grade? $32 + 63 = x$ $x - 63 = 32$	The 4th grade held a vote to decide where the 95 students in the grade should go for their annual field trip. 32 students voted to go to the ice skating rink. The rest chose the local park. How many voted to go to the park? $32 + x = 95$ $x = 95 - 32$	The 4th grade held a vote to decide where the 95 students in the grade should go for their annual field trip. Some students voted to go to the ice skating rink and others voted to go to the local park. What are some possible combinations of votes? $x + y = 95$ $95 - x = y$

Note: These representations for the problem situations reflect our understanding based on a number of resources. These include the tables in the Common Core State Standards for mathematics (Common Core Standards Initiative, 2010), the problem situations as described in the Cognitively Guided Instruction research (Carpenter, Hiebert, & Moser, 1981), and other tools. See the Appendix and companion website for a more detailed summary of the documents that informed our development of this table.

ACTIVE SITUATIONS

	Result Unknown	Change Addend Unknown	Start Addend Unknown	
Add-To	Paulo counted out 75 crayons and put them in the basket. Then he found 23 more crayons under the table. He added them to the basket. How many crayons are now in the basket? $75 + 23 = x$ $23 = x - 75$	Paulo counted out 75 crayons and put them in the basket. Then he found some more crayons under the table. He added them to the basket and now there are 98 crayons in the basket. How many crayons were under the table? $75 + x = 98$ $x = 98 - 75$	Paulo was organizing the crayons at his table. He found 23 crayons under the table and added them to the basket. When he counted, there were 98 crayons in the basket. How many crayons were in the basket before Paulo looked under the table for crayons? $x + 23 = 98$ $98 - 23 = x$	
Take-From	There are 26 students in Mrs. Amadi's class. After lunch, 15 left to get ready to play in the band at the assembly. How many students are not in the band? $26 - 15 = x$ $26 = 15 + x$	There are 26 students in Mrs. Amadi's class. After the band students left the classroom for the assembly, there were 11 students still in the classroom. How many students are in the band? $26 - x = 11$ $x + 11 = 26$	After lunch, 15 band students left Mrs. Amadi's class to get ready to play in the assembly. There were 11 students still in the classroom. How many students are in Mrs. Amadi's class? $x - 15 = 11$ $15 + 11 = x$	

RELATIONSHIP (NONACTIVE) SITUATIONS

	Total Unknown	One Part Unknown	Both Parts Unknown
Part-Part-Whole	The 4th grade held a vote to decide where to go for the annual field trip. 32 students voted to go to the ice skating rink. 63 voted to go to the local park. How many students are in the 4th grade? $32 + 63 = x$ $x - 63 = 32$	The 4th grade held a vote to decide where the 95 students in the grade should go for their annual field trip. 32 students voted to go to the ice skating rink. The rest chose the local park. How many voted to go to the park? $32 + x = 95$ $x = 95 - 32$	The 4th grade held a vote to decide where the 95 students in the grade should go for their annual field trip. Some students voted to go to the ice skating rink and others voted to go to the local park. What are some possible combinations of votes? $x + y = 95$ $95 - x = y$
	Difference Unknown	**Greater Quantity Unknown**	**Lesser Quantity Unknown**
Additive Comparison	Jessie and Roberto both collect baseball cards. Roberto has 53 cards and Jessie has 71 cards. How many fewer cards does Roberto have than Jessie? $53 + x = 71$ $71 - 53 = x$	Jessie and Roberto both collect baseball cards. Roberto has 53 cards and Jessie has 18 more cards than Roberto. How many baseball cards does Jessie have? $53 + 18 = x$ $x - 18 = x$	Jessie and Roberto both collect baseball cards. Jessie has 71 cards and Roberto has 18 fewer cards than Jessie. How many baseball cards does Roberto have? $71 - 18 = x$ $x + 18 = 71$

online resources — Full chart available for download at **http://resources.corwin.com/problemsolving3-5**

Sandbox Notes

To recognize the difference between relationship situations and Take-From or action situations, be sure to fully enter the Explore phase of problem solving and bring in the physical mode of representation for problems (see Figure 3.3). Use the work space provided to show a solution for each of the problems. Try several physical manipulatives and some hand-drawn picture models or diagrams that reflect the story in the word problem, finding ways to show a relationship or action. Revisit your restatement and specify where you can see each quantity in the problem in the models you have created. Think about how your work expresses your understanding of the problem situation:

- *Think about the quantities in each situation. What do they represent? What work do they do?*

- *How can you represent the quantities in the word problems in your manipulatives or pictures?*

- *What number sentence best shows what is happening in each story?*

Remember, if you find yourself rushing to compute the answers right away, try rereading the problems without considering numbers and instead focus on the story.

The problems in Figures 3.1 and 3.2 highlight the difference between active problem situations and those that show a relationship. Keep this in mind as you formulate the problems in your own words. And, remember, your work here isn't to come up with an answer to the problems but to explore the problem situation by engaging in and thinking about multiple representations.

FIGURE 3.1   **FIGURE 3.2**

There are 26 students in Mrs. Amadi's class. 15 left to get ready to play in the band at the assembly. How many students remain in the classroom?	There are 26 students in Mrs. Amadi's class. 15 play in the concert band. The rest sing in the choir. How many are in the choir?

ENTER THE PROBLEM

FIGURE 3.3   A MODEL FOR MATHEMATIZING WORD PROBLEMS

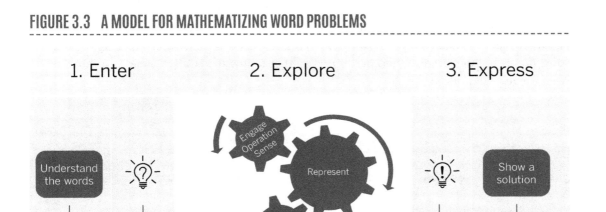

STUDENTS AND TEACHERS THINK ABOUT THE PROBLEMS

Now that you've had a chance to think about your own approach, look at the student work in Figures 3.4 and 3.5 and consider how the students described or drew what is happening in each word problem. Then read the teacher responses that follow the student work and think about what the teacher noticed.

FIGURE 3.4

STUDENT WORK

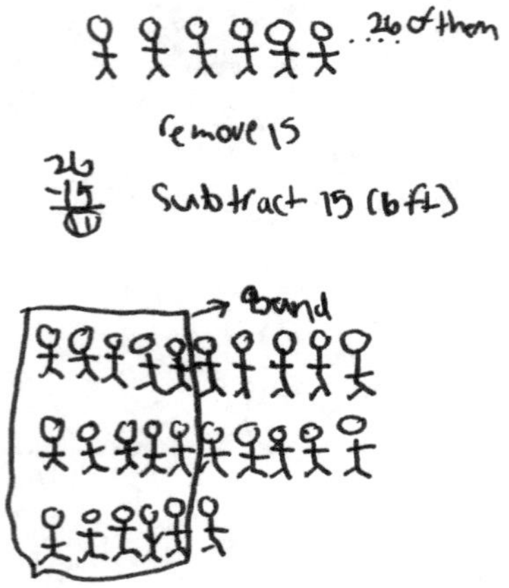

TEACHER RESPONSE

When I approached this student, I noted that he had not drawn all of the figures: he had drawn 6 figures and ellipses (. . .) to show that he meant more figures. I wanted to see more of his thinking so I asked him to draw it again and emphasized that I wanted to see a full model of his thinking.

The second model is much more complete. I was curious how he would show the students leaving the classroom. The loop and arrow are pretty effective!

VIDEO

Video 3.1

Leaving for Band Practice With Counters

resources.corwin.com/problemsolving3-5

FIGURE 3.5

STUDENT WORK

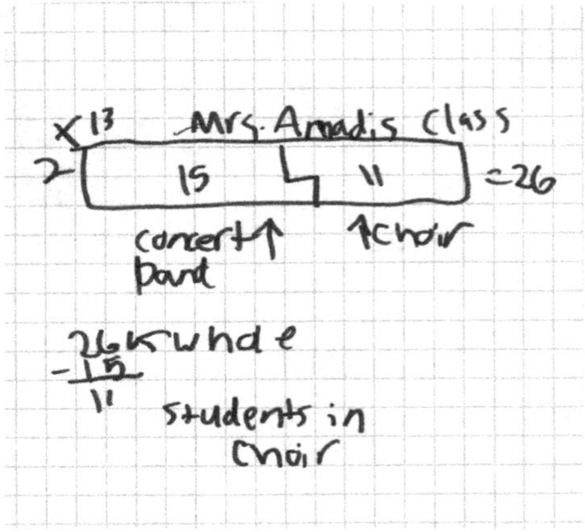

TEACHER RESPONSE

It's interesting to me that this student's drawing looks a little like an area or bar model, but the irregular line in the middle is a curious addition. It clearly shows two parts though.

VIDEO

Video 3.2

Dressing for Band and Choir With Counters

resources.corwin.com/problemsolving3-5

TAKE-AWAY ACTION Look back at your own work. How did you model the "take-away" action of students leaving the band room? Did you draw some kind of marks to show that motion? The work sample in Figure 3.4 captured that same kind of action in two ways, pictorially and verbally, by circling and pointing with an arrow, and using the word *left* to describe the action. (Unlike a key word in a problem, the student introduced this word into his solution.) The student work became even more clear after the teacher directed the student to elaborate on the model by drawing all 26 of the figures. As we saw in Chapter 2, this kind of problem is referred to as a Take-From problem situation, and it can be clearly modeled with pictures or manipulatives that display action and show a visible quantity removed.

PART-PART-WHOLE RELATIONSHIPS By contrast, the solution to the choir-band problem in Figure 3.5 shows 15 students in the concert band and 11 students in the choir, represented using 26 squares on graph paper. This is effective because it immediately shows that there are two groups of students. As with the take-away problem, the verbal representation is also important, clarifying that this is a description of a relationship and not the result of any action. Each group of students represents one *part* of the whole class. This problem situation is called Part-Part-Whole. Sometimes it's referred to as Put Together/Take Apart, which can cause confusion because it may suggest action where there isn't any. We prefer Part-Part-Whole because it emphasizes the relationship.

Part-Part-Whole: A problem situation that describes the relationship between subgroups (parts) and the entire collection (whole).

DEFINING THE PART-PART-WHOLE SITUATION

In this chapter we chose to contrast the Take-From and the Part-Part-Whole problem situations because this distinction is particularly challenging for students (and adults) to understand. For example, when we ask teachers to describe the differences between the two problems at the beginning of the chapter, they say things like this:

> *In the first one, something happened but in the second one nothing happened: the problem just described something.*
> *The first one is normal and, I can't describe it, but the second one is different. It's more complicated. The first one is very straightforward.*

Though teachers can tell there is something different about the choir-band problem in Figure 3.2, they struggle to find the words to describe it. Acting out problems using physical objects makes sense for modeling the band problem, but it just doesn't seem as effective with the choir-band type of problem. The choir-band problem is an example of a Part-Part-Whole problem, and it describes the relationship between the parts of the problem situation. It doesn't describe an action like the Take-From band problem does.

Before we explore how to model these relationships to improve student understanding, take a moment to consider some of the Part-Part-Whole situations that might be familiar to your students. Figure 3.6 lists some possible "wholes." What parts or subgroups might be included in them? Also listed are some examples of parts. What whole might include them? (Note that Part-Part-Whole problems can have an unlimited number of parts.) The figure includes some examples to get you started, and then there are rows of empty cells so that you can think up more examples to use with your students.

FIGURE 3.6 PART-PART-WHOLE SITUATIONS

WHOLE	PARTS OF THE WHOLE
Class	Boys, girls
The American flag	Red stripes, white stripes
Pets in the house	Dogs, cats, fish
Colors	
	Soccer, baseball, swimming

MODELING RELATIONSHIPS VERSUS ACTION

The images in Figures 3.7 and 3.8 are representations of the same problems we saw in Figures 3.1 and 3.2. Rather than using two samples of student work this time, we are demonstrating the difference between representations of the Take-From and Part-Part-Whole problem situations using images that are nearly identical. The two-color counters are particularly useful for this demonstration because they allow us to show the two different parts of the whole, in this case, the class of 26 students.

FIGURE 3.7   FIGURE 3.8

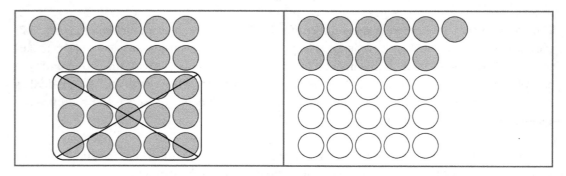

Watch the model of the Take-From band problem in Video 3.1. How does the video answer change or add to your interpretation of the student's representation and his response in general? Does the action in the video make you see the action in the problem differently than you see it in the illustration in Figure 3.4?

Video 3.2 shows the choir-band Part-Part-Whole problem from Figure 3.5, also using a set of two-color counters. The two-color counters are particularly effective for showing the difference between two parts of the whole class. Note that each video models what *happens* in the problem, not just the answer. If you are reading this with a group, now is a good time to stop and discuss, or simply reflect on your own if you're reading this independently: what is the difference between modeling an answer and modeling what happens in a problem?

IMPROVING THE ACCURACY OF STUDENT MODELS

As students begin to explore modeling subtraction and addition problem situations, it's important to encourage them to create models that represent problem situations as fully and as accurately as possible. Models are powerful learning tools, and seriously engaging with them will strengthen your students' understanding. In one study, researchers observed kindergarten students modeling problem situations that included not just addition and subtraction but also multiplication and division (Carpenter, Ansell, Franke, Fennema, & Weisbeck, 1993). The young students were able to do this because they directly represented exactly what happened in the problem story. The researchers didn't claim that these youngsters could write a matching equation or use the correct symbols in an equation, but they noted that the students could act out the story in the problem and arrive at an accurate quantity. We don't expect very young children to do this all the time, but the lesson is clear: in the beginning of learning an operation—in this case, subtraction or addition—we can monitor students' models of problem situations and encourage direct representation to build students' problem-solving capacity. Here are some things to look for and ask yourself:

1. If the problem situation is a Take-From, does the student re-create the take-from action either by actively removing an object, or, in pictures, crossing out objects, or in some other way by showing removal of the objects?

2. If the problem situation is a Part-Part-Whole, can you distinguish the attribute of one kind of object in the group from the others? Does the student use color, or shape, or another distinguishing attribute that allows you to see the relationship between one part and the other part(s) and the whole?

3. If you aren't sure what action or relationship the students are trying to model, ask them to describe their thinking. Ask for more details, just as the teacher in Figure 3.4 did. What other questions could you ask to gather this information?

Writing Equations: Addition or Subtraction?

The student work samples in Figures 3.4 and 3.5 include a subtraction equation (or calculation) to compute the answer. But, as we noted in Chapter 2, the operation used for computation does not define the problem situation. The Take-From problem and the Part-Part-Whole problem can be computed using subtraction or addition. Writing equations for Part-Part-Whole problem situations can be especially challenging because the problem situation describes a relationship between the parts and the whole, which does not match what most of us think about when using addition and subtraction symbols. This is likely because we have an intuitive model of subtraction as an operation associated with removal, and our intuitive model for addition is a joining action. But subtraction and addition can do so much more! To make matters even more interesting, a relationship problem situation can also be represented by equations with either addition or subtraction symbols. This is true because addition and subtraction are inverse operations, which generally means that one will "undo" the other. In active problems, an inverse operation shows that actions can be undone or reversed. In nonactive problem situations, the two operations are more likely to show multiple ways to describe the same situation.

As you read the Part-Part-Whole word problem in Figure 3.9, think about the equation that best represents the relationships in the problem. Again, do not rush to find an equation that would simply work to calculate an answer. Instead, start by focusing on the relationships in the problem and write one that would be the best illustration of these relationships.

FIGURE 3.9

Tyler's job was to empty all of the 95 trash and recycling bins at the amusement park. He emptied 63 trash cans. How many recycling bins are there at the amusement park?

Look at the models in Figures 3.10 and 3.11 and think about what equations might most closely match each student's interpretation of the problem situation. After studying the student work, read the teacher's comments and consider what is challenging the teacher's thinking.

FIGURE 3.10   FIGURE 3.11

STUDENT WORK		
	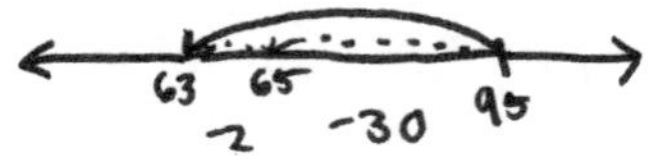	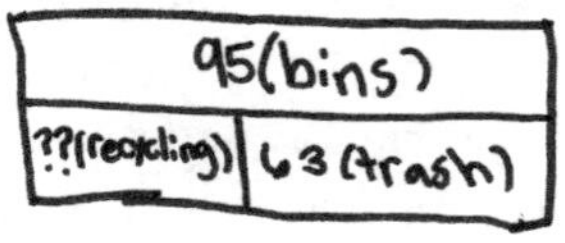 $$95 = x + 63$$
TEACHER RESPONSE	Mimi is particularly fond of open number lines. We learned them earlier this year, and now she uses them for nearly every problem. I believe that her open number line here reflects the trash and recycling problem, but I wonder how she would write the equation.	Since we started introducing Part-Part-Whole problems, Kelsey has started using the bar model to make sense of many different types of problems. Some of them don't make sense, but this one does. I particularly like how her equation expresses the relationship in the problem in nearly exactly the same way that her bar model does.

The bar model that Kelsey used (Figure 3.11) is a good fit for Part-Part-Whole situations because it visibly shows the relationship between the parts (the lower, partitioned bar) and the whole (the upper, full-length bar). It is particularly flexible because the bar can be partitioned into any number and size parts depending on the problem situation. Indeed, many instructional resources recommend bar models for any subtraction or any addition situation. But remember that our goal in this book is to maintain focus on using representations to show *what happens* in the problem situation, rather than on effective computation strategies. Since bar models do not show any kind of action, we suggest reserving them for Part-Part-Whole problem situations when the focus is on understanding context in word problems.

When students' intuitive model of subtraction is limited to "take-away," it limits their thinking. In reality, subtraction is also a good operation for representing the difference between two related quantities and the whole. In the case of the trash and recycling problem in Figure 3.9, subtraction shows the difference between the whole (number of bins) and one part (number of trash bins). To fully understand the relationship between addition and subtraction, and to model situations from the real world effectively, it is important that students be able to use both addition and subtraction equations to represent a variety of situations.

Often children will let the order in which the numbers are presented in the problem guide the structure of their equations. In this case, students would be more likely to present the 95 first, followed by the 63 trash bins, and then the rest. With this thinking, the equation would look like this:

$$\text{total bins} = \text{trash bins} + \text{recycling bins}$$
$$95 = 63 + x$$

Notice that the equation could also show that students are focused first on the two kinds of bins rather than on the total number of bins. For a student who sees the situation this way, this equation might make more sense:

$$\text{trash bins} + \text{recycling bins} = \text{total bins}$$
$$63 + x = 95$$

A student who writes the following equation is likely looking ahead to an efficient computational strategy, recognizing that an efficient way to calculate a One Part Unknown problem like this one is to subtract:

$$\text{total bins} - \text{trash bins} = \text{recycling bins}$$
$$95 - 63 = x$$

An open number line like the one in Figure 3.10 can also help students find an efficient computation strategy. After all, each of the preceding equations can be represented by the same number line, with only a change in the direction of an arrow indicating subtraction or addition. The key here is to match the equation to the problem, allowing the context—and the students' understanding of the context—to be the guide to what the equation should look like. Because this problem is a Part-Part-Whole, the bar model in Figure 3.11 captures the meaning of the problem situation better than the number line can.

At the beginning of this chapter we asked you to write the equation that you felt best represented the two problems in Figures 3.1 and 3.2. In the recycling-trash problem, we saw that the *best* equation might not be a single version. The *best* equation may vary from student to student, but the *best* equation should represent the student's understanding of the context. When students write equations, ask about the reasoning for their choices, whether they look accurate to you or not. Their reasoning may surprise you!

Moving Beyond Whole Numbers

One of the benefits of focusing on context and relationships in a word problem is that it provides everyone access to the problem at the outset, whether they have learned to calculate the numbers or not. Thus, students who haven't mastered the calculation of fractions or decimals can still take a problem into the mathematizing sandbox, find the story, and express it through different representations. In this section we explore problems involving fractions and decimals, which represent the new categories of numbers introduced in grades 3–5.

Warning: The next page includes student examples of these problem situations. If you find it difficult to resist looking forward while practicing in the sandbox, consider covering the facing page with a sheet of paper.

As you pause and enter the sandbox and look for models that closely represent the Part-Part-Whole problem situation, think about whether and how the introduction of fractions affects your exploration. For example, do the fractions in the problem context affect your choice of model: discrete, linear, or area?

Remember to revisit the Sandbox Notes earlier in the chapter for suggestions and guiding questions.

FIGURE 3.12   **FIGURE 3.13**

ENTER THE PROBLEM	Mixed packages of juice bottles are sold four to a pack at the grocery store. There are two types of juice: apple juice and grape juice. Mary has $3\frac{3}{4}$ packages of juice left in her refrigerator. $1\frac{1}{4}$ of a package is apple juice. How much grape juice is there?	Jorge has two pieces of licorice rope, which are $3\frac{3}{4}$ feet long in total. The red licorice is $1\frac{1}{4}$ feet long while the rest is black. How long is the rope of black licorice?
EXPLORE		

STUDENTS AND TEACHERS THINK ABOUT THE PROBLEMS

Sometimes student thinking surprises us because they think of things that we ourselves might never have thought of. The work samples shown in Figures 3.14 and 3.15 surprised the teacher who was reading them. Now that you've had a chance to solve this problem yourself, look at these solutions and the teacher responses and consider what is similar to your thinking and what is different.

One of the challenges with using fractions in Part-Part-Whole situations is that the word *whole* has more than one meaning. There is the *whole* of Part-Part-Whole—the total quantity when all the parts are combined—and the *whole* of the fractions—which is one unit partitioned to identify fractional parts. To simplify matters, when discussing fractions, we use the term *whole* with some kind of modifier to distinguish it from the *whole* in Part-Part-Whole. The problem in Figure 3.12, for example, shows that a "4-pack" becomes the **unit whole**. The fraction $\frac{1}{4}$ refers to one of four equal pieces of the unit whole: this relationship should be a key feature of any representation created to solve this problem. In Figure 3.13, the unit whole is one foot of licorice, represented by a length of one unit on the number line. In general, when focusing on the meaning of the problem, the choice of representation should reflect the details in the problem. In this case, the context-focused representation of the juice problem should show a package that contains four items. We see that in the student work in Figure 3.14. The more linear licorice is represented on a (linear) number line.

Unit whole: The whole that is partitioned into fractions and is the piece to which each fractional piece relates.

FIGURE 3.14   **FIGURE 3.15**

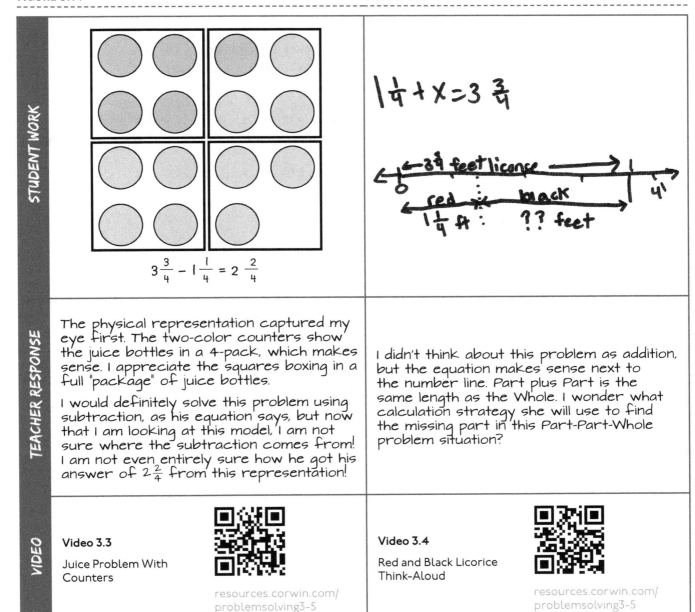

STUDENT WORK

$3\frac{3}{4} - 1\frac{1}{4} = 2\frac{2}{4}$

$1\frac{1}{4} + X = 3\frac{3}{4}$

3¾ feet licorice

red ⋮ black

1¼ ft ⋮ ?? feet

4'

TEACHER RESPONSE

The physical representation captured my eye first. The two-color counters show the juice bottles in a 4-pack, which makes sense. I appreciate the squares boxing in a full "package" of juice bottles.

I would definitely solve this problem using subtraction, as his equation says, but now that I am looking at this model, I am not sure where the subtraction comes from! I am not even entirely sure how he got his answer of 2¼ from this representation!

I didn't think about this problem as addition, but the equation makes sense next to the number line. Part plus Part is the same length as the Whole. I wonder what calculation strategy she will use to find the missing part in this Part-Part-Whole problem situation?

VIDEO

Video 3.3

Juice Problem With Counters

Video 3.4

Red and Black Licorice Think-Aloud

resources.corwin.com/ problemsolving3-5

resources.corwin.com/ problemsolving3-5

FINDING THE EQUATION IN THE MODEL

Equations, of course, are simply one form of representation, and as such there is value to writing equations so that they closely represent the problem situation. These may look different from equations whose sole purpose is to provide the most efficient path to calculating the answer. But both are useful.

The models in Figures 3.14 and 3.15 show a discrete and a linear model, respectively, both of which do a good job of reflecting the context of the word problem they represent. In both work samples, we see a quantity of four in the representations, in the form of four "packages." The work sample in Figure 3.14 uses color to identify the different juices, and the illustration in Figure 3.15 is labeled "red" and "black" for the colors of licorice. Similarly, since both problems are of the Part-Part-Whole variety, the color labels serve a dual purpose—they help us sort out the two parts of the problem context.

Now let's consider how the student whose work is shown in Figure 3.14 translated the physical model into an equation. In the absence of verbal cues, labels, or other forms of representation, we look to the equation here for insight into the student's thinking:

$$\text{all juice} - \text{grape juice (blue)} = \text{apple juice (gray)}$$

$$3\tfrac{3}{4} - 1\tfrac{1}{4} = x$$

This equation is an effective representation of the relationship between the whole collection of juice and the apple juice part. But let's consider the value of using another option, an addition equation, like this one:

$$\text{grape juice (blue)} + \text{apple juice (gray)} = \text{all juice}$$

$$1\tfrac{1}{4} + x = 3\tfrac{3}{4}$$

or even in this form:

$$\text{all juice} = \text{grape juice (blue)} + \text{apple juice (gray)}$$

$$3\tfrac{3}{4} = 1\tfrac{1}{4} + x$$

Such addition equations are described as having a *missing addend*. Rather than immediately translating this form into a subtraction equation, there are some calculation benefits to the missing addend approach. For example, it prompts a *counting-on* calculation strategy that can also reinforce standards related to adding fractions with like denominators, one that is typically found in most fourth-grade standards. The counting-on strategy encourages students to add up to "friendly numbers," or ones that involve easier calculations. Figure 3.16 shows how this might work in the licorice problem context, both in equation and in diagram form. You can see and hear this thinking in Video 3.3.

FIGURE 3.16 USING THE COUNTING-UP STRATEGY

red licorice + black licorice = all of the licorice

$$1\tfrac{1}{4} + x = 3\tfrac{3}{4}$$

$$1\tfrac{1}{4} + \tfrac{3}{4} = 2 \quad (\text{add}\ \tfrac{3}{4}\ \text{to get to}\ 2)$$

$$2 + \tfrac{4}{4} = 3 \quad (\text{add}\ \tfrac{4}{4}\ \text{to get to}\ 3)$$

$$3 + \tfrac{3}{4} = 3\tfrac{3}{4} \quad (\text{add}\ \tfrac{3}{4}\ \text{to get to}\ 3\tfrac{3}{4})$$

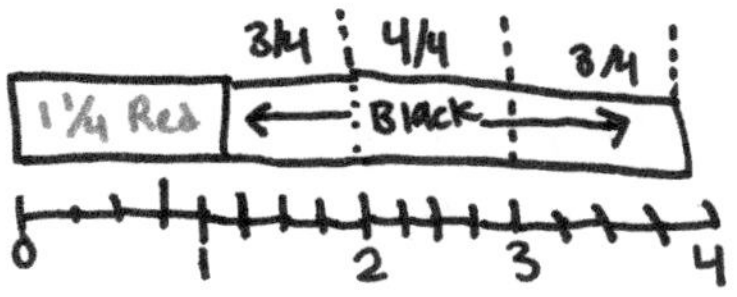

Up to grade 4, when grade-level standards typically specify adding with like denominators, it is entirely reasonable, often preferable, to add values represented as fourths and leave the solution as $\tfrac{10}{4}$ or $2\tfrac{2}{4}$ feet. Not only does this reemphasize that four of those fourths make one ($\tfrac{4}{4}=1$), but it also helps students connect their adding to counting on the $\tfrac{1}{4}$ tick marks of a number line representation.

Part-Part-Whole situations can be easily represented by either addition or subtraction equations. Since finding and describing the relationship between the parts and the whole with subtraction or addition does not match our most primitive ideas of what subtraction or addition are (primarily as a removal or a joining operation, respectively), either interpretation will challenge learners for different reasons. One benefit of representing the relationship as subtraction is that it sets up a calculation strategy that is familiar to many of us as teachers. But a benefit of an addition equation representation is that it gives students the opportunity to engage in counting-on calculation strategies, not just with fractions but also with friendly numbers in whole number problems as well. Either way, we emphasize again that addressing calculating strategies or computing an answer has little or no impact on students' understanding of the relationships expressed in the Part-Part-Whole problem situation. The calculation strategies make up a separate yet still important skill set.

MODELING MEASUREMENT PROBLEMS

Measurement is a natural setting for building student understanding of non-whole-number values. Rulers provide visual markers for identifying and naming the lengths or weights or volumes that measure between two whole numbers. For example, think about the representations you might choose to identify the values for the length of a tiger (Figure 3.17).

One of the challenges in the intermediate grades is in making sense of a variety of different models and tools for representing numbers. When learning to work with fractional values, students learn to coordinate the relationship between the numerator and the denominator while working with area or discrete models (fractions as a part/unit whole). By contrast, a number line encourages students to recognize a fraction as representing a single value with a unique point on the number line (fractions as numbers). These activities require different ways of thinking about a fraction, and both are important. While working with values written in decimal form, students can use their place value understandings and the additional models and tools to build on those understandings. However, as we discuss here, the approaches students use can influence their understanding of the problem situation and how that connects to the real-world context. Figures 3.18 and 3.19 illustrate how two students modeled the problem in Figure 3.17.

FIGURE 3.17

A female Siberian tiger is 2.53 meters long, from its nose to the tip of its tail. If the tail is 1.1 meters long, how long is the tiger's body?

FIGURE 3.18

STUDENT WORK

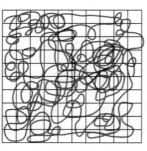 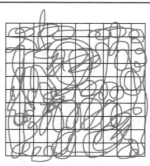 

2+1+0.53+0.1=3.63

The tiger is 3.63 meters long.

TEACHER RESPONSE

We started our decimal operations unit using 100-grids as a tool for understanding, so I am pleased to see this student using the grid.

She's got a good strategy for adding. She put all the ones, tenths, and hundredths together and added them up by place value just like we did in class. It took me a while to figure out how she got the wrong answer. I know that sometimes kids just add up the numbers they see, but I heard her talking about her 100-grids with her neighbor and she understood that the problem was about a tiger and her tail.

I wonder if the process of calculation somehow got in the way of really understanding the problem?

FIGURE 3.19

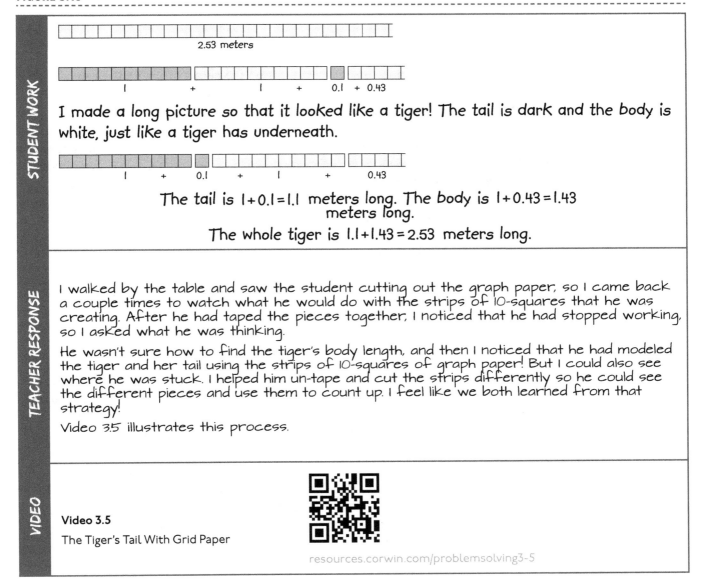

STUDENT WORK

2.53 meters

1 + 1 + 0.1 + 0.43

I made a long picture so that it looked like a tiger! The tail is dark and the body is white, just like a tiger has underneath.

1 + 0.1 + 1 + 0.43

The tail is 1+0.1=1.1 meters long. The body is 1+0.43=1.43 meters long.

The whole tiger is 1.1+1.43=2.53 meters long.

TEACHER RESPONSE

I walked by the table and saw the student cutting out the graph paper, so I came back a couple times to watch what he would do with the strips of 10-squares that he was creating. After he had taped the pieces together, I noticed that he had stopped working, so I asked what he was thinking.

He wasn't sure how to find the tiger's body length, and then I noticed that he had modeled the tiger and her tail using the strips of 10-squares of graph paper! But I could also see where he was stuck. I helped him un-tape and cut the strips differently so he could see the different pieces and use them to count up. I feel like we both learned from that strategy!

Video 3.5 illustrates this process.

VIDEO

Video 3.5

The Tiger's Tail With Grid Paper

resources.corwin.com/problemsolving3-5

Often we see measurement story problems in more active problems, representing situations where something is changing. It might be an Add-To, when a tree grows, or a Take-From, when a piece of something is cut away. But as we see in Figure 3.17, measurement problems can also be nonactive, making comparisons in the problem, describing a part of a whole, a tiger and the length of one its prominent features: its very long tail. Tigers are known for their exceptionally long tails, and trying to understand how long the tail is as part of the tiger's overall length is a naturally interesting real-world context for students. What we are striving for are models that most accurately reflect that context. As the student examples in Figures 3.18 and 3.19 reveal, it is possible to solve the problem using models with varying degrees of accuracy. Let's look at these two solutions and see what might be lost in focusing just on getting the answer.

Figure 3.18 is an example of a representation that matches a computational strategy but is less successful at matching the problem context. While the equation the student gives shows effective use of the properties of operations, it also unnaturally breaks up the lengths of the tiger and her tail into ones, tenths, and hundredths:

$$2\,(\text{tiger}) + 1\,(\text{tail}) + 0.53\,(\text{tiger}) + 0.1\,(\text{tail}) = 3.63$$

Perhaps it's no surprise that the student lost focus on the details of the problem situation too quickly before moving to do the calculation. But as the teacher noted, the student was aware of the problem situation, and we can see in the representation that the student had identified the tiger length and the tail length accurately. What we don't know is whether the student had a clear understanding that the tiger's tail is included in the length. This may be an error not necessarily related to a reading of the problem, but related to the challenge of the One Part Unknown version of the Part-Part-Whole situation in general. It may just be a matter of asking the student, "How long is the tiger?" and seeing how she addresses the fact that she has two answers: 2.53 meters in the problem and 3.63 meters in her answer.

In the One Part Unknown version, it may be helpful to focus students on the equation that represents the problem context. The student work in Figure 3.19, for example, does this effectively with the context equation that matches not only the student's own pictorial representation but also the problem context in general:

$$1.1 + x = 2.53$$
$$\text{tail length} + \text{body length} = \text{tiger's length}$$

The equation in turn shows the structure of the problem situation. While it's true that the student who modeled the tiger's length as an actual length had a greater challenge calculating his answer, it is also more likely that he understands and is working within the problem context. As noted earlier, for students who are just starting to focus on problem solving separately from computation, it is beneficial to intentionally match the problem type and the relationship in the problem to the representation used to find a solution. This supports students' operation sense as they learn to build meaning of the four major operations. The two student work samples in Figures 3.18 and 3.19 were done using the same common tool: graph paper. But only one student cut it into strips to mimic the length-measuring situation in the problem. Consider what tool you might make available to students to help them make sense of this problem situation.

THE SPECIAL CASE OF BOTH PARTS UNKNOWN

A Part-Part-Whole word problem typically has only one element unknown, either one of the parts or the whole, but the addition and subtraction problem types table at the beginning of the chapter also includes a fourth column labeled "Both Parts Unknown." A Part-Part-Whole problem with both parts unknown is less like the other varieties and more like an open-ended task: with any given whole (or sum), there are many combinations of parts possible. This task is not only a good problem-solving task, but it also provides good practice in organizing information and practicing calculation. It is not, however, typically useful for focusing on context. In the problems provided in Figure 3.20, we give suggestions for keeping the focus on the problem's context. In the early primary grades, teachers give students 10 two-color counters and ask them to pour out the counters and make as many combinations of 10 as they can find. Students in later grades can do a similar task with decimals, with one as the unit whole. Consider the examples in Figure 3.20 for grades 3–5.

FIGURE 3.20 STAYING FOCUSED ON A PROBLEM'S CONTENT: DECIMALS AND FRACTIONS

Decimals   Using $1.00 as the whole, challenge students to make combinations of money that make one dollar:

> You and your friend have $1.00 between you to share. You decide to buy chocolates and sour candies. Find 10 different ways you might spend $1.00 on chocolates and sour candies.

Choose one of the possible combinations and write a story telling why you spent your money that way.

Fractions: Using 1 as the unit whole, ask students to create combinations of fractions using the same denominator:

> You and a friend have decided to make a trail mix for a hike from raisins and peanuts. Raisins and peanuts are sold $\frac{1}{16}$ pound at a time. Find as many combinations of 1 pound of trail mix as possible.

Choose one of the possible combinations and write a story telling why you chose that trail mix combination.

KEY IDEAS

1. Part-Part-Whole problem situations are nonactive. There is no beginning or end of a story because no changes are taking place.

2. The Part-Part-Whole problem situation describes a relationship, rather than an action, between the parts and the whole.

3. A Part-Part-Whole situation can be represented by either an addition or a subtraction equation without changing the meaning of the problem.

4. Effective models and representations of Part-Part-Whole problem situations have an attribute that helps distinguish one "part" from another "part." This may be color, size, or pattern, or another discernible attribute.

5. The "whole" in Part-Part-Whole is not the same as the "whole" in the part/unit whole interpretation of a fraction.

6. Students don't need to focus on classifying problem situations, but one research team discovered that using simple language like "something happened" to describe active problems and "altogether" to describe Part-Part-Whole problem situations was helpful (Rudnitsky et al., 1995).

IDENTIFY THE PROBLEM SITUATION

Look at the following problems and decide which ones have action (Take-From or Add-To) and which ones are about relationships (Part-Part-Whole). Draw a picture or make a concrete model for each situation:

1. There were 571 fans at the concert. 250 of the fans were children and the rest were adults. How many adult fans were at the concert?

2. There are pennies and nickels in the piggy bank totaling $1.56. What are the possible values of pennies and nickels in the piggy bank?

3. There were 446 vehicles at the antique car show. After the 104 antique motorcycles were driven off, how many vehicles were left at the show?

4. The farmer sold $3\frac{1}{2}$ pounds of apples and $2\frac{1}{4}$ pounds of cherries at the market. How many pounds of fruit did the farmer sell?

5. There were 856 books donated for the used book sale. After 149 of them were sold, how many books were left in the sale?

WRITE THE PROBLEM

Create two word problems that could be represented and/or solved by each equation below. One word problem should be a Take-From situation and one should be a Part-Part-Whole situation.

1. $7\frac{1}{3} - 2\frac{1}{2} = x$

2. $12{,}462 - x = 8{,}548$

3. $x + 2.5 = 4.75$

4. $300 - 246 = x$

5. $1\frac{3}{4} + 2\frac{1}{2} = x$

6. $16.99 - 2.49 = x$

BRANCH OUT

In the book *This Plus That: Life's Little Equations*, the author cleverly uses equations to write stories about life (Rosenthal, 2011). Although there are no quantities in these equations, they still tell stories. Ask students to write their own equations, encouraging them to write equations with different elements missing. Here are some examples. $\alpha + \text{pool} = \text{summer}$ or $\alpha + \text{recess} = \text{loud}$, even Saturday afternoon $- \alpha = \text{fun}$.

REFLECT

1. In this chapter we emphasized the distinction between problem situations that include action and those that are about the relationship between quantities. What classroom routines can help your students notice this distinction in their everyday lives?

2. Part-Part-Whole situations where both addends are unknown are excellent opportunities to develop number sense as students compose and decompose numbers to make various combinations. What situations can you use in your classroom to extend this experience from the classic "ways to make 10" to experiences that include fraction and decimal values?

3. Using a copy of the Addition and Subtraction Problem Situations table from the beginning of this chapter, from the appendix, or from the companion website (http://resources.corwin.com/problemsolving3-5), search the textbook you use for addition and subtraction word problems. Classify each word problem you find as *active* or *nonactive*. If the problem is a nonactive Part-Part-Whole problem type, decide what is missing: one part, both parts, or the whole.

CHAPTER FOUR

Additive Comparisons
Another Kind of Relationship

Thinking About Additive Comparison Situations

In Chapter 3 we explored Part-Part-Whole problem situations and highlighted the difference between these problem types, which describe relationships, and those such as Add-To and Take-From that describe actions. Now we turn to Additive Comparison problems, which also describe relationships. Comparisons are the last of the addition and subtraction problem types.

Addition and Subtraction Problem Situations

	Difference Unknown	Greater Quantity Unknown	Lesser Quantity Unknown	
Additive Comparison	Jessie and Roberto both collect baseball cards. Roberto has 53 cards and Jessie has 71 cards. How many fewer cards does Roberto have than Jessie? $53 + x = 71$ $71 - 53 = x$	Jessie and Roberto both collect baseball cards. Roberto has 53 cards and Jessie has 18 more cards than Roberto. How many baseball cards does Jessie have? $53 + 18 = x$ $x - 18 = 53$	Jessie and Roberto both collect baseball cards. Jessie has 71 cards and Roberto has 18 fewer cards than Jessie. How many baseball cards does Roberto have? $71 - 18 = x$ $x + 18 = 71$	

ACTIVE SITUATIONS

	Result Unknown	Change Addend Unknown	Start Addend Unknown	
Add-To	Paulo counted out 75 crayons and put them in the basket. Then he found 23 more crayons under the table. He added them to the basket. How many crayons are now in the basket? $75 + 23 = x$ $23 = x - 75$	Paulo counted out 75 crayons and put them in the basket. Then he found some more crayons under the table. He added them to the basket and now there are 98 crayons in the basket. How many crayons were under the table? $75 + x = 98$ $x = 98 - 75$	Paulo was organizing the crayons at his table. He found 23 crayons under the table and added them to the basket. When he counted, there were 98 crayons in the basket. How many crayons were in the basket before Paulo looked under the table for crayons? $x + 23 = 98$ $98 - 23 = x$	
Take-From	There are 26 students in Mrs. Amadi's class. After lunch, 15 left to get ready to play in the band at the assembly. How many students are not in the band? $26 - 15 = x$ $26 = 15 + x$	There are 26 students in Mrs. Amadi's class. After the band students left the classroom for the assembly, there were 11 students still in the classroom. How many students are in the band? $26 - x = 11$ $x + 11 = 26$	After lunch, 15 band students left Mrs. Amadi's class to get ready to play in the assembly. There were 11 students still in the classroom. How many students are in Mrs. Amadi's class? $x - 15 = 11$ $15 + 11 = x$	

RELATIONSHIP (NONACTIVE) SITUATIONS

	Total Unknown	One Part Unknown		Both Parts Unknown
Part-Part-Whole	The 4th grade held a vote to decide where to go for the annual field trip. 32 students voted to go to the ice skating rink. 63 voted to go to the local park. How many students are in the 4th grade? $32 + 63 = x$ $x - 63 = 32$	The 4th grade held a vote to decide where the 95 students in the grade should go for their annual field trip. 32 students voted to go to the ice skating rink. The rest chose the local park. How many voted to go to the park? $32 + x = 95$ $x = 95 - 32$		The 4th grade held a vote to decide where the 95 students in the grade should go for their annual field trip. Some students voted to go to the ice skating rink and others voted to go to the local park. What are some possible combinations of votes? $x + y = 95$ $95 - x = y$

	Difference Unknown	Greater Quantity Unknown	Lesser Quantity Unknown	
Additive Comparison	Jessie and Roberto both collect baseball cards. Roberto has 53 cards and Jessie has 71 cards. How many fewer cards does Roberto have than Jessie? $53 + x = 71$ $71 - 53 = x$	Jessie and Roberto both collect baseball cards. Roberto has 53 cards and Jessie has 18 more cards than Roberto. How many baseball cards does Jessie have? $53 + 18 = x$ $x - 18 = 53$	Jessie and Roberto both collect baseball cards. Jessie has 71 cards and Roberto has 18 fewer cards than Jessie. How many baseball cards does Roberto have? $71 - 18 = x$ $x + 18 = 71$	

Note: These representations for the problem situations reflect our understanding based on a number of resources. These include the tables in the Common Core State Standards for mathematics (Common Core Standards Initiative, 2010), the problem situations as described in the Cognitively Guided Instruction research (Carpenter, Hiebert, & Moser, 1981), and other tools. See the Appendix and companion website for a more detailed summary of the documents that informed our development of this table.

online resources Full chart available for download at http://resources.corwin.com/problemsolving3-5

Sandbox Notes

As you enter the mathematizing sandbox (Figure 4.3) to model and solve these problems, make sure you have a number of manipulatives available. For each problem, try several of the physical manipulatives and some hand-drawn picture models with the goal of choosing one that most accurately represents each story to record in the workspace provided. Think about the features of the models you have chosen. What makes them a good choice?

Before moving on to the student work and teacher responses for these problems, take a moment to consider the similarities and differences between the two stories. Based on what you have learned so far about problem types, how might you categorize each of these problems? How are they similar to and different from the other problem types discussed in Chapters 2 and 3?

Again, here are the questions to guide your thinking:

- *Think about the quantities in each situation. What do they represent? What work do they do?*
- *How can you represent the quantities in the word problems with your manipulatives or pictures?*
- *What number sentence best shows what is happening in each story?*

As you read through the problems in Figures 4.1 and 4.2 and work to restate them in your own words, think about the relationships in the problems. How might your restatements help you clarify the nature of these relationships?

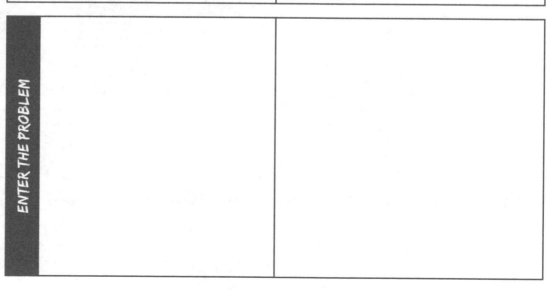

FIGURE 4.1

FIGURE 4.2

| Jessie and Roberto both collect baseball cards. Roberto has 53 cards and Jessie has 18 more cards than Roberto. How many baseball cards does Jessie have? | Lilliana has read 71 books so far this school year. She has read 18 nonfiction books, and the rest of her books are fiction. How many fiction books has she read? |

ENTER THE PROBLEM

FIGURE 4.3   A MODEL FOR MATHEMATIZING WORD PROBLEMS

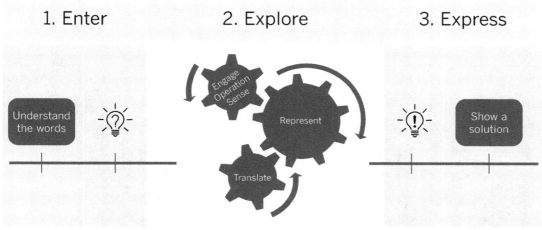

STUDENTS AND TEACHERS THINK ABOUT THE PROBLEMS

Take a look at the student work in Figures 4.4 and 4.5 and think about how the student representations are used to address the problem situations.

FIGURE 4.4   **FIGURE 4.5**

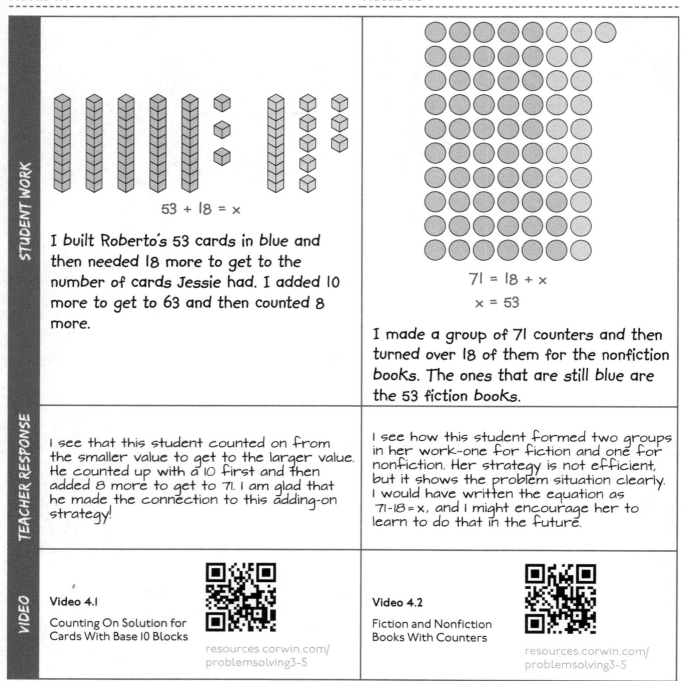

STUDENT WORK

$53 + 18 = x$

I built Roberto's 53 cards in blue and then needed 18 more to get to the number of cards Jessie had. I added 10 more to get to 63 and then counted 8 more.

$71 = 18 + x$

$x = 53$

I made a group of 71 counters and then turned over 18 of them for the nonfiction books. The ones that are still blue are the 53 fiction books.

TEACHER RESPONSE

I see that this student counted on from the smaller value to get to the larger value. He counted up with a 10 first and then added 8 more to get to 71. I am glad that he made the connection to this adding-on strategy!

I see how this student formed two groups in her work-one for fiction and one for nonfiction. Her strategy is not efficient, but it shows the problem situation clearly. I would have written the equation as $71 - 18 = x$, and I might encourage her to learn to do that in the future.

VIDEO

Video 4.1

Counting On Solution for Cards With Base 10 Blocks

resources.corwin.com/ problemsolving3-5

Video 4.2

Fiction and Nonfiction Books With Counters

resources.corwin.com/ problemsolving3-5

Let's start by considering the student representations. Without even thinking about the quantities or the stories in both problems, what is immediately apparent when you compare the representations? If you noticed that in Figure 4.4 there are two separate groups, while in Figure 4.5 there is a whole group comprising two parts, you would have identified the key difference between the two problem types. The book problem represents a Part-Part-Whole relationship, which is clear because the two parts (fiction and nonfiction books) are easy to see. The cards problem, however, represents a comparison problem, because it compares two separate quantities. The concrete use of base 10 blocks in two colors helps the student differentiate between how many cards Roberto has and how many Jessie has: The teacher's comment recognizes that the student has identified the lesser and greater quantities, reflecting the relationship that is always present in an **Additive Comparison** relationship. You can see and hear solutions to these problems in Videos 4.1 and 4.2.

Pause for a moment to think about situations in which your students would encounter Additive Comparison problems. What quantities might they compare? What kinds of questions might they pose and answer? Figure 4.6 provides space for you to list potential Additive Comparison situations in the first column and possible difference and quantity combinations to match the situations. We have listed a few to get you started, but then think about and add more problem contexts that you could use with your students.

> Additive Comparison: A problem situation that describes the absolute difference in value between two quantities.

FIGURE 4.6 ADDITIVE COMPARISON SITUATIONS

CONTEXT	LESSER QUANTITY	DIFFERENCE	GREATER QUANTITY
Weight of pets	17 pounds	5 pounds	x
Baking temperature	325° F	x	350° F
Snowfall	x	3.1 inches	12.6 inches
Money saved			
Pounds of recycling collected			
Length of inchworm			

LANGUAGE CAN GET TRICKY

As with each of the problem situations we have examined so far, there are variations of Additive Comparison problems based on which of the three terms is unknown in the given problem. In Figure 4.6, the unknown terms are referred to as *lesser, greater,* and *difference,* but you will commonly see the terms *smaller* and *bigger* (or sometimes *higher* and *lower*) used in word problems as well. *Smaller* and *bigger* (and *higher* and *lower*) refer to physical attributes, but since *lesser* and *greater* describe a quantity we will use these terms whenever possible. Where these unknowns fall and how they are expressed in the language of the problem can greatly affect students' understanding. Consider another variation of the baseball card problem: *Jessie and Roberto both collect baseball cards. Roberto has 53 cards, 18 fewer than Jessie. How many baseball cards does Jessie have?* Does this new version seem more difficult or less difficult than the original problem in Figure 4.1?

For many students, a problem may be more challenging because of the language used to present the situation (de Koning, Boonen, & van der Schoot, 2017). For example, the word *less* in a word problem might indicate subtraction to students who are taught to use key words as clues. Students may also write equations based on the order in which information is shared (De Corte & Verschaffel, 1987). If you combine both the word *less* and the tendency to write equations relying on the order in which the numbers appear in the problem, it is nearly guaranteed that some students will generate the following equation: $53 - 18 = x$. Because 53 is the first number given in the problem above, and 18 is the second, followed by the word *fewer*, students are likely to create an incorrect equation. Have you observed students rushing to create an equation like this one and for these reasons?

Instead of jumping to quick conclusions, let's think about the problem in terms of operation sense rather than key words, focusing on the relationships expressed in the words—"more than" or "greater than" and "less than" or "fewer than"—rather than on key words. As we have noted throughout this book, by engaging in exploration and modeling a problem situation, students can develop a sense of what is actually happening in a problem. Although many representations can be used to effectively express the Additive Comparison problem situation, bar models are particularly useful in highlighting the relationships in these problems. Figure 4.7 illustrates how a bar model would be used.

FIGURE 4.7 USING A BAR MODEL

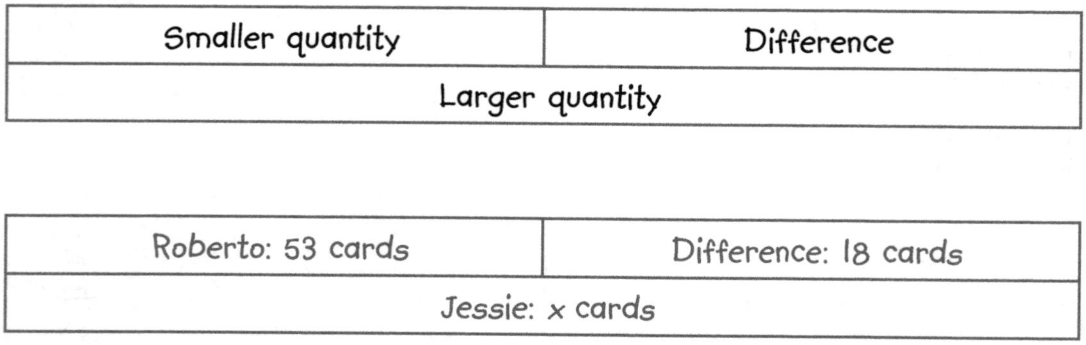

Smaller quantity	Difference
Larger quantity	

Roberto: 53 cards	Difference: 18 cards
Jessie: x cards	

Displaying quantities in a bar model offers a visual structure that makes it easier for students to see that the difference (18 cards) combined with the smaller quantity (53 cards) makes the larger quantity (x cards). In this way the bar model offers a structure that supports thinking about the mathematical relationships within the context of the story. The structure also helps clarify a problem situation, even if the way we say it in English might make it harder to understand. For example, we say, "18 less than 71," but mathematically this is written as 71 − 18. Have you ever noticed that in this type of problem, the two numbers (in this case, 18 and 71) change places in the English sentence compared to the math sentence? This is a pretty common use of language in word problems. Overall the language challenge is one of the difficulties of Additive Comparison problems, and it illustrates a risk of relying on key word strategies for helping students to solve word problems: Sometimes they simply don't work, and sometimes key word strategies are downright deceptive. Focusing on the relationships in the problem situation sidesteps the language complications and instead focuses on meaning.

It is important for students to see Additive Comparison problems written in a variety of ways. Straightforward language such as the wording used in the original version of the baseball card problem (Figure 4.1) might be considered "friendly language" because the phrase "more than" is included in the problem and it matches the action of adding two quantities. More complex language, as in the rewrite represented in Figure 4.7, might be considered "less-friendly language." These are the problems many students find tricky, but it's important to include both friendly and less-friendly versions of problems in your lessons. Recognize that most standards call for mastery of the friendly version in first grade and the less-friendly version in second grade (McCallum, Daro, & Zimba, n.d.). You might expect that your students would master them in a similar order using the calculations appropriate to their grade level. With experience, students can learn to focus on what these expressions mean and apply a structure like the bar model to support their thinking.

As Figure 4.8 illustrates, using both "more than" and "less than" language means that students might see as many as six possible word problems derived from a single relationship. The figure offers another Additive Comparison problem, first sharing an example of the potentially tricky "less than" language. Use the blank spaces to write the other versions students might encounter based on the same story.

FIGURE 4.8 PRACTICE WITH THE LANGUAGE OF ADDITIVE COMPARISON PROBLEMS

	"More than" language	"Less than" language
Greater Quantity Unknown		Frank's dog weighs 17 pounds. That is 5 pounds less than Scott's dog. How much does Scott's dog weigh?
Lesser Quantity Unknown		
Difference Unknown	Scott's dog weighs more that Frank's dog. Frank's dog weighs 17 pounds and Scott's dog weighs 22 pounds. How much more than Frank's dog does Scott's dog weigh?	

Once you have crafted these variations, talk with your colleagues about how your students might respond to them. Which ones will your students consider most straightforward? Which are likely to be more challenging? You may decide to ask your students to rewrite a problem using "less than" rather than "more than" to express the same relationship, as we did here. Or you may speak directly to students about the use of language in "less than" word problems. What support will *your* students need to recognize related problems and represent them accurately?

BUILDING MODELS FOR COMPARISONS

In the second of the two problems in Figures 4.9 and 4.10, we revisit the comparison words in a problem situation related to measurement (short*er*, long*er*, bigg*er*, etc.) and ask students to find "how much bigger?" Compare this with the problem in Figure 4.8, which asks, "how many," because it refers to a quantity of discrete objects. As you read, think of tools student might use in the mathematizing sandbox to make sense of these problems.

FIGURE 4.9

In one minute, Gretchen completed 34 jumping jacks, 5 more than Melinda. How many jumping jacks did Melinda complete?

FIGURE 4.10

Rahul and Sandy measured their height in centimeters. Rahul is 142 cm tall and Sandy is 131 cm tall. How much shorter is Sandy than Rahul?

What do you see when you look at the student work models in Figures 4.11 and 4.12? Ask yourself: Have the students made the Additive Comparison elements (lesser quantity, greater quantity, difference) and their relationship evident in their representations?

FIGURE 4.11

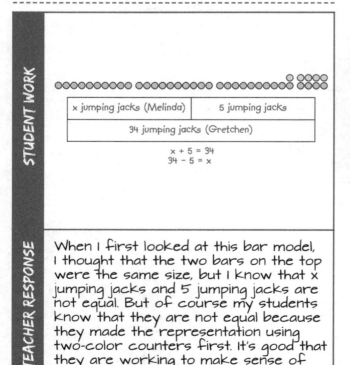

STUDENT WORK

x jumping jacks (Melinda)	5 jumping jacks
34 jumping jacks (Gretchen)	

$$x + 5 = 34$$
$$34 - 5 = x$$

TEACHER RESPONSE

When I first looked at this bar model, I thought that the two bars on the top were the same size, but I know that x jumping jacks and 5 jumping jacks are not equal. But of course my students know that they are not equal because they made the representation using two-color counters first. It's good that they are working to make sense of the problem first.

FIGURE 4.12

STUDENT WORK

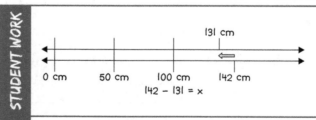

$$142 - 131 = x$$

TEACHER RESPONSE

I was happy that so many of my students wanted to get out tape measures and meter sticks to measure their own height. When I set up this problem, I intentionally used students' names so that the problem would engage them. It turns out that the exact numbers I used for Sandy and Rahul were different from their actual height but that didn't matter. The connection to their own height measurement really helped them create meaningful models. This double number line model was a collaborative effort. I appreciate that it shows the difference and a directional arrow that shows why they wrote a subtraction equation.

As the teacher's response indicates, the bar model in Figure 4.11 is not drawn proportionally. For some students, these models may be more useful if they are drawn more proportionally, as shown in Figure 4.13. Because operation sense is about the relationships themselves, not the computation, a physical model like two-color counters will show the relationship in either case. A more proportional form of the bar model may be more helpful for keeping track of the relative sizes. In a proportional bar model, the bars for the difference and the smaller quantity are not necessarily equal but, instead, show their relative sizes. In this case the bar for 5 jumping jacks is approximately $\frac{1}{7}$ the size of the larger quantity. In general, when students use the bar model, we want them to recognize that the smaller quantity plus the difference is the same as (is equal to) the larger quantity. (Note that the student in this case also recognized the subtraction version of this relationship: $34 - 5 = x$.)

FIGURE 4.13

lesser quantity + difference = greater quantity

$$x + 5 = 34$$

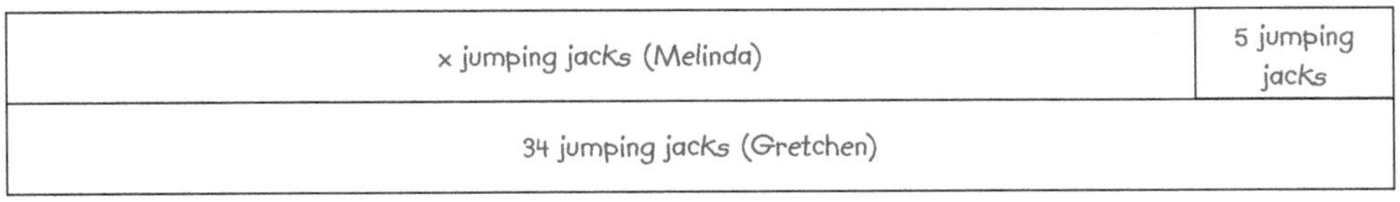

x jumping jacks (Melinda)	5 jumping jacks
34 jumping jacks (Gretchen)	

The double number line in Figure 4.12 is a diagram that is closer to proportional. Not only can we see the difference between Rahul's and Sandy's heights, but we can also see that, compared to their overall heights, the difference isn't all that much. The directional arrow serves as a reminder that the larger quantity minus the smaller quantity is equal to the difference between Rahul's and Sandy's heights. The representation this student has chosen shows clearly how the term *difference* can make sense as the solution to a subtraction problem:

larger quantity – smaller quantity = difference

$$142\,cm - 131\,cm = 9\,cm$$

Both of these examples use representations that clearly show the relationships within additive comparisons. By focusing on the relative size of the two quantities, students are able to see the relationship and their computation options without becoming caught up in the specific language of the problem, whether friendly or unfriendly. Both the bar model (Figure 4.11) and the double number line (Figure 4.12) show the difference filling the gap between the smaller and larger quantities.

If you are reading this book with colleagues, now would be a good time to try out the bar model on another problem. Use the dog weight problem presented in Figure 4.8. Start with the basic structure of two bars on top and a single bar below. The longer bar below will always represent the greater quantity. The upper bar is a little more flexible. But, adhering to the reading convention of reading from left to right, we present our model with the lesser quantity aligned to the left. The difference fills the empty space that remains. Note that in the general model in Figure 4.14, the two upper bars are equal. This is a good goal for a general problem structure, but while students are working on more and different problems you may ask them to focus on some degree of proportionality. Modeling for the purpose of mathematizing a problem situation is not a place for precision in measurement, but reasonable estimates should be encouraged. Understanding the structure of the comparison problem situation is more important when learning this model. Use the blank bars in Figure 4.15 for your work.

FIGURE 4.14

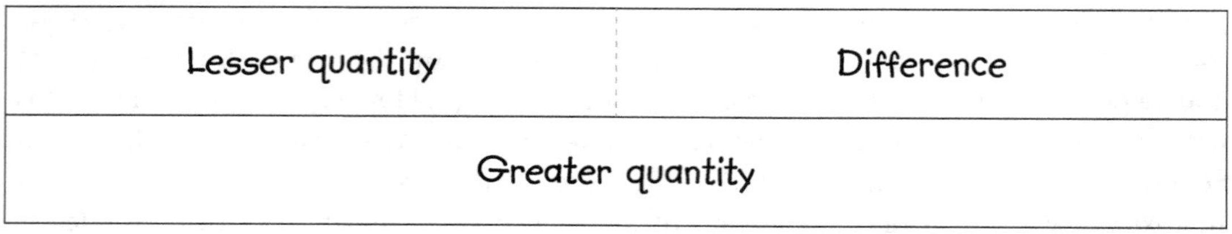

Lesser quantity	Difference
Greater quantity	

FIGURE 4.15

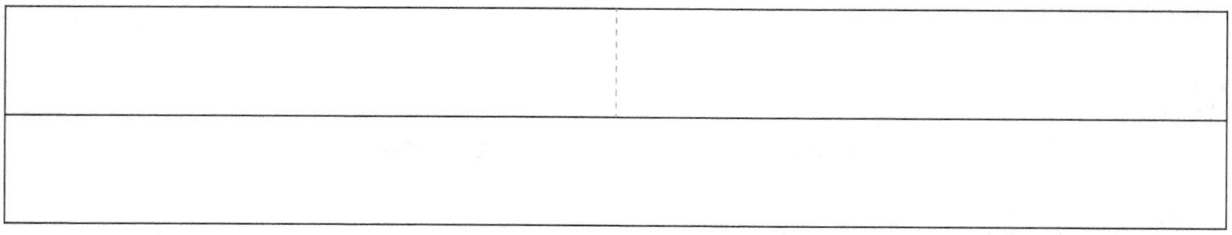

How can this structure help your students consistently see the mathematical relationships in Additive Comparison problems?

KNOWING WHEN TO ADD AND WHEN TO SUBTRACT

As we noted in Chapters 2 and 3, addition and subtraction are inverse operations, which generally means that one will "undo" the other. In active problems, an inverse operation shows that actions can be undone or reversed. In nonactive problem situations, the two operations are more likely to show multiple ways to describe the same situation. Writing different versions of a comparison word problem can help students understand this inverse relationship.

Earlier we showed how the information in the baseball card problem could be organized in a bar model (Figure 4.7). Figure 4.16 includes four versions of the same relationship, each expressing the relationship between the quantities with a different word problem, or with a different unknown, or using a different comparative word (for example, *less, more*). Despite all of these differences, the relationship remains the same as in the bar model discussed previously. Mathematically, each equation is a valid representation of each of the word problems because the underlying structure of the word problem consists of the relationship between the number of baseball cards Roberto and Jessie each have. However, some equations better match the language of the word problem or the question the problem is asking.

The example word problem in the matching exercise in Figure 4.16 matches the equation opposite it. The rest are mixed. Connect the word problem to the equation that best matches it in the opposite column. There will be one equation left at the end. For that one, you can craft your own word problem to match it.

All of these equations reflect the relationships among the smaller quantity, larger quantity, and difference. By isolating different variables, each equation shows a different perspective on the relationship. Once these relationships are clear, students can use them to work through any Additive Comparison problem, no matter how complex the language. As long as students can identify the three elements and the relationships among them, they can write an accurate equation and solve the problem.

FIGURE 4.16 MATCHING WORD PROBLEMS TO THE EQUATIONS THAT FIT BEST

Example	Roberto has 53 cards and Jessie has 18 more cards than Roberto has. How many baseball cards does Jessie have?		$53 + 18 = x$ (smaller + difference = larger)
1.	Jessie has 71 cards and Roberto has 53 cards. How many fewer cards does Roberto have than Jessie?	a.	$71 = x + 18$ (larger = smaller + difference)
2.	Roberto has 53 cards. That is 18 cards fewer than Jessie has. How many cards does Jessie have?	b.	$71 - 53 = x$ (larger − smaller = difference)
3.	Jessie has 71 cards. Roberto has cards, too, but Jessie has 18 more than Roberto. How many baseball cards does Roberto have?	c.	$53 = x - 18$ (smaller = larger − difference)
4.		d.	$x + 18 = 71$ (smaller + difference = larger)

A Note About Equations

Generating equations is not a natural outcome of recognizing relationships within a problem situation. When students do write equations, they may initially produce equations that exactly match the action in the problem. This is completely reasonable and acceptable, except in cases where it conflicts with the "typical" equation that a teacher expects to see. For example, in Figure 4.5, the equation that best matched the student's thinking is $71 = 18 + x$. The student recognizes the 71 total books, identifies the 18 that are nonfiction, and notes that the rest are fiction ($x = 53$). From a contextual point of view, this equation is ideal. But notice the teacher's comment that follows. She is uncomfortable with this version of the equation and would like the student to learn another, more standard, version, which is $71 - 18 = x$.

Why do we, as teachers, expect the subtraction version? Perhaps it's because we have experience in algebra, where solving this equation requires solving for x. Maybe it is because we recognize right away that this problem can be interpreted as a difference and think that it has to be a subtraction problem. Maybe you didn't even have the uncomfortable feeling that this teacher did. In essence, this is the point. As long as we recognize that a simple situation like this one can be represented by at least four different varieties of equation, we can be aware that there is more than one choice. Because we are focused on context in this book, our preference is to target the equations that best match the context of the problem, but we recognize that flexibility is always important. Furthermore, as students learn to work with the abstract symbols, we can expect that their understanding of symbols such as variables, operators ($+$, $-$, $\times$, $\div$), and the equals sign will vary from the mature adult version (Gutstein & Romberg, 1995), similar to the way students' understanding of punctuation needs time to mature. The best strategy is to focus on students' understanding of the equation within the context of their work. Make sure that the equations they write reflect what *they* think they are saying and build to more formal versions over time.

Warning: The next page includes student examples of these problem situations. If you find it difficult to resist looking forward while practicing in the sandbox, consider covering the facing page with a sheet of paper.

Moving Beyond Whole Numbers

Most of this chapter explores the relationships contained in Additive Comparison problems using structures like a bar model to highlight these relationships. In this section, as we move into problems involving fractions and decimals, we consider strategies that students can learn in order to model their understanding of additive comparisons and open up problems to find solutions.

Before we do, take the two Additive Comparison problems in Figures 4.17 and 4.18 into the mathematizing sandbox by trying out different physical and pictorial models. As you restate the problems and then engage in your explorations in the work space provided, consider this question: What is similar between the two problems, and what is different?

FIGURE 4.17

FIGURE 4.18

ENTER THE PROBLEM	Kevin earned $93.50 mowing lawns one weekend. Chris earned $35 more than Kevin. How much did Chris earn that weekend?	Aisha sold $128.50 in strawberries at the farmer's market. She also sold asparagus and earned $35 less. How much did Aisha earn selling asparagus?
EXPLORE		

STUDENTS AND TEACHERS THINK ABOUT THE PROBLEMS

How does the student work in Figures 4.19 and 4.20 compare to your own solution strategies?

FIGURE 4.19 **FIGURE 4.20**

STUDENT WORK	+$35 $93.50 $128.50 Kevin Chris Right away I knew that Kevin made $93.50. I also knew that the difference between them was $35, but I wasn't sure who made more money. Then we talked about it at my table and I knew how to do it. $93.50 + 35 = x$	asparagus $ | $35 Strawberries $128.50 I was sure that Aisha sold less $$$ in asparagus, but I didn't know what else to do. Then I thought about the bar model and then I knew what to do. $128.50 - x = 35$
TEACHER RESPONSE	The kids are responding well to this open number line strategy. They identify one value and then use their understanding of the problem to go either up or down.	I see how this student organized her thinking with the bar model. She figured out right away that less money was made on asparagus and the bar model scaffolded her thinking to find the rest.
VIDEO	**Video 4.3** Money Earned Mowing With a Number Line resources.corwin.com/ problemsolving3-5	**Video 4.4** Money Earned at the Market With a Bar Model resources.corwin.com/ problemsolving3-5

THE ANCHOR-JUMP STRATEGY AND BAR MODELS

The solution shown in Figure 4.19 draws on a strategy we have yet to discuss, although we saw it demonstrated: the **Anchor-Jump strategy**. Before this strategy can be employed, students must identify the three essential elements:

$$\text{smaller quantity} + \text{difference} = \text{larger quantity}$$
$$93.50 + 35 = x$$

Anchor-Jump strategy: A problem-solving strategy in which you identify one quantity in the problem situation, mark (anchor) it, and then move back or forward (jump) to the other quantity.

The open number line visual is effective because it allows students to focus on one quantity in the problem situation first. First *anchor* one value. In Figure 4.19, the problem is anchored on $93.50 (Kevin's earnings), so it is the first point placed on the open number line. Next, students reason about whether the comparing quantity is greater than or less than the first one. The next sentence in the problem reveals the next move: Chris made more, so the difference of $35 *jumps* to a higher value. Once the anchor point and the jump are labeled, the relationship is now translated into a visual form that students can use as a model for thinking about the comparison. The student can make decisions about the best calculation strategy using the open number line as a source of information. Video 4.3 shows this thinking in action.

Like the Anchor-Jump strategy, a bar model begins with labeling and categorizing the known quantities in the problem. Figure 4.20 and Video 4.4 demonstrate this strategy, which we also touched on earlier in the chapter. Although the student seems to have chosen to start with the quantity of asparagus sales and then moved to the rest, what's important is that the relationships among the quantities reflect the problem situation.

Both of these comparison problems—like all comparison problems—follow the same basic structure, which includes two different values and the difference between them. The bar model and the Anchor-Jump strategy help students focus on the relationships between the quantities in the problem and gives them a structure to organize their understandings, which helps them make sense of the language in the problems.

MODELING THE DIFFERENCE IN COMPARISON SITUATIONS

Difference, one of the three quantities of all Additive Comparison problems, can sometimes be challenging to model and visualize. Let's look at the two problems in Figures 4.21 and 4.22 to consider how. First, as you read the problems consider what is similar between the two problems and what is different. How would you represent the difference in each? Then look at the representations included in the sample solutions in Figures 4.23 and 4.24.

FIGURE 4.21   **FIGURE 4.22**

| The soccer (futbal) coach had $2\frac{3}{4}$ pounds of green grapes for snacks after practice. He also had $1\frac{1}{4}$ pounds of red grapes. How many more pounds of the grapes are green? | After today's practice, the team drank $1\frac{1}{4}$ gallons of water. That is $1\frac{1}{2}$ gallons less than they drank on the hottest day of the season. How much did the team drink on the hottest day? |

FIGURE 4.23   **FIGURE 4.24**

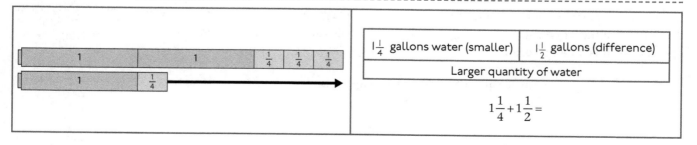

First a note on fraction bars. The benefits of building a model using a set of objects like fraction bars is that students can visualize the actual quantity difference between the smaller and the larger quantities. Because such models represent specific quantities, they are by definition proportional, unlike the more abstract diagrams in bar models and open number lines. Of course, because color is used to indicate the value of each piece, it then can't be used also to distinguish the elements of the problem (smaller quantity, difference, larger quantity) as was done with two colors of base 10 blocks in Figure 4.4 or using the two-color counters in Figure 4.5. Students will have to find other ways to highlight the different elements of the problem.

But for now, let's consider how the single element of difference can be modeled. Perhaps you noticed in Figure 4.23 that the difference was not represented as a stand-alone quantity with its own set of fraction blocks but by an arrow. One of the reasons comparisons can be challenging is because the difference between the two quantities being compared can only be imagined—the difference doesn't exist as a physical object. For example, you can also see it in the drawing of the two children in Figure 4.25. The line shows that the difference between their two heights is measurable, yet the difference is not part of the shorter child, nor is it part of the taller child. It is the gap between the two quantities.

FIGURE 4.25 DIFFERENCE: AN IMAGINARY QUANTITY

Source: MicrovOne/iStock.com

When modeling comparison problems, filling, counting, and measuring this space can be difficult. This problem points to the benefits of having students engage in multiple representations. The bar model in Figure 4.24, by contrast, focuses on relationships among the quantities named in the problem, which does not treat the difference as an imaginary quantity. The bar model instead helps build a conceptual understanding of the underlying problem structure. Think about how powerful these models are together!

When we make instructional decisions on providing access to manipulatives and structural models, we are also obligated to make sure that students have a variety of experiences and can make these decisions based on their own understandings. When students are encouraged to create representations that reflect their own thinking about a comparison relationship, the potential for great variety in the classroom increases. In this chapter alone we have seen an extensive collection of concrete models, pictorial models, and mathematical structures that not only can help students make sense of problem situations but also can spark discussion and productive mathematical discourse as students make sense of each other's models. The result is a more engaging and productive classroom environment.

Problem Posing as an Instructional Strategy

As educators we often ask students to solve word problems. When we do this, we are asking them to make sense of a context that someone else presents to them. We may also focus their attention on real-life situations, and sometimes focusing on imaginative situations can achieve the same goal. A group of educators noted how often we pose problems to students but wondered what would happen if the students posed the problems themselves (English, 1998).

Some notable results to this experiment can help you gain perspective on students' problem-solving mindset. Despite the formal instruction, most of the problem types the students generated were one-step problems, primarily missing the whole or total value. This means that if they wrote an Add-To problem, the result was overwhelmingly the unknown. If they wrote a Part-Part-Whole problem, the whole was mostly the unknown. When the students were asked to write "harder" problems, they made problems that included more steps. In other words, they created multistep problems that followed the same pattern as their one-step problems. What the students did *not* do was create problems with more relationships between elements of the problem. This is exactly the kind of thinking that Additive Comparison problems ask students to do—to set up relationships between different elements.

Interestingly, the second most useful tidbit from this study is that there is one strategy that most inspired students to think about and write their own problems: reading picture books. So, here is an idea to try. Read a book, any book that you and your students enjoy, and engage students in problem posing. Ask them to write word problems based on the story. Start with Add-To, Take-From, and Part-Part-Whole problems, but also focus their attention on Additive Comparison problems. For example, challenge them to make Additive Comparison problems based on the characters, plot, and setting of the story, even making up specific quantities if the book does not include them. Focus on the relationships between the quantities. This is also a great way to practice estimating and measuring.

KEY IDEAS

1. Abstract models (or diagrams) of Additive Comparison problems can be proportional or nonproportional, and there are advantages and disadvantages for each type of model.

2. Comparisons are a nonactive problem situation. They describe a relationship, not an action.

3. The language in an Additive Comparison problem can be a roadblock. Exposing students to many different ways to talk about comparisons can help them sort out the root relationship.

4. Additive comparisons (the constant difference in value discussed in this chapter) are different from multiplicative comparisons (discussed in Chapter 7).

5. The bar model, number line, and double number line structures can help students organize the relationships among the quantities in a comparison.

6. The Anchor-Jump strategy can help students identify one quantity and consider its relationship to the other quantities in a problem.

7. The difference between two quantities is a value that does not correlate with anything concrete. It measures a space between two real objects but is not real itself. This can sometimes make it challenging for students to recognize it.

8. Problem-posing activities can help students identify and mathematize examples of comparisons in their own environment.

TRY IT OUT!

IDENTIFY THE PROBLEM SITUATION

Decide if each of the following is an example of a Part-Part-Whole or Additive Comparison problem type. Draw a bar model or other picture to represent the situation. Remember to explain the reasoning for your decision.

1. Mom put jelly beans in both of her girls' baskets. Kimmy counted 22 jelly beans in her basket. Lauren is older so she got 15 more jelly beans than Kimmy got. How many jelly beans did Lauren get?

2. The front patio measures 300 square feet. The back patio measures 830 square feet. How much tile is needed to cover both patios?

3. The cafeteria at school expects to sell 350 cartons of milk each day. They normally sell 210 chocolate milk cartons and the rest are cartons of plain milk. How many cartons of plain milk do they sell?

(continued)

(continued)

WRITE THE PROBLEM

For practice, write an Additive Comparison word problem for each of the following bar models. As you consider the quantities in the problem, redraw the line in the upper bar to reflect the actual difference between the quantities:

2.46 seconds	x seconds
2.78 seconds	

x pounds	$2\frac{3}{4}$ pounds
$12\frac{1}{4}$ pounds	

12,974 people	2,490 people
x people	

Now, use the three contexts given under "Identify the Problem Situation" and write a different situation for each. For example, if you decided that the problem situation is Part-Part-Whole, write an Additive Comparison situation using the same information found in the problem. As before, make a bar model or draw a visual to match your problem situation:

1. Jelly beans in a basket

2. Front and back patio tiles

3. Chocolate and plain milk sales

BRANCH OUT

1. Ask students to figure out how many days old they are. (You can structure this lesson as a rigorous task-based lesson as well.) Record their responses and ask groups of students to make additive comparisons about their ages: *Mary is z days older than Franco.*

2. Give students a number and tell them that it is the difference between two quantities. The students then name the unit being counted and two numbers with that difference. Ask students to create visual and/or concrete representations for their comparisons.

3. The book *Actual Size* (Jenkins, 2011) shows actual size illustrations of body parts of interesting animals. Pass out rulers and ask students to make additive comparisons between, for example, the width of their eye and the width of the eye of the giant squid!

REFLECT

1. When children pose problems, they like to make them "harder" by adding more steps (English, 1998). However, posing problems that instead require additive comparisons may be even harder for them. Think of some contexts in your classroom or school that can encourage students to compare quantities regularly. Build up to comparing multiple quantities.

2. The bar model is a useful tool for students to add structure to an Additive Comparison problem. Think of ways you can introduce the bar model as a tool to understand these problem situations. How can you help students use a bar model for both Part-Part-Whole and Additive Comparison problems but still recognize the problem situations as different?

3. Scan the textbook you use for Additive Comparison word problems. What kinds of contexts do the textbook authors include? How can you create contexts more familiar to your students and have additional problems for them to solve? How can you encourage your students to write their own Additive Comparison word problems?

PART TWO

Multiplication and Division

ASYMMETRICAL (NONMATCHING) FACTORS

	Product Unknown	Multiplier (Number of Groups) Unknown	Measure (Group Size) Unknown	
Equal Groups (Ratio/Rate)*	Mayim has 8 vases to decorate the tables at her party. She places 3 flowers in each vase. How many flowers does she need? $8 \times 3 = x$ $x \div 8 = 3$	Mayim has some vases to decorate the tables at her party. She places 3 flowers in each vase. If she uses 24 flowers, how many vases does she have? $x \times 3 = 24$ $x = 24 \div 3$	Mayim places 24 flowers in vases to decorate the tables at her party. If there are 8 vases, how many flowers will be in each vase? $8 \times x = 24$ $24 \div 8 = x$	
	Resulting Value Unknown	**Scale Factor (Times as Many) Unknown**	**Original Value Unknown**	
Multiplicative Comparison	Amelia's dog is 5 times older than Wanda's 3-year-old dog. How old is Amelia's dog? $5 \times 3 = x$ $x \div 5 = 3$	Sydney has $15 to spend on dog treats. Her best friend has $5. Sydney has how many times more dollars than her friend has? $x \times 5 = 15$ $5 = 15 \div x$	Devonte has 15 dog toys on the floor in his living room. That is 3 times the number of toys in the dog's toy basket. How many toys are in the toy basket? $3 \times x = 15$ $15 \div 3 = x$	

SYMMETRICAL (MATCHING) FACTORS

	Product Unknown	One Dimension Unknown	Both Dimensions Unknown
Area/Array	Mrs. Bradley bought a rubber mat to cover the floor under the balance beam. One side of the mat measured 5 feet and the other side measured 8 feet. How many square feet does the mat measure? $5 \times 8 = x$ $x \div 8 = 5$	The 40 members of the student council lined up on the stage in the gym to take yearbook pictures. The first row started with 8 students and the rest of the rows did the same. How many rows were there? $8 \times x = 40$ $x = 40 \div 8$	Mr. Donato is arranging student work on the wall for the art show. He started with 40 square entries and arranged them into a rectangular arrangement. How many entries long and wide could the arrangement be? $x \times y = 40$ $40 \div x = y$
	Sample Space (Total Outcomes) Unknown	**One Factor Unknown**	**Both Factors Unknown**
Combinations** (Fundamental Counting Principle)	Karen makes sandwiches at the diner. She offers 3 kinds of bread and 7 different lunch meats. How many unique sandwiches can she make? $3 \times 7 = x$ $3 = x \div 7$	Evelyn works at the ice cream counter. She says that she can make 21 unique and different ice cream sundaes using just ice cream flavors and toppings. If she has 3 flavors of ice cream, how many kinds of toppings does Evelyn offer? $3 \times x = 21$ $21 \div 3 = x$	Audrey can make 21 different fruit sodas using the machine at the diner. How many different flavorings and sodas could there be? $x \times y = 21$ $x = 21 \div y$

*Equal Groups problems, in many cases, are special cases of a category that includes all ratio and rate problem situations. Distinguishing between the two categories is often a matter of interpretation. The Ratio and Rates category, however, becomes a critically important piece of the middle school curriculum and beyond, so the category is referenced here. It will be developed more extensively in the grades 6–8 volume of this series.

**Combinations are a category addressed in middle school mathematics standards. They are introduced briefly in chapter 8 for illustration purposes only and will be developed more extensively in the grades 6–8 volume of this series.

CHAPTER FIVE

Equal Groups Multiplication
Two Factors, Different Jobs

Thinking About Equal Groups Situations

Having explored addition and subtraction problem types in Part 1, we turn now to multiplication and division. Instead of looking for action or relationships, the problem types in the table at the beginning of this chapter are differentiated based on the work that each factor does in the multiplication operation. This will be true for division as well, since division is the inverse operation of multiplication, something we explore further in Chapter 6. In this chapter, we look at Equal Groups multiplication.

Multiplication and Division Problem Situations

	Product Unknown	Multiplier (Number of Groups) Unknown	Measure (Group Size) Unknown	
Equal Groups (Ratio/Rate)*	Mayim has 8 vases to decorate the tables at her party. She places 3 flowers in each vase. How many flowers does she need? $8 \times 3 = x$ $x \div 8 = 3$	Mayim has some vases to decorate the tables at her party. She places 3 flowers in each vase. If she uses 24 flowers, how many vases does she have? $x \times 3 = 24$ $x = 24 \div 3$	Mayim places 24 flowers in vases to decorate the tables at her party. If there are 8 vases, how many flowers will be in each vase? $8 \times x = 24$ $24 \div 8 = x$	

*Equal Groups problems, in many cases, are special cases of a category that includes all ratio and rate problem situations. Distinguishing between the two categories is often a matter of interpretation. The Ratio and Rates category, however, becomes a critically important piece of the middle school curriculum and beyond, so the category is referenced here. It will be developed more extensively in the grades 6–8 volume of this series.

Note: These representations for the problem situations reflect our understanding based on a number of resources. These include the tables in the Common Core State Standards for mathematics (Common Core Standards Initiative, 2010), the problem situations as described in the Cognitively Guided Instruction research (Carpenter, Hiebert, & Moser, 1981), in Heller and Greeno (1979) and Riley, Greeno, & Heller (1984), and other tools. See the Appendix and companion website for a more detailed summary of the documents that informed our development of this table.

ASYMMETRICAL (NONMATCHING) FACTORS

	Product Unknown	Multiplier (Number of Groups) Unknown	Measure (Group Size) Unknown	
Equal Groups (Ratio/Rate)*	Mayim has 8 vases to decorate the tables at her party. She places 3 flowers in each vase. How many flowers does she need? $8 \times 3 = x$ $x \div 8 = 3$	Mayim has some vases to decorate the tables at her party. She places 3 flowers in each vase. If she uses 24 flowers, how many vases does she have? $x \times 3 = 24$ $x = 24 \div 3$	Mayim places 24 flowers in vases to decorate the tables at her party. If there are 8 vases, how many flowers will be in each vase? $8 \times x = 24$ $24 \div 8 = x$	
	Resulting Value Unknown	**Scale Factor (Times as Many) Unknown**	**Original Value Unknown**	
Multiplicative Comparison	Amelia's dog is 5 times older than Wanda's 3-year-old dog. How old is Amelia's dog? $5 \times 3 = x$ $x \div 5 = 3$	Sydney has $15 to spend on dog treats. Her best friend has $5. Sydney has how many times more dollars than her friend has? $x \times 5 = 15$ $5 = 15 \div x$	Devonte has 15 dog toys on the floor in his living room. That is 3 times the number of toys in the dog's toy basket. How many toys are in the toy basket? $3 \times x = 15$ $15 \div 3 = x$	

SYMMETRICAL (MATCHING) FACTORS

	Product Unknown	One Dimension Unknown	Both Dimensions Unknown
Area/Array	Mrs. Bradley bought a rubber mat to cover the floor under the balance beam. One side of the mat measured 5 feet and the other side measured 8 feet. How many square feet does the mat measure? $5 \times 8 = x$ $x \div 8 = 5$	The 40 members of the student council lined up on the stage in the gym to take yearbook pictures. The first row started with 8 students and the rest of the rows did the same. How many rows were there? $8 \times x = 40$ $x = 40 \div 8$	Mr. Donato is arranging student work on the wall for the art show. He started with 40 square entries and arranged them into a rectangular arrangement. How many entries long and wide could the arrangement be? $x \times y = 40$ $40 \div x = y$
	Sample Space (Total Outcomes) Unknown	**One Factor Unknown**	**Both Factors Unknown**
Combinations** (Fundamental Counting Principle)	Karen makes sandwiches at the diner. She offers 3 kinds of bread and 7 different lunch meats. How many unique sandwiches can she make? $3 \times 7 = x$ $3 = x \div 7$	Evelyn works at the ice cream counter. She says that she can make 21 unique and different ice cream sundaes using just ice cream flavors and toppings. If she has 3 flavors of ice cream, how many kinds of toppings does Evelyn offer? $3 \times x = 21$ $21 \div 3 = x$	Audrey can make 21 different fruit sodas using the machine at the diner. How many different flavorings and sodas could there be? $x \times y = 21$ $x = 21 \div y$

online resources ⌖ Full chart available for download at **http://resources.corwin.com/problemsolving3-5**

Sandbox Notes

The key to understanding multiplication and division problem situations is identifying the work each factor does. Keep this in mind as you experiment with different representations of the problems in Figures 5.1 and 5.2. Use the workspace provided to try physical, pictorial, symbolic, and verbal representations. Think about how your work expresses each problem situation.

Again, here are the questions to guide your thinking:

- *Think about the numbers in each situation. What do they represent? Which are quantities? Which are not? What work do they do?*

- *How can you represent the quantities in the word problems with your manipulatives or pictures?*

- *What number sentence best shows what is happening in each story?*

As in previous chapters, as you do the initial work of restating the problems in Figures 5.1 and 5.2 in your own words, focus on comparing the problems. Where do you see differences? Similarities? Remember that the strategy of replacing quantities with the word *some* is always available and may be helpful in identifying similarities.

FIGURE 5.1

FIGURE 5.2

| Mayim has 8 vases to decorate the tables at her party. She places 3 flowers in each vase. How many flowers does she need? | Kwon wants to fill 3 bags with collectible cards for his party guests. He put 8 cards in each bag. How many cards does he need? |

ENTER THE PROBLEM

FIGURE 5.3 A MODEL FOR MATHEMATIZING WORD PROBLEMS

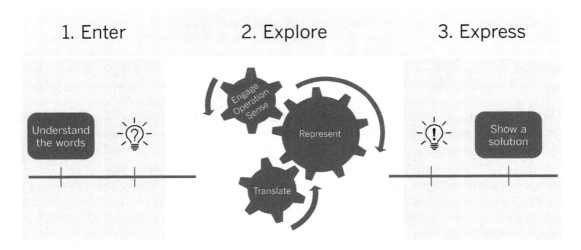

STUDENTS AND TEACHERS THINK ABOUT THE PROBLEMS

When we ask teachers to talk about these problems, we hear things like this:

The math in the problems is the same—they both have an answer of 24.

They're both about groups, but one has 8 vases and one has 3 bags. The total number of items, flowers or cards, is the same.

These teachers recognize that the computation in these problems is the same: The product of 3 and 8 is 24. The second teacher sees that they're both about groups of objects but the number of groups in each situation is different.

The concrete models in the student work in Figures 5.4 and 5.5 also make these distinctions clear. In these problem situations, the 3 and 8 in each word problem do different "work." The 3 in Figure 5.1 tells "how many in one group" (vase), while the 3 in Figure 5.2 tells "how many groups" (bags) there are. The models also make clear the key similarity: Both problems require that objects be separated into groups of equal size, with each container holding the same number of objects. This is why they are called **Equal Groups** problem situations. How did you represent the containers and the objects in each problem?

Equal Groups: A multiplication problem situation in which one of the factors states the number of groups and the other factor states how many objects are in each group.

FIGURE 5.4   **FIGURE 5.5**

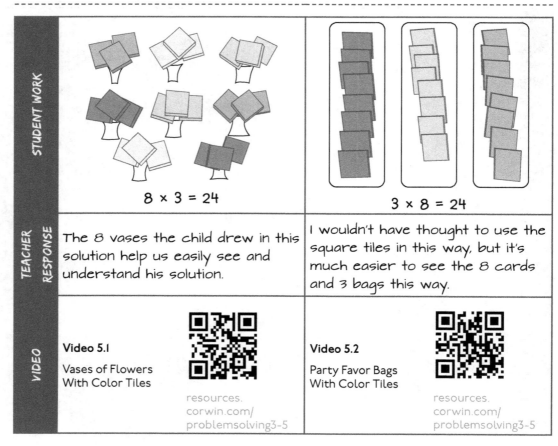

| | STUDENT WORK | $8 \times 3 = 24$ | $3 \times 8 = 24$ |

| TEACHER RESPONSE | The 8 vases the child drew in this solution help us easily see and understand his solution. | I wouldn't have thought to use the square tiles in this way, but it's much easier to see the 8 cards and 3 bags this way. |

| VIDEO | **Video 5.1** Vases of Flowers With Color Tiles | resources. corwin.com/ problemsolving3-5 | **Video 5.2** Party Favor Bags With Color Tiles | resources. corwin.com/ problemsolving3-5 |

MULTIPLIER AND MEASURE FACTORS

Keeping our focus on the factors, let's look more closely at how each factor operates in Equal Groups problems. As with the problems in Figures 5.1 and 5.2, often the groups are defined as "containers" (one of the factors) holding an equal numbers of "objects" (the other factor). Because containers function differently in the real world from objects, much of the time the two factors cannot be meaningfully swapped and make sense in context. Consider the following order of flowers for a wedding:

> *The florist delivered 8 vases. There are 3 flowers per vase, for a total of 24 flowers.*

What if this happened instead?

> *The florist delivered 3 vases. There are 8 flowers for each vase, for a total of 24 flowers.*

The florist could argue: "There are still 24 flowers. Why is this a problem?" This example makes it clear that the "work" done by the factors 8 and 3 differs meaningfully. We started calling the factors "container" and "object" to describe the work they do, but, of course, groups aren't always defined as containers, as in the following example:

> *7 children each have 4 pencils.*

So what do we call the factor that defines the number of groups? We use the term **multiplier factor**, a term that appears in many mathematics textbooks. The other factor, which we called "objects" is the quantity that we can repeatedly add to find the product. We will refer to that factor as the **measure factor**. This is also often referred to as the *multiplicand* in many circumstances, but that word is somewhat clumsy. We use the term *measure* because it clearly represents an amount that can be measured or counted out into groups. For the pencil situation, the multiplier factor is 7 (children) and the measure factor is 4 (pencils) because 7 children will each hold a quantity of 4 pencils.

Multiplier factor: The factor in an Equal Groups problem situation that answers the question "How many groups?"

Measure factor: The factor that describes how many are in a group in an Equal Groups problem situation.

When the two factors are doing different work, as in Equal Groups problems, we call this *asymmetric multiplication* (Kouba & Franklin, 1993). (In later chapters we will explore symmetric multiplication problems, where the factors do the same work.) In Figure 5.6, we begin the work of creating problem situations that distinguish the multiplier from the measure factor. Try inserting quantities (values and units) that make sense for the situations. If you are working with a group of colleagues, this is a good time to stop and discuss your problem situations.

FIGURE 5.6 EQUAL GROUPS SITUATIONS

MULTIPLIER NUMBER OF GROUPS	MEASURE NUMBER IN A GROUP	PRODUCT
7 children	4 pencils (per child)	28 pencils
2 baskets	25 strawberries (per basket)	50 strawberries
3 families	4 children (per family)	12 children
8 vases	3 flowers (per vase)	24 flowers
3 bags	8 cards (per bag)	24 cards
		24 jelly beans
		12 basketballs
3 teachers		
5 cars		
	5 cars	
	3 dimes	

Which factor typically comes first? Does it matter? The Common Core State Standards set up the expectation that the first factor in a multiplication expression is the *multiplier factor* (National Governors Association Center for Best Practices and Council of Chief State School Officers, 2010). This makes sense in English because when we talk about multiplication we say, "4 times 7," which to most Americans means "7, 4 times." In this case, 4 is the multiplier factor and 7 is the measure factor. But, this isn't a hard and fast rule! As a matter of fact, much of the scientific world and many countries around the globe do the opposite: The first factor is the measure factor, and the second factor, the multiplier, tells how many are needed (Anghileri, 1989; Watanabe, 2003)!

Like many other people, you may not have ever distinguished between 4×7 and 7×4 in a meaningful way. You may even be surprised to read that there is an expected order! Keep in mind that for young problem solvers, the position of the factor is *not* the most important detail—it's more important that our students understand the *work* the factor does. Does the factor describe how many groups there are or does it tell how big each group is? Can students describe the meaning or "work" of each factor? In other words, is the factor a multiplier factor or a measure factor? This is true for whole numbers as well as for factors that are fractions or decimals.

EQUAL GROUPS AND THE COMMUTATIVE PROPERTY

Starting in third grade, students start making sense of the commutative property of multiplication. The commutative property has the advantage of reducing the number of basic multiplication facts that students must learn. Students with a full understanding of the property recognize that $3 \times 2 = 2 \times 3$ and can use one known fact to extend their family of known facts. For example, most students learn their multiples of five earlier than their multiples of seven, so $7 \times 5 = 35$ is well known. The student with an understanding of the power of the commutative property can extend this understanding to include $5 \times 7 = 35$, one of the set of multiples of seven.

It's not surprising that most standards focus student attention on the commutativity of multiplication as a focus for understanding the meaning of multiplication. This is an important algebraic understanding for students to have, as it is vitally important for mastering the flexibility the commutative property brings to computation strategies and later to algebraic manipulation. However, this focus on the commutative property as a pathway to understanding multiplication does not necessarily help students develop a deep understanding of operation sense, how multiplication is used to solve and make sense of real-world problems. In fact, it might actually interfere. Consider the problem in Figure 5.7, a perfect example of this situation. It describes a task in which learners are asked to think more deeply about the work of the factors in a multiplication problem.

FIGURE 5.7

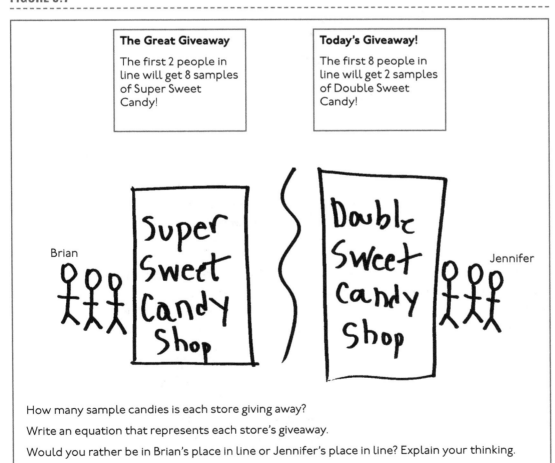

The Great Giveaway

The first 2 people in line will get 8 samples of Super Sweet Candy!

Today's Giveaway!

The first 8 people in line will get 2 samples of Double Sweet Candy!

How many sample candies is each store giving away?

Write an equation that represents each store's giveaway.

Would you rather be in Brian's place in line or Jennifer's place in line? Explain your thinking.

As you read through the students' solutions in Figures 5.8 and 5.9, notice how the commutative property helped the student whose work is represented in Figure 5.8 find the product of 2 and 8 but does not help her solve this problem.

FIGURE 5.8   **FIGURE 5.9**

STUDENT WORK	Each store is giving away the same number of candies. They are giving 16 candies, so it's the same I can write it like this 2×8 or like this 8×2 I know my twos so I don't have to know my eights to figure it out! See, each store gave away 16 candies so Brian and Jennifer will get the same amount. I want to be Jennifer, because she is a girl.	The stores are different. Brian is sad because he will not get any candies because they will be all gone before it's his turn. 8+8=16
TEACHER RESPONSE	This student has written accurate expressions about the problem situation. I don't think she recognizes that the stores are different. She thinks both Jennifer and Brian will get candies.	This student sees that Brian, as the third person in line, will not get candies when the candies are given out to 2 people, in groups of 8 candies. I don't know whether this student can write a multiplication equation, however.

Although understanding that $2 \times 8 = 8 \times 2$ is commutative, and that it is an efficient strategy for recalling a fact, the *situations themselves are not commutative*. Super Sweet candy will be given away in groups of eight pieces to the first two visitors. Brian is third in line and the student's response in Figure 5.9 shows keen awareness that Brian will lose out. Although the solution in Figure 5.8 accurately recognizes the equality of 8×2 and 2×8, unlike the solution in Figure 5.9, it does not recognize that Jennifer has made the better choice of candy shops! When the candy is passed out in groups of two pieces to the first eight people in line, Jennifer is comfortably within the group who will receive a sample.

How useful is the commutative property? How much should we focus on it? Interestingly, several anthropologists have also explored the use of the commutative property in Africa and South America, interviewing individuals with limited or no formal schooling (Petitto & Ginsburg, 1982; Schliemann, Araujo, Cassundé, Macedo, & Nicéas, 1998). Overall, the property is rarely used, and when it is, the flexible use of factors is used only when the difference in calculation efficiency is significant. An example of an efficient use is when 100×2 is abandoned in favor of 2×100, for example. In other words, the commutative property is a learned skill, one that more likely develops with schooling rather than as an intuitive understanding. Interestingly, Japanese textbooks do not explicitly present the commutative property until after students have explored the basic multiplication facts, primarily because there is a focused distinction between the multiplier factor and the measure factor in their textbooks (Watanabe, 2003).

Does this mean that we should avoid the commutative property of multiplication during instruction? Not at all! It means that we should recognize the power of the property as a useful tool for computing and relating numbers outside of problem contexts. Quantities, in most Equal Groups situations and real-world problems, are not interchangeable. When we engage in problem-solving-focused instruction, our goal might be to avoid the use of the commutative property during the comprehension and sense-making stages of problem solving. Recognizing this distinction, we can save the flexibility of the commutative property for computation once quantities and relationships in a problem are well established. If you would like to think more about this idea, check out Donna Boucher's lively blog post entitled "Are 6×5 and 5×6 the same?" Be sure to read the user comments that follow as they demonstrate a wide range of views on the matter (Boucher, 2014).

REPRESENTING LARGER QUANTITIES

Up to this point, we have shared problems in which the numbers are easy to represent with manipulatives and pictures. The pair of problems in Figures 5.10 and 5.11 are similar but with numbers of greater values. How might this impact student representations? Are there new challenges in finding the multiplier and measure factors?

FIGURE 5.10

FIGURE 5.11

| Every month Jeremy spends a day at the food pantry putting together bags of food to give away. Today he put 5 pounds of rice in each of the 36 bags on the table. How much rice did he pack up today? | Every month Jeremy spends a day at the food pantry putting together bags of food to give away. Five of the families have young infants who need formula. He put a 36 ounce can of formula in each of their bags. How much formula did he pack up today? |

Numbers often influence the choice of representation or the tool we use to represent an operation in a context. In the problem in Figure 5.10, 5 pounds is the measure factor and 36 bags is the quantity represented as the multiplier factor. Representing this situation with a physical model is challenging because it requires either strategic grouping of units or a collection of 180 individual units of some kind. In neither of the student work models (Figures 5.12 and 5.13) is a single unit used as the sole manipulative, which is a reasonable expectation when students are multiplying quantities this great.

FIGURE 5.12   **FIGURE 5.13**

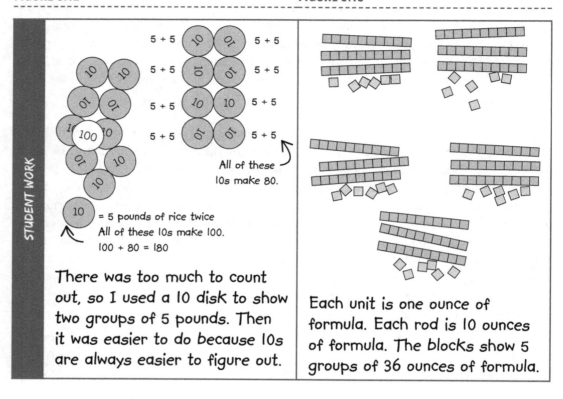

There was too much to count out, so I used a 10 disk to show two groups of 5 pounds. Then it was easier to do because 10s are always easier to figure out.

Each unit is one ounce of formula. Each rod is 10 ounces of formula. The blocks show 5 groups of 36 ounces of formula.

The model in Figure 5.12 groups two 5-pound bags of rice into a 10, which is represented by a 10-place value disk. A student may have chosen to use nickels or a five-frame, but as you likely have discovered, there are rarely enough of any tool to go around for each student to be able to use even 36 units to represent a problem like this one. Some students will need to do this, though, and it is perfectly acceptable to provide them with the collection (and time) they need to put this together. However, most students by third or fourth grade are able to unitize groups of 10 in order to make fewer groups to arrive at 36 fives. The student in Figure 5.12 has even demonstrated that she sees that 10 of the tens makes 100, which is shown by the extra 100-place-value disk set on top and her annotations. This solution gives some convincing evidence that the student understands the context because she has given us a key to see why she is using the 10-place-value chip: 10 = 5 pounds of rice, twice. If this key had not been present we would not know if the student was strategically selecting the tool or simply re-presenting the answer of 180 using the closest tool available. Thus it is useful to prompt students to offer windows into their thinking, through additional verbal or symbolic representations.

Figure 5.13 models a different context, one in which the factors have changed roles. The measure factor is 36 ounces of formula, and since there are five families receiving this amount, the multiplier factor is 5. A student might make the case that the model used in Figure 5.12 could be used again to represent the work. After all, multiplication is commutative. In this case it is important to note that they may not be representing the actual context and the quantities but rather are *representing only the numbers* in the problems, and not the context. Computing with the numbers and not solving the actual problem *decontextualizes* the calculation. If it is done too early, or without recognition of the context, the student may not be developing the robust operation sense needed to solve novel problems or to tackle modeling tasks. Similarly, the quantities in an Equal Groups problem are not interchangeable. For example, the base-10 blocks in Figure 5.13 are a grouped (or unitized) model that allow the student to represent 36 quickly. The student has to create a group only five times, unlike the previous example, which required five to be copied 36 times.

Earlier in the chapter, we showed that the power of the commutative property of multiplication can backfire when it comes to helping students develop a strong operation sense. As students create models of problem contexts, take a moment to note whether their representations accurately reflect the context of the word problem they are modeling. If students are representing only numbers and operators, redirect their attention to the quantities, which include the values, the units, and the role of each factor in the context. This will continue to direct their focus to the context of the problem and building operation sense.

Moving Beyond Whole Numbers

Look at the two problems in Figures 5.14 and 5.15, both Equal Groups problems involving decimals or fractions. Again, as you state the problems in your own words, also describe where they are similar and different. As with Figures 5.1 and 5.2 in this chapter, keep these differences and similarities in mind while you enter the mathematizing sandbox and try out different representations in the workspace provided. Consider how having quantities expressed in fractions and decimals might influence your representations.

FIGURE 5.14

FIGURE 5.15

Shweta wants to ride the FreeFall coaster at the amusement park 4 times. Each ticket costs $2.50. How much will Shweta's rides cost in all?	Shweta and her friends are eating popcorn. Each bag contains 4 cups of popcorn. Shweta and her friends eat $2\frac{1}{2}$ bags of popcorn. How many cups of popcorn did they eat?

ENTER THE PROBLEM

EXPLORE

STUDENTS AND TEACHERS THINK ABOUT THE PROBLEMS

Take a look at the student work in Figures 5.16 and 5.17 and notice how the students describe or draw what is happening in the word problems. Then look below at the teacher commentary that follows the student work and consider what the teachers noticed in the student work.

FIGURE 5.16

FIGURE 5.17

STUDENT WORK	I saw the problem said in all so I knew I had to add. I found the numbers and added them together. $4 + 2.50 = 6.50$	 I drew three bags of popcorn and put 4 pieces in for each cup. They ate two whole bags and one half of a bag so I counted 10 cups they ate.
TEACHER RESPONSE	I can see this student likely did not think about the context of the problem. She just used a key word. That means she added the numbers incorrectly. Adding $2.50 four times, or multiplying, would have solved the problem. I don't think she knows what the 4 means here.	This student appears to understand the problem and shows his thinking clearly. I can't tell if he knows how multiplication relates to this problem. He found a way to solve it by counting.
VIDEO	Video 5.3 FreeFall Ride Think-Aloud resources.corwin.com/ problemsolving3-5	Video 5.4 Eating Popcorn Sketch resources.corwin.com/ problemsolving3-5

EQUAL GROUPS AND REPEATED ADDITION

For the four rides problem (Figure 5.16), the student makes it clear in her statement that she is using a key word strategy, identifying the words *in all* as a sign she should move to addition. As the teacher notes, although addition *could* be used to solve this problem, the number sentence reveals that this student does not know what the numbers used in the problem mean. What questions could we ask here to help the student return to the mathematizing sandbox? How do we help her pause and focus on the action in the story, not just the numbers? We might ask her to read the problem without any numbers and talk about what is happening in the problem:

> *Shweta wants to ride the FreeFall coaster a bunch of times. Each ticket costs some money. How much will the rides cost in all?*

Then, put the price of a ticket, $2.50, back in the problem. What if Shweta wants to ride only once, what is the cost? Twice? Three times? This conversation brings the student back to focus on the structure of the problem, $2.50 for each ride Shweta takes. This might lead to a number sentence with addition, $2.50 + 2.50 + 2.50 + 2.50$ (for the original four rides), but then we can ask the student to write a multiplication expression describing the same problem situation. Recognizing that four is a multiplier factor and not a measure factor might also come from creating a concrete model. Repeated addition can arrive at the same *answer* as the related multiplication sentence, but it will never have the same brute power that multiplication does. To learn more about the relationship between multiplication and repeated addition, read the blog post entitled "Multiplication Ain't No Repeated Addition" (Devlin, 2008). Although it makes sense to help students access multiplication through repeated addition in Equal Groups problem situations, over the long term, transitioning to multiplicative thinking is the goal. In fact, most fourth-grade standards begin the transition from repeated addition to multiplicative thinking with a standard related to one of multiplication's most important jobs: finding how many "times as many." We will address this concept in depth in Chapter 7.

UNDERSTANDING A PORTION OF A GROUP

The second student, with pictorial representations of popcorn (Figure 5.17), solved the problem accurately but we cannot know if the student understands that this is an example of multiplication ($2\frac{1}{2}$ bags $\times 4$ cups per bag) or if he sees it as addition (4 cups $+ 4$ cups $+ 2$ cups). This is not a trivial distinction. Recall the questions we introduced in the "Sandbox Notes" and use them as a guide to lead the student back to the mathematizing sandbox and help this student continue thinking about this problem as multiplication:

How does your picture show what is happening in the story?

Where are the numbers in the problem, 4 and $2\frac{1}{2}$, shown in your picture?

How could you write a multiplication expression for this problem?

The bar model is accurate, but as drawn, it creates an addition or counting situation. The student's caption explains that the three full bags of popcorn correspond to the three sections of the rectangle. Each set of four pieces of popcorn represents four cups in each bag. A dotted line shows half of the third bag, and the caption echoes the same idea. Yet we do not see an equation demonstrating that the student recognizes that $2\frac{1}{2} \times 4 = 10$ as a grade-appropriate symbolic representation of this context. We are not entirely sure that they would be able to conceptualize $2\frac{1}{4}$ bags of popcorn or $2\frac{1}{8}$ bags of popcorn in the same manner. In other words, what if the fractional portion wasn't readily visible?

This is an important transition for students as they learn about fractions and decimals. Repeated addition, and multiplication, are not as straightforward when the multiplier factor is not a whole number. A fraction of some quantities (of a bag of popcorn, for example) makes sense, whereas a fraction of other quantities (half of a child holding pencils, for example) does not. As students transition from seeing multiplication only as a shortcut for repeated addition, to identifying multiplier and measure factors, to understanding situations with a portion of an object or a group of objects, they are moving into multiplicative reasoning, a critical step on the journey to the proportional reasoning essential for middle school.

STARTING WITH AN EXPRESSION TO BUILD MULTIPLICATIVE REASONING

Let's explore what happens when students are challenged to write word problems that could be represented by the expression in Figure 5.18. Before looking at the examples in Figures 5.19 and 5.20, think about what problem you might write and whether it represents an Equal Groups multiplication situation.

FIGURE 5.18

Write a word problem that can be represented by the following expression:

$$\frac{2}{3} \times 6$$

Use pictures or concrete objects to show how you would find a solution.

Before discussing these responses, think about the openness of this task. Asking students to create a word problem from only an expression gives us the opportunity to assess how they interpret the operation and how they create models of their mathematical thinking about an operation. It's a different perspective that could reveal another view on their understanding.

FIGURE 5.19   **FIGURE 5.20**

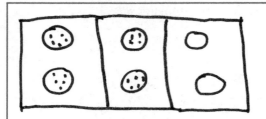

I have 6 cookies. $\frac{2}{3}$ of the cookies are oatmeal raisin. How many oatmeal raisin cookies do I have?

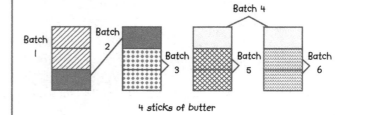

4 sticks of butter

$\frac{2}{3}$ of a stick of butter is needed to bake one batch of brownies. How many sticks of butter are needed to make six batches of brownies?

Both examples intentionally created a context in which it matters whether the factor is the multiplier factor or the measure factor. If you haven't done so already, look again at Figures 5.19 and 5.20 and decide what role the factor $\frac{2}{3}$ plays in each problem context. If you are working with a team of colleagues, this is a good time to stop and share your observations.

WHEN THE MULTIPLIER FACTOR IS LESS THAN ONE In Figure 5.19, $\frac{2}{3}$ is the multiplier factor because it tells how many groups (or measures) of six cookies are oatmeal raisin. In this case the fraction can also be called an *operator* (Kieren, 1976; Lamon, 2012). In the representation shown, there are six cookies and a fractional part of them is identified. The student has separated the cookies into three equal groups, which is shown by the two vertical lines. Two of the three groups ($\frac{2}{3}$) are dotted with raisins while the remaining third has no dots. The product of 4 can be seen in the four cookies total that have raisins. It may seem somewhat difficult to think of "$\frac{2}{3}$ of the cookies" as saying "number of groups" because in whole number Equal Groups problems "number of groups" means to make more and more copies. But, multiplication with a multiplier factor less than one appears to violate that rule. In reality it was never a rule that multiplication *always* makes numbers larger! That rule "expires" when multiplying by a factor less than one (Karp, Bush, & Dougherty, 2014). The multiplier factor also makes *less than one* (or a portion of one) copy of the measure factor! In other words, it's *less than one* group.

Modeling $\frac{2}{3}$ as a multiplier factor can be a challenging exercise that requires a deep understanding of models of partitioned fractions. Before we move on to discuss the example in Figure 5.20, let's consider another problem in which the multiplier factor is less than one. For the problem in Figure 5.21, we use a discrete manipulative model so that we can make the problem more approachable.

> $\frac{7}{8}$ *of the students in the class are staying after school to work on a project that is due tomorrow. If there are 24 students in the class, how many will be staying after school.*

FIGURE 5.21

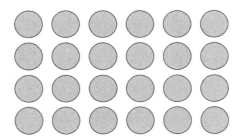

Although $\frac{7}{8}$ is not immediately visible in the arrangement shown in Figure 5.21, we can encourage students to look for eight equal units. Flipping the chips to create contrast can help make the eight equal groups visible, as seen in Figure 5.22. The loops highlight seven of the eight units of three.

FIGURE 5.22

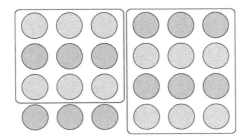

7 units × 3 chips = 21, or in terms of the original problem, $\frac{7}{8} \times 24 = 21$, or seven out of eight equal groups found in a group of 24 is 21. Video 5.5 shows this thinking.

WHEN THE MEASURE FACTOR IS LESS THAN ONE Figure 5.20 shows a change in the roles of the factors. In this case, $\frac{2}{3}$ cup is the amount of butter needed to bake one batch of brownies, making it the measure factor. The quantity 6 represents the number of batches of brownies to be baked, which is the multiplier factor. In story form, this can be restated as six groups of $\frac{2}{3}$ of a stick, which reveals the familiar Equal Groups structure. The representation in Figure 5.20 shows a single stick

Video 5.5

Staying After School With Two-Color Counters

resources.
corwin.com/
problemsolving3-5

of butter, partitioned into three equal pieces: The stick of butter is the *unit whole*. The first group of two-thirds is shaded in gray and the second group of two-thirds is taken from both the first stick and the second stick, and is shaded in [blue], and so on. By the end of the process, the six measures of butter ($\frac{2}{3}$ of a stick each) are equivalent to four full sticks (unit wholes) of butter.

Content standards and textbooks may not distinguish $6 \times \frac{2}{3}$ and $\frac{2}{3} \times 6$ from each other: Each may be equally part of the same standard. But as we saw in the representations given in Figures 5.19 and 5.20, the models for each expression are quite different and require students to make sense of a different interpretation of $\frac{2}{3}$ and a different interpretation of 6. Moving from whole number multiplier factors to fractional multiplier factors marks a significant change in how students need to make sense of what a multiplier factor does. In the Equal Groups problem type, the multiplier tells us *how many* groups we have. Making sense of and modeling $\frac{2}{3}$ of a group, or $2\frac{1}{2}$ groups, or even 0.4 groups is a significant shift in modeling practice. For that reason, it is all the more important to encourage modeling what happens in the problem context and picking the right tools for the job. To read more, visit the Math Minds blog that addresses a similar set of problems (Gray, 2015).

MOVING THE MISSING TERM

In the problems in the preceding section, both of the factors are known quantities. In this final pair (Figures 5.23 and 5.24), the missing element in the problem is one of the factors; we have moved away from the first cell in this row to one of the other cells, where the multiplier or measure is missing. As you look at the problems and student work (Figures 5.25 and 5.26), think about what is given and what you are asked to find.

Take a moment to determine which of the factors in these problems is the multiplier factor and which is the measure factor. The table in Figure 5.27 can help you organize your thinking. Consider the clues in the context or in the language of the problem that helped you make those decisions. If you are reading this book with a group, take a moment here to discuss how you made your decisions. Identifying the work that each factor—indeed each number—is doing in the problem makes it much easier to find the problem's story. When students are able to find the story narrative in a word problem, they have more tools available to help them select the appropriate operation.

FIGURE 5.23

Shweta wants to ride the FreeFall coaster at the amusement park more than once. She handed the cashier $10 and got 4 ride tickets. How much was each ticket?

FIGURE 5.24

Shweta and her friends are at the amusement park. The 10 of them lined up to get on the FreeFall ride. The ride seats 4 people at a time. How many cars will it take for their whole group to ride?

FIGURE 5.25

FIGURE 5.26

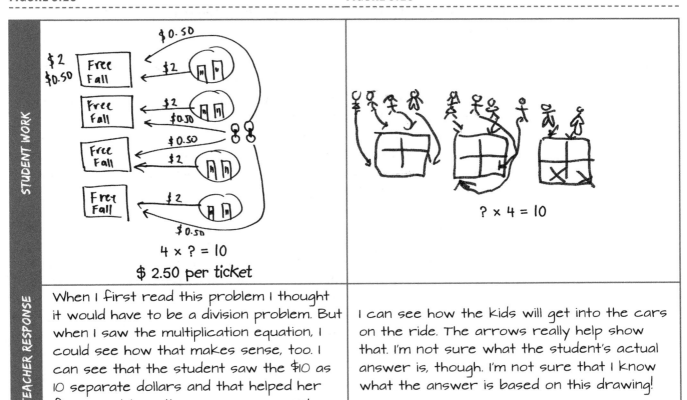

STUDENT WORK

TEACHER RESPONSE

When I first read this problem I thought it would have to be a division problem. But when I saw the multiplication equation, I could see how that makes sense, too. I can see that the student saw the $10 as 10 separate dollars and that helped her figure out how the money was spent.

I can see how the kids will get into the cars on the ride. The arrows really help show that. I'm not sure what the student's actual answer is, though. I'm not sure that I know what the answer is based on this drawing!

FIGURE 5.27 IDENTIFYING THE NUMBERS IN A WORD PROBLEM

	MULTIPLIER FACTOR	MEASURE FACTOR	PRODUCT
Tickets Problem (Figure 5.23)			
Riders in Cars Problem (Figure 5.24)			

Mathematical story:
A retelling of the action
or relationships in a
word problem or other
problem context in a
way that highlights the
important mathematical
details over any other
information.

In problem situations where the placement of the unknown, in this case the missing factor, might make it a bit more challenging for students to sort through the problem, it can be helpful to zero in on the problem's **mathematical story**. As we discussed in previous chapters, the story is a bare-bones verbal statement expressing only the relationships between the necessary quantities. It goes beyond simply restating the problem in your own words to focus only on the essentials. The story of the problem in Figure 5.23 could be stated as follows:

> *4 tickets for some dollars each, cost $10.*

This version of the problem directly translates to a multiplication equation. The problem in Figure 5.24 can be translated as

> *I am not sure how many cars it will take for 10 of us to go, 4 at a time, on the ride.*

The language in these versions is contrived to emphasize the process of mathematizing, but these situations are not unusual. They are the kind of situations that people face in their daily lives. We may not routinely consider how to mathematize these situations into working equations, but with practice we easily could. One take-away from this set of responses is the value of encouraging students to practice a routine of translating a problem situation into a distilled form of language that gets closer to the action or relationships in the problem (*a story*).

One final note about this set of problems is the contrasting forms of the solutions. The missing measure factor in Figure 5.23 is a money quantity and is best represented as a decimal value ($2.50). But the missing factor in Figure 5.24 is a multiplier with an unclear exact value. Numerically, the answer is $2\frac{1}{2}$, but is there really such a thing as $\frac{1}{2}$ of an amusement park coaster car? Of course not. The contextual answer is that it would take three cars for all of the friends to ride the coaster, with two extra seats in the final car. This is one of the reasons it is challenging to write real-life Equal Groups problems with a fractional multiplier. The ones we presented here are extremely contrived because real-life problems have constraints, like the four-seater car in the roller coaster problem. Finally, real life is flexible. Numbers can be expressed in multiple ways, for example, as fractions or decimals. The curricula we use likely are not as flexible. Knowing that creating appropriate word problems has built-in challenges may help you be less critical of the contrived situations, but it also may help you look to life in your classroom to find better and more contextualized examples. In Chapter 6, we will continue thinking about missing factor situations as we explore division from an Equal Groups perspective.

KEY IDEAS

Equal groups multiplication problems are situations in which there are two factors, one representing the size of the group (the measure) and one representing the number of groups (the multiplier). These are some of the key ideas we want you to remember and share with your students as you learn about equal groups multiplication problems:

1. Equal groups multiplication is related to repeated addition, but it is not the same thing.

2. Equal groups are asymmetric multiplication problems; the two factors do two different jobs in the problem.

3. One factor represents the size of the group (the measure) and one factor represents the number of groups (the multiplier).

4. When the multiplier factor is less than one, the product will be less than the starting value of the measure factor in the problem. To find the product, the measure factor will need to be partitioned into fractional pieces. Modeling with the right tools or pictures will help students make sense of the new value.

5. When the measure factor is less than one, students need to model a single measure and iterate it (make copies of it). Modeling with the right tools or pictures will help students make sense of the new value.

6. The commutative property can help students find the solution to a multiplication problem, but the meaning of the problem can change when the factors are reversed.

7. The equation that shows the problem situation best might be different from the computation equation that helps find the solution.

IDENTIFY THE FACTOR

For each of the following typical word problems, identify the multiplier factor and the measure factor. Write the multiplication equation that represents each situation. After each, make a note of the evidence you used to make your decision about the factors.

1. Brian made packages of 3 cookies in a bag to sell at the school bake sale. He hopes to sell all 9 packages before the bake sale ends. How many cookies does he hope to sell?

2. Michael was in charge of selling shirts at the school basketball game. He is planning how to stack 48 shirts on the table in stacks that are all the same size. What are some ways he could stack the shirts?

3. Haylea used the whole package of 45 beads to make her necklace. Her pattern used the same number of red, white, and blue beads. How many beads of each color did she use?

4. Gabriella agreed to create 4 interesting graphs for each edition of the school newspaper. When she got home she told her mom that she needed to start work on 40 graphs! Then her mom asked, "How many times is the newspaper going to be published?" What was Gabriella's answer?

5. Matthew estimated that it would take 0.45 pounds of lunch meat to make each sandwich. 30 people have been invited to the luncheon. How much lunch meat should Matthew order?

6. Edward was hired to pass out samples of a new trail mix at the grocery store. His manager gave him a package with 200 ounces of trail mix and said each person should get a 1.5 ounce sample. How many people got a sample of trail mix from Edward?

7. Eleanor loves to make eggnog each year during the holidays. She has an old recipe that calls for $1\frac{1}{2}$ dozen eggs. How many eggs does she need?

8. Debbie is coordinating snacks for the field trip. She purchased a 46.5 ounce bag of pretzels. Describe 3 ways she could equally divide up this bag into reasonable snack sizes for the students.

WRITE THE PROBLEM

For each of the following equations, write a word problem that matches. Include a representation that corresponds to the situation.

1. $3 \times 7 = 21$

2. $7 \times 3 = 21$

3. $4 \times 52 = 208$

4. $52 \times 4 = 208$

5. $\frac{1}{3} \times 36 = 12$

6. $36 \times \frac{1}{3} = 12$

7. $\frac{3}{5} \times 20 = 12$

8. $20 \times \frac{3}{5} = 12$

BRANCH OUT

1. Brainstorm situations in your own classroom that can be mathematized with Equal Groups situations. Consider situations related to daily tasks such as lunch counts, transportation to and from school, in-school clubs and activities, assemblies, and the like. The school environment is rich with examples!

2. Identify picture books your students enjoy that include Equal Groups multiplication situations. Read the stories and then mathematize them by talking about them in terms of multiplier and measure factors. Here are two examples to get you started:

   a. The book *One Is a Snail, Ten Is a Crab* (Sayre & Sayre, 2003) presents students with a variety of fun beach situations in which they can identify the multiplier and measure factors. For example, "ten is a crab" means that the number of crabs is the multiplier and the number of legs (per crab) is the measure factor.

   b. *The Doorbell Rang* by Pat Hutchins (1986) takes students on a fun journey sharing cookies with visitors. Reading the book with students can help them distinguish between the multiplier and measure factors, particularly when they distinguish between, for example, 4×6 and 6×4 in the story.

REFLECT

1. Understanding the commutative property is an important part of student learning in grades 3–5. How does distinguishing between the two factors in an Equal Groups multiplication problem change your thinking about the commutative property?

2. $\frac{2}{3} \times 6$ and $6 \times \frac{2}{3}$ are often taught in the same unit, presented as multiplication of a whole number by a fraction. How does this chapter change your thinking about how you present multiplication of fractions to students?

3. Refer to the Multiplication and Division Problem Situations table at the beginning of this chapter (you can download a copy from http://resources.corwin.com/problemsolving3-5). Examine the textbook you use and look for examples of Equal Groups multiplication word problems. For each problem, decide which factor is the measure factor and which is the multiplier factor. You will likely encounter some problems that are not the Equal Groups type. The opportunity to classify the remaining word problems will come in later chapters.

CHAPTER SIX

Equal Groups Division
When a Factor Is Missing

In Chapter 5, we thought about multiplication in the case of Equal Groups situations with a focus on the role of the factors while finding the unknown product. With one factor showing the number of groups (the multiplier) and one factor showing the size of the groups (the measure), clarifying these roles serves as an entry for students to develop stronger operation sense, including a richer understanding of multiplication. In this chapter, we will continue to explore the Equal Groups situation but this time from the perspective of division: when you know the product and one factor but must find the other factor. This leads us into two different models of division: partitive and measurement division.

Multiplication and Division Problem Situations

	Product Unknown	Multiplier (Number of Groups) Unknown	Measure (Group Size) Unknown	
Equal Groups (Ratio/Rate)*	Mayim has 8 vases to decorate the tables at her party. She places 3 flowers in each vase. How many flowers does she need? $8 \times 3 = x$ $x \div 8 = 3$	Mayim has some vases to decorate the tables at her party. She places 3 flowers in each vase. If she uses 24 flowers, how many vases does she have? $x \times 3 = 24$ $x = 24 \div 3$	Mayim places 24 flowers in vases to decorate the tables at her party. If there are 8 vases, how many flowers will be in each vase? $8 \times x = 24$ $24 \div 8 = x$	

*Equal Groups problems, in many cases, are special cases of a category that includes all ratio and rate problem situations. Distinguishing between the two categories is often a matter of interpretation. The Ratio and Rates category, however, becomes a critically important piece of the middle school curriculum and beyond, so the category is referenced here. It will be developed more extensively in the grades 6–8 volume of this series.

Note: These representations for the problem situations reflect our understanding based on a number of resources. These include the tables in the Common Core State Standards for mathematics (Common Core Standards Initiative, 2010), the problem situations as described in the Cognitively Guided Instruction research (Carpenter, Hiebert, & Moser, 1981), in Heller and Greeno (1979) and Riley, Greeno, & Heller (1984), and other tools. See the Appendix and companion website for a more detailed summary of the documents that informed our development of this table.

ASYMMETRICAL (NONMATCHING) FACTORS

	Product Unknown	Multiplier (Number of Groups) Unknown	Measure (Group Size) Unknown	
Equal Groups (Ratio/Rate)*	Mayim has 8 vases to decorate the tables at her party. She places 3 flowers in each vase. How many flowers does she need? $8 \times 3 = x$ $x \div 8 = 3$	Mayim has some vases to decorate the tables at her party. She places 3 flowers in each vase. If she uses 24 flowers, how many vases does she have? $x \times 3 = 24$ $x = 24 \div 3$	Mayim places 24 flowers in vases to decorate the tables at her party. If there are 8 vases, how many flowers will be in each vase? $8 \times x = 24$ $24 \div 8 = x$	
	Resulting Value Unknown	Scale Factor (Times as Many) Unknown	Original Value Unknown	
Multiplicative Comparison	Amelia's dog is 5 times older than Wanda's 3-year-old dog. How old is Amelia's dog? $5 \times 3 = x$ $x \div 5 = 3$	Sydney has $15 to spend on dog treats. Her best friend has $5. Sydney has how many times more dollars than her friend has? $x \times 5 = 15$ $5 = 15 \div x$	Devonte has 15 dog toys on the floor in his living room. That is 3 times the number of toys in the dog's toy basket. How many toys are in the toy basket? $3 \times x = 15$ $15 \div 3 = x$	

SYMMETRICAL (MATCHING) FACTORS

	Product Unknown	One Dimension Unknown	Both Dimensions Unknown
Area/Array	Mrs. Bradley bought a rubber mat to cover the floor under the balance beam. One side of the mat measured 5 feet and the other side measured 8 feet. How many square feet does the mat measure? $5 \times 8 = x$ $x \div 8 = 5$	The 40 members of the student council lined up on the stage in the gym to take yearbook pictures. The first row started with 8 students and the rest of the rows did the same. How many rows were there? $8 \times x = 40$ $x = 40 \div 8$	Mr. Donato is arranging student work on the wall for the art show. He started with 40 square entries and arranged them into a rectangular arrangement. How many entries long and wide could the arrangement be? $x \times y = 40$ $40 \div x = y$
	Sample Space (Total Outcomes) Unknown	One Factor Unknown	Both Factors Unknown
Combinations** (Fundamental Counting Principle)	Karen makes sandwiches at the diner. She offers 3 kinds of bread and 7 different lunch meats. How many unique sandwiches can she make? $3 \times 7 = x$ $3 = x \div 7$	Evelyn works at the ice cream counter. She says that she can make 21 unique and different ice cream sundaes using just ice cream flavors and toppings. If she has 3 flavors of ice cream, how many kinds of toppings does Evelyn offer? $3 \times x = 21$ $21 \div 3 = x$	Audrey can make 21 different fruit sodas using the machine at the diner. How many different flavorings and sodas could there be? $x \times y = 21$ $x = 21 \div y$

online resources ▷ Full chart available for download at **http://resources.corwin.com/problemsolving3-5**

Sandbox Notes

The instinct to jump into computation is strong, but, of course, we ask you to wait and explore first (Figure 6.3). Here again are the questions to focus your thinking:

- *Think about the numbers in each situation. What do they represent? Which are quantities? Which are not? What work do they do?*

- *How can you represent the quantities in the word problems with your manipulatives or pictures?*

- *What number sentence best shows what is happening in each story?*

Gather your materials and act out each problem to slow down your thinking. Even if you don't have 52 counters or a 52 inch piece of string, use what you have to role play each problem situation.

Thinking About Equal Groups Division

The two problems in Figures 6.1 and 6.2 are fairly straightforward. Still, we ask you to take a pause before engaging in your active exploration. Restate the problems in your own words, adding a sentence or two describing how they are similar and different.

FIGURE 6.1

FIGURE 6.2

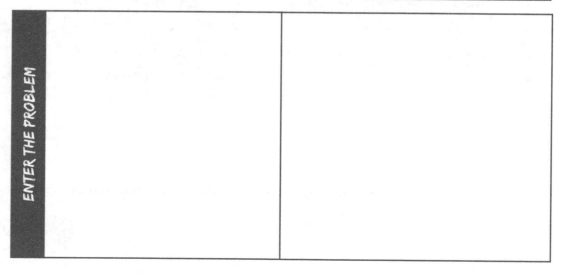

| ENTER THE PROBLEM | Enrique's family brought a large bag of 52 packaged snacks to share during a camping trip. There are 4 people in the family. How many snacks will each person get? | Francisco bought a 52-inch long rope of licorice for the car ride to the campground. Every time someone wanted a piece, he cut off a 4-inch piece and handed it to them. How many times could he share a piece of licorice? |

FIGURE 6.3 A MODEL FOR MATHEMATIZING WORD PROBLEMS

STUDENTS AND TEACHERS THINK ABOUT THE PROBLEMS

Take a look at the student work in Figures 6.4 and 6.5 and how the students describe or draw what is happening in the given word problems. Then look at the teacher commentary that follows the student work and consider what the teachers noticed.

FIGURE 6.4

FIGURE 6.5

	FIGURE 6.4	FIGURE 6.5
STUDENT WORK	 $4 \times 10 = 40$ $4 \times 3 = 12$ $\overline{52}$ The rod is 10 snacks and each cube is another snack. That means that each person in the family gets 13 snacks.	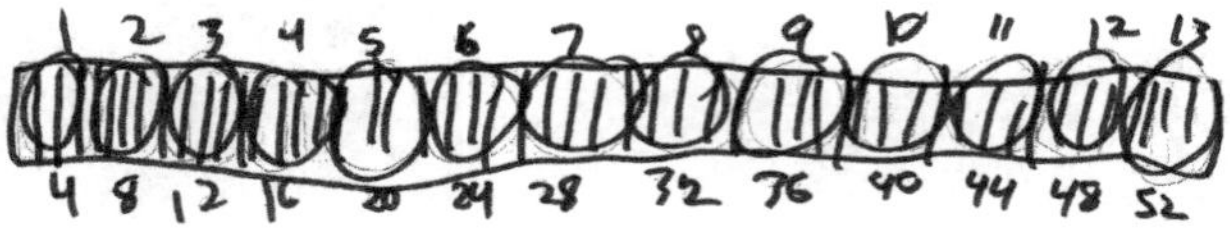 He gave away four inches at a time.
TEACHER RESPONSE	I see four circles. That must represent the four people in the family. It's interesting that she approached this problem using multiplication.	I can almost imagine that this is a rope of licorice! He explained to me that the numbers along the bottom of the bar represent the inches that are taken off each time. The numbers along the top represent the number of times the father could pass out a serving of licorice. I wouldn't have thought to use both sets of numbers, but it really helped me understand what's going on in the student's solution strategy. It reminds me of a double number line.
VIDEO	**Video 6.1** Sharing Snacks With a Base 10 Block Sketch resources.corwin.com/ problemsolving3-5	**Video 6.2** Cutting Pieces of Licorice resources.corwin.com/ problemsolving3-5

PARTITIVE DIVISION

Partitive division: Also known as fair-share division, most commonly represented by the equal distribution of objects into a known number of sets.

Most people are familiar with the model of division in the Figure 6.1 problem, and we often refer to it informally as *fair-share* division. Students will often use circles, or something like them to form groups, or containers, to hold the items being distributed. This model of division is called **partitive division** and the action of distributing the objects in the set is called *partitioning*. Acting out partitive division situations is an important precursor to the partitioning skills required for making equal parts with fractions because in both tasks it is essential that the parts created be equal.

For this reason, it is important to watch for equal parts as students do fair-share activities to make equal groups. In the early stages, they may not distribute the items equally and may even justify their decisions with nonmathematical answers. For example, it isn't unusual for a student to justify an unequal distribution with a comment such as "My dad is hungrier, so he got more snacks." Of course, this thinking makes sense in a real-world context, and it's important to honor the sentiment. But as a mathematical goal, we want students to distribute equally when they fair share.

You may have noticed that the student response to the first problem (Figure 6.4) used base 10 blocks to show an answer. As she began to distribute a fair share to each of the circles, it appears that she may have anticipated how many snacks each person would get in their fair share. For example, each circle has a rod inside it and an expression off to the right indicates that she is likely showing $4 \times 10 = 40$ to match the blocks. Three more cubes follow, likely representing single snacks and corresponding to the equation $4 \times 3 = 12$. Video 6.1 illustrates this approach to solving the problem.

FIGURE 6.6 EARLY PARTITIVE DIVISION STUDENT WORK

Students with an emerging understanding of fair share may not unitize 10 snacks with a rod because they are not yet able to anticipate how much is in a fair share. Contrast the work in Figure 6.4 with the work in Figure 6.6. The drawing in Figure 6.4 shows unitizing because the student confidently chose a rod, which is a grouping of 10 units. In Figure 6.6 the student uses individual marks to distribute the quantity to each person. Both approaches are appropriate for partitive (fair-share) division but at varying levels of sophistication. Although the student does not use tallies conventionally by using a cross bar for the fifth tally in the series, the fact that the numbers are in groups of five shows that there may be some evidence of unitizing quantities.

Partitive division is the first model of division that most students learn from school textbooks, but Jere Confrey, primary author and researcher behind turnonccmath.org, insists that partitive thinking starts at a much earlier age, even before students learn to count (Confrey & Smith, 1995). It isn't hard to imagine a toddler who can successfully separate, or partition, a pile of cookies into two equal groups or a preschooler who can fair share a pile of pennies amongst the four siblings in her family. These are early examples of partitioning and are a precursor to understanding division. Of course, you probably engage in partitive thinking every day doing routine management activities in your classroom. Perhaps you have six table groups in your classroom and while passing out a pile of scratch paper you give each table roughly one-sixth of the pile. As you separate math manipulatives into table boxes, maybe you put some in each box but then come back for a second pass, mentally partitioning the remaining blocks into six equal groups so that each table still receives about the same amount. This is all partitive thinking, even though the quantities may not always be precisely equal. Your intention is to give fair shares.

It is important for students to understand a partitive model of division in part so that they learn to mathematically represent a fair share. The fair-share skill is critically important when learning to identify, create, and name fractions. One key skill to understanding fractions is recognizing that a fraction, for example $\frac{1}{8}$, can be called $\frac{1}{8}$ only if all of the eight pieces of the whole are equivalent.

MEASUREMENT (QUOTITIVE) DIVISION

Measurement division: A model of division focused on the formation of equal portions of a known size. This model is sometimes thought of as *repeated subtraction*.

We often ask teachers in workshops to write a division word problem as they walk in and settle at their tables. Typically, 80 percent of the word problems they produce are best described as partitive division, whereas **measurement division**, also known as quotitive division, makes up a large proportion of the other 20 percent. This is the model of division shown in Figure 6.5, often describing situations in which the division could be represented by repeated subtraction. In the problem context in Figure 6.2, the father gives out pieces of licorice that are four inches long. Although the work in this sample doesn't explicitly call this repeated subtraction, it could be interpreted as such. The narration in Video 6.2 makes this repeated subtraction more explicit, repeatedly subtracting groups of four, which are circled and numbered in the diagram. On the bottom of the rectangular representation, the numbers of inches are shown in groups of four. On top of the rectangle, the servings of licorice given out are shown counting up by one as the rope of licorice decreases in length.

$$52 - 4 = 48 \quad \text{Rope length } - 4 \text{ in} = 48 \text{ in } 1 \text{ serving}$$
$$48 - 4 = 44 \quad \text{Rope length } - 4 \text{ in} = 44 \text{ in } 2 \text{ servings}$$
$$44 - 4 = 40 \quad \text{Rope length } - 4 \text{ in} = 40 \text{ in } 3 \text{ servings}$$

Discrete objects: Objects that each represent a whole and are not partitioned into fractional values.

As with partitive division, children who have not been introduced to measurement division exhibit an intuitive understanding of how to solve such problems but often run into issues with modeling and keeping track. In one study, young students (2nd and early 3rd graders) were given measurement division problem situations and **discrete objects** to model them (Mulligan & Mitchelmore, 1997). Of course, they were not told the problems were division situations nor were they taught to use the $\div$ symbol, so they had to rely on other problem-solving skills. The students were able to reliably remove equal groups until the set was exhausted, even if they may not have been able to produce an equation or tell the interviewer how many total objects were in the set. Still, some were not able to identify the "answer" or quotient because they lost track of the number of times they gave away objects! In the case of our problem situation with the licorice, this would look like losing track of

Continuous objects: Objects that can be partitioned into infinitely more and smaller pieces. Continuous objects are typically measured rather than counted.

the number of times Francisco gave away a **continuous object**, that is, a 4 inch length of licorice. Offering students a strategy for keeping track of how many times they take away a measure can be a big help in supporting their growing understanding of division. In Figure 6.5, the numbers along the top of the bar tell how many groups of 4 inches are given away. An organized table, a set of counters, or tallies are other strategies to help students keep track of the groups they are taking away. The solution strategy in Figure 6.5 makes it easier to see how measurement division could also be called *repeated subtraction*. Repeated subtraction is the opposite (or inverse) of repeated addition, which, as mentioned in Chapter 5, is the way we typically introduce multiplication to students.

Classrooms contain many opportunities for real-life measurement division. Perhaps students are doing some origami animals or other paper-folding activity. You direct a helper to pass out five squares of origami paper to each of their classmates. As you look at your stack of papers, you might wonder how many students can get five sheets of origami paper before opening a new package. This is measurement division thinking (rather than partitive thinking) because your goal is to pass out an exact quantity to each individual, rather than give each student a fair share. At home, and trying to encourage healthful eating, you might pack lunches using the same quotitive thinking: Each child gets three mini carrots in their lunch bag. You might wonder how many lunches your family will be able to pack with one big bag of carrots. Both of these, actions and thoughts, point to measurement division–like thinking. Like the classroom situation mentioned earlier, the numbers need not be precise to engage in measurement division–like thinking. The problem contexts we ask students to engage with will likely be more precise, but it's important to recognize the partitive and quotitive tendencies that already permeate our everyday lives.

THE UNKNOWNS IN PARTITIVE AND MEASUREMENT DIVISION

When modeling division situations, it is helpful to focus attention on what information is missing in a problem situation. Because the dividend is typically known in a division calculation, we focus attention only on the divisor and the quotient and their role in the problem situation. But first, note that the *divisor* and the *quotient* refer to a number's role in a *calculation*: We divide by the divisor in order to find the answer, or the quotient.

$$\text{dividend} \div \text{divisor} = \text{quotient}$$

Since multiplication and division are related—inverse—operations, we can, and we will, represent the same division using words that are familiar in multiplication:

$$\text{product} \div \text{factor} = \text{factor}$$

However, none of these words describes the *context* of the problem situation. Since Chapter 5, we have focused on whether a factor is a multiplier factor or a measure factor. This is even true for division problems, except now the factors are either in the *divisor or quotient positions*. In Figure 6.7, look for patterns that can help clarify the differences between partitive and measurement division situations.

FIGURE 6.7 PARTITIVE AND MEASUREMENT DIVISION SITUATIONS

PRODUCT (DIVIDEND)	MULTIPLIER FACTOR	MEASURE FACTOR	FAIR SHARE OR REPEATED SUBTRACTION?	PARTITIVE OR MEASUREMENT DIVISION
28 pencils	7 children	? pencils (per child)	Fair Share	Partitive
50 berries	? baskets	25 berries (per basket)	Repeated Subtraction	Measurement
12 children		4 children (per family)		
15 puppies	5 breeders			
24 flowers	? bouquets	? flowers (per bouquet)	Fair Share	
30 candies	? boxes	? candies (per box)	Repeated Subtraction	
20 pages				Partitive
32 paper plates				Measurement

Partitive problem situations typically represent fair-sharing activities, with attention to making sure that a set of objects is equally distributed to a predetermined number of places. For example, in distributing 28 pencils, we make sure to give an equal number of pencils to each of 7 children, without knowing how many each will get:

$$28 \div 7 = x$$
28 pencils ÷ 7 children = x pencils (per child)

Measurement problem situations are focused on the distribution of objects (or some other measure) in repeated subtraction, and it is clear how much is being shared in each distribution. What we don't know is how many portions will be given out:

$$50 \div 25 = x$$
50 berries ÷ 25 berries = x baskets

You may have noticed a pattern in the units, which is highlighted in color above. In partitive situations, the units in the dividend and the quotient are the same (pencils). In the measurement situation, the dividend and the divisor share the same unit (berries). Distilling the problem into a story and determining units, we can figure out which is partitive division (multiplier factor is known) and which is measurement division (measure factor is known). Take a moment to discuss with your colleagues why this might be true.

REMAINDERS

You will notice that all of our examples turn out neatly; there are no remainders. We made this choice in order to focus on the work of division in an Equal Groups context without the added complication of remainders. As we move into real-world situations, however, remainders are a reality. Our focus here is on how students understand problem situations so that they can decide which operation best does the work that needs to be done. In other words, our focus is on how we know when we need to divide.

As you and your students work with division in more realistic situations, there will be remainders. As students recontextualize an answer back into the problem situation, there are typically four possibilities for remainders (examples are provided with each of the possibilities):

- We can put aside the remainder and use the whole number part of the result as the answer.
  There are 45 flowers. Each bouquet requires 10 flowers. How many full bouquets can be made? (4)

- We can use the next highest whole-number value.
  There are 75 children going on the field trip. Each bus carries 30 children. How many buses are required for the trip? (3; Who wants to ride on half a bus?)

- We can include the remainder as a partial quantity, represented as a fraction or decimal.
  John can read about 40 pages in an hour. How long will it take him to read a 60-page book? ($1\frac{1}{2}$ or 1.5 hours)

- The remainder is the solution.
  Mrs. King has 25 books to give to 8 students for summer reading. If each student gets the same number of books, how many will she have left? (1)

As you and your students work with division problems, first focus on identifying problem situations where division is helpful. Then divide, finding an answer that might include a remainder. Then use the preceding list to help decide how to handle the remainder in the given context.

MATCHING MODELS TO CONTEXTS

Take a look at the problem in Figure 6.8 and how the student describes and draws what is happening in the given situation.

FIGURE 6.8

> Enrique's family is the last to arrive at the campground. Now there are 48 people checked in who all have to share 4 campfire pits. How many people are at each campfire pit that evening?

FIGURE 6.9 CAMPFIRE PROBLEM—DOES THE MODEL MATCH THE SITUATION?

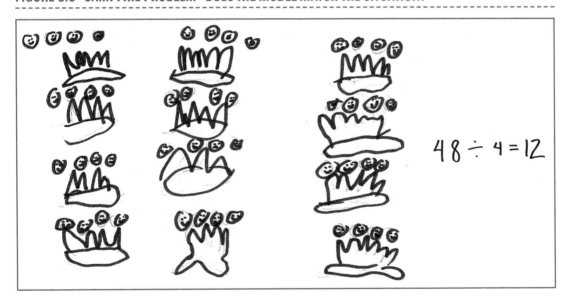

Look closely at Figure 6.9 and try to make sense of this student's thinking. What do you notice? If you are reading this book as part of a book study, this is a good time to stop and discuss the student's answer and the representation that accompanies it with your collaborative team. If you are not reading this as part of a study group, compare your response to the student's response. Where do you see 4? What is the unit? Where do you see 12? What is the unit?

The student work in Figure 6.9 shows 48 people gathered around campfires, and it also shows the correct answer for 48 ÷ 4. Both of these details are accurate. However, the student's drawing does not match the given problem situation! Instead of 12 campfires, an accurate representation would show 4 campfires, the multiplier factor, and 12 people in each group, the measure factor, but this student's work has these quantities in the factors flip-flopped.

What questions could we ask to help this student understand how the picture and the problem are different? In this case, focusing on the quantities is key:

> *What quantities from the problem are important? (campfires and people)*
> *How many campfires are at the campground? How does your picture show this?*
> *How many people are at the campground? How does your picture show this?*

Questions like these can help students pause to mathematize; they help students not only to identify the numbers in the story (4 and 48) but also to think about the relationship between them.

FIGURE 6.10 CAMPFIRE PROBLEM—A MORE ACCURATE MODEL

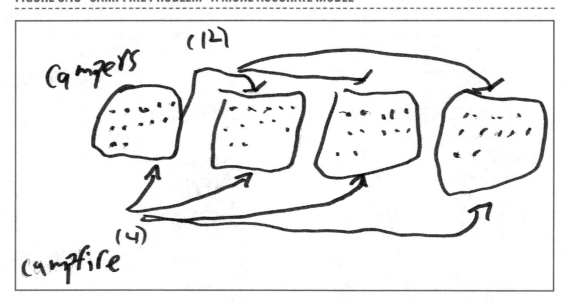

Figure 6.10 is less entertaining, but it is still a more accurate representation of the situation. Each square represents a campfire. At each campfire are 12 campers.

So, if the student's answer in Figure 6.9 is correct, why is it a problem that the representation does not match the problem situation? The simple answer is this: Not matching the problem situation reveals that the student has not displayed operation sense in the solution, which is far more important in the long term than arriving at the right answer. Remember that operation sense is understanding all of the "work" that each operation can do or, in other words, the kinds of problems an operation can solve. Operation sense also extends to the use of appropriately drawn representations for the action (or relationships) in the problem so that it represents an appropriate understanding of the situation, which we see in Figure 6.3, in the mathematizing sandbox. This is key for students to make sense of word problems and other problem situations that can be mathematized. Students are better able to recognize the actions and relationships in a problem context and translate them into mathematical symbols and equations when they have a solid operation sense. In this respect the answer is far less important than strong mathematizing skills.

Moving Beyond Whole Numbers

Like multiplication, division problems present their own challenges when involving fractions and decimals. As we noted in Chapter 5, when factors involve numbers that are less than one, the results can be confusing. But by bringing a strong understanding of the operation and the models that are appropriate for these operations to their problem solving, students can stay focused on the problem situation and avoid the confusion that results when they make snap judgments about answers.

Let's look at the two problems in Figures 6.11 and 6.12 and again consider how they are similar and different. Write your restatements in the spaces provided.

FIGURE 6.11

FIGURE 6.12

| Amenda is building a 3-yard track to test her new model train. She is able to build a $\frac{1}{4}$-yard length of track each day after school. How many days will it take her to finish the track? | Amenda is trying to figure out if she has enough glue to build her track. It takes $\frac{1}{4}$ of a bottle of glue to put together 3 pieces of track. How many pieces of track can you build with one bottle of glue? |

ENTER THE PROBLEM

How would you solve these problems? Use the spaces below to draw pictures or sketch the concrete representations you created.

EXPLORE

STUDENTS AND TEACHERS THINK ABOUT THE PROBLEMS

Take a look at the student work in Figures 6.13 and 6.14 and notice how the students describe or draw what is happening in the given word problems. Then look at the teacher commentary that follows the student work and consider what the teachers noticed in the student work.

FIGURE 6.13   **FIGURE 6.14**

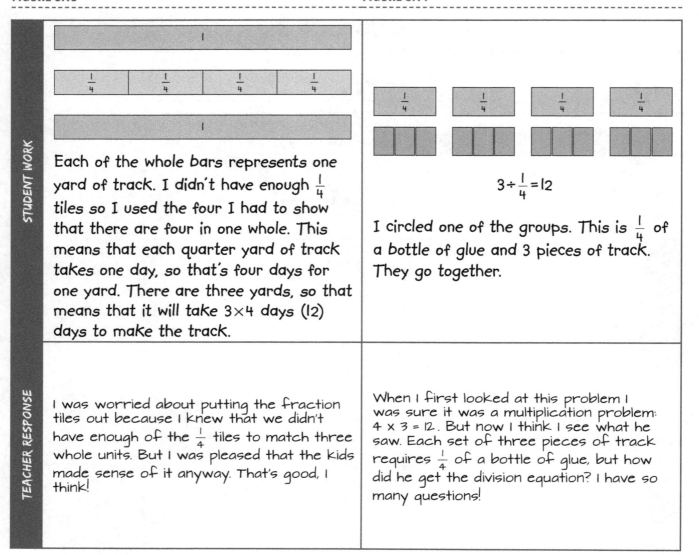

STUDENT WORK

Each of the whole bars represents one yard of track. I didn't have enough $\frac{1}{4}$ tiles so I used the four I had to show that there are four in one whole. This means that each quarter yard of track takes one day, so that's four days for one yard. There are three yards, so that means that it will take 3×4 days (12) days to make the track.

$3 \div \frac{1}{4} = 12$

I circled one of the groups. This is $\frac{1}{4}$ of a bottle of glue and 3 pieces of track. They go together.

TEACHER RESPONSE

I was worried about putting the fraction tiles out because I knew that we didn't have enough of the $\frac{1}{4}$ tiles to match three whole units. But I was pleased that the kids made sense of it anyway. That's good, I think!

When I first looked at this problem I was sure it was a multiplication problem: 4 × 3 = 12. But now I think I see what he saw. Each set of three pieces of track requires $\frac{1}{4}$ of a bottle of glue, but how did he get the division equation? I have so many questions!

ENTERING CHALLENGING DIVISION PROBLEMS

The track construction problem in Figure 6.11 may or may not be perceived as a division situation by students, or even by teachers themselves! One strategy for entering such a problem is to analyze it to identify the mathematical story in the problem situation. Armed with definitions and experience, students can recognize this as a measurement division model by

1. Recognizing that the problem is asking how many groups (multiplier factor): There are 3 yards of track. How many groups of $\frac{1}{4}$ yard are in 3 yards?

    and

2. Recognizing that the size of each group ($\frac{1}{4}$ yard, the measurement factor) is the known factor; and the number of groups (multiplier factor) is the unknown.

    and

3. Understanding that such problems are measurement division problems.

Another good strategy is to continue the exploration of a challenging word problem by making repeated connections among the five representations introduced in Chapter 1 (Figure 6.15).

FIGURE 6.15

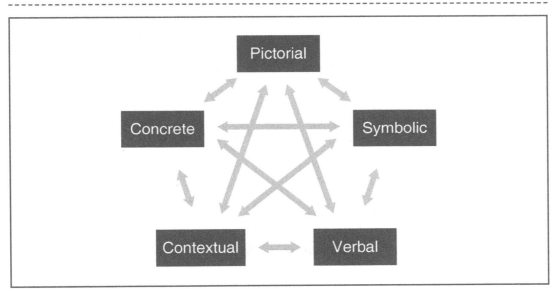

Source: Lesh, Post, & Behr (1987).

Figure 6.16 shows how the track-building problem in Figure 6.11 can be represented using all five of the representations we introduced in Chapter 1. For example, the pictorial representation looks much like a number line, showing an endpoint of 3 and separate jumps that increase by $\frac{1}{4}$. This is the same $\frac{1}{4}$ that is the measure factor in the division equation $3 \div \frac{1}{4} = n$, which is a symbolic representation of the problem. Can you see other connections between the equation (symbolic) and the number line (pictorial)? If you are working with a group, take some time to make even more connections among the multiple representations. As the model in Figure 6.15 illustrates, and as we discussed in Chapter 1, these representations are interrelated. The symbolic representation can be translated into a pictorial representation and vice versa. Consider how the work of translating deepens your understanding of the problem situation. Video 6.3 explores some of the connections summarized in the figure.

Video 6.3

Lesh Model Connections/ Translations for Track Problem

resources. corwin.com/ problemsolving3-5

FIGURE 6.16 FIVE MODES FOR REPRESENTING A WORD PROBLEM

REPRESENTATION	EXAMPLE
Contextual	Amenda is building a 3-yard track to test her new model train. She is able to build a $\frac{1}{4}$-yard length of track each day after school. How many days will it take her to finish the track?
Pictorial	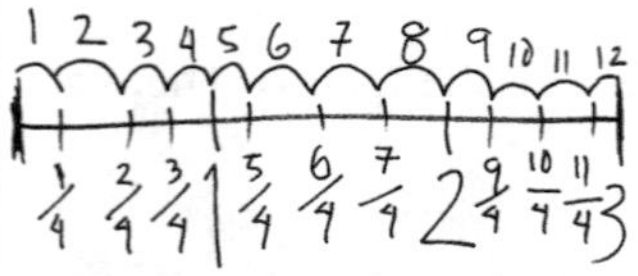
Concrete	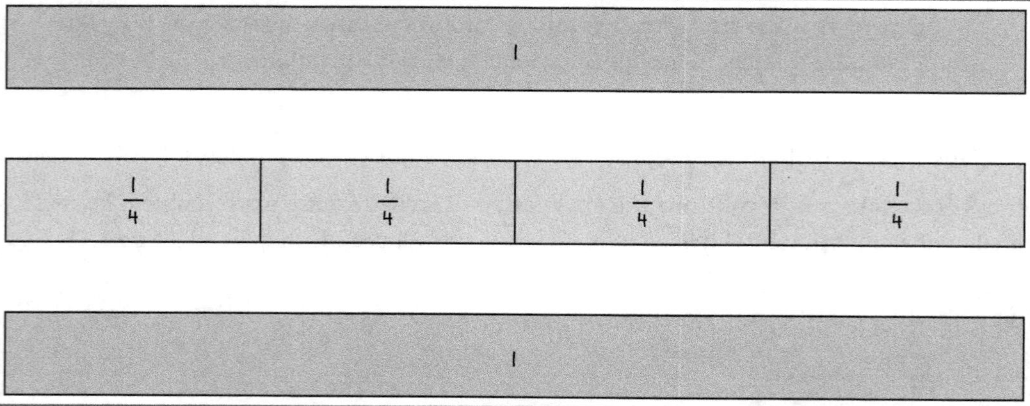
Verbal	Each of the blue bars represents one yard of track. I didn't have enough $\frac{1}{4}$ tiles so I used the four "I had to show that there are four in one whole. This means that each quarter yard of track takes one day, so that's four days for one yard. There are three yards, so that means that it will take 3×4 days (12 days) to make the track."
Symbolic (Equation)	$?\left(\text{days}\right) \times \frac{1}{4}\left(\text{yards of track per day}\right) = 3\left(\text{yards of track}\right)$ $\frac{1}{4}n = 3$ $3\left(\text{yards of track}\right) \div \frac{1}{4}\left(\text{yards of track per day}\right) = ?\left(\text{days}\right)$ $\frac{3}{\frac{1}{4}} = n \text{ or } 3 \div \frac{1}{4} = n$

TRANSLATING THE FIVE REPRESENTATIONS: TRY IT OUT

Now let's turn to the track and glue problem in Figure 6.12, best represented by a partitive division model. Creating a story for the problem, and entering the problem by starting with a verbal representation, could distill the problem as follows:

3 pieces of track go with $\frac{1}{4}$ of a bottle of glue. It's like the track pieces get a fair share of the glue.

Before diving into the work of moving through multiple representations on your own, we would like to say more about verbal representations and writing stories. Verbal representations can come in many shapes and forms and be used at various points to clarify and define. Sometimes they are used to explain and add meaning to other representations. As we have suggested throughout the book, a story that distills the problem into its essentials or an effort to restate the problem in your own words provides a verbal representation and serves as a useful beginning. Translating it to other representations—pictorial, concrete, and the like—moves you down the path of exploration. By later translating those representations into a different verbal representation, you are clarifying and honing your understanding even further.

Now dive deeply into this problem context, using the table in Figure 6.17 to create and connect five different representations of the problem in Figure 6.12. The opening problem and the student's representation are included to give you a start. The student who created this visual representation, however, did not include a description of the strategy used, nor did the student include any symbols, like an equation or labels of the units. Complete the student's response including a representation for all five categories. Be sure to make connections among the five representations. How are the particular elements in one representation expressed in the others?

FIGURE 6.17 TRY IT OUT: FIVE MODES FOR REPRESENTING A WORD PROBLEM

REPRESENTATION	EXAMPLE
Contextual	Amenda is trying to figure out if she has enough glue to build her track. It takes $\frac{1}{4}$ of a bottle of glue to put together 3 pieces of track. How many pieces of track can you build with one bottle of glue?
Pictorial	
Concrete	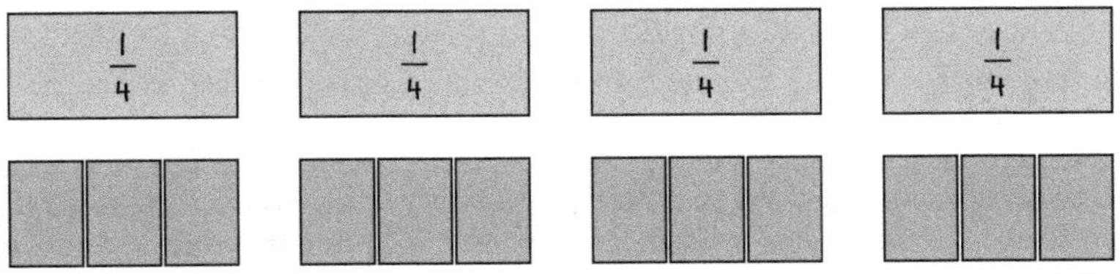
Verbal	
Symbolic (Equation)	

Both railroad track problem situations illustrate why it is important to understand the partitive and measurement models of division. In partitive division, the value of $\frac{1}{4}$ is not a quantity we can measure. When we say that Amenda uses $\frac{1}{4}$ of a bottle of glue to build three tracks, we recognize that $\frac{1}{4}$ is the multiplier factor—it doesn't have a unit of measure by itself. The concrete representation in Figure 6.17 makes a model to show the relationship, but that's not the same as its being a unit. The multiplier factor essentially tells us what to do, so we are left to ask *How big or how much?* At the same time, the $\frac{1}{4}$ in a measurement division context is an actual measure, a length of track, and is represented in Figure 6.16 by the same $\frac{1}{4}$ tile. It tells us how big a group is. We then have to ask *How many can I get?*

These same questions will help find a solution when looking at division outside of a meaningful context. Consider the division problem $2,678 \div 4$. This is a calculation with no reference to a context, but students can call on their division model understanding and ask *How many groups of 4 can I get from 2,678?* This is measurement division thinking. As you consider more possible partial products, they ask *Can I make 10 groups of 4?* (Yes) *Can I make 100 groups of 4?* (Yes) *Can I make 1,000 groups of 4?* (No) *Can I make 200?* (Yes) Most students can learn to do this in larger and more efficient chunks! If students do not have a strategy to model a context-free problem like this one, the strategy they then use to calculate this quotient is a memorized procedure. Memorized procedures may not always be reliable. If students can apply one of the two models of division to a problem, they can use manipulatives or pictures to create a representation to help model and find the quotient.

TRACKING THE UNIT WHOLE AND THE REFERENT WHOLE

One of the challenges of fraction division is keeping track of the unit whole. Although the two problems in Figures 6.18 and 6.19 appear to be whole number division, they have fractional quotients, which leads to many questions about what constitutes the "whole." Read and think about this pair of problems. What pictures or concrete representations would you use initially to represent the whole numbers in these problems. As you work on a solution, does your choice of the best model for these problems change?

FIGURE 6.18

FIGURE 6.19

On Saturday there were 4 dogs at the shelter. Jian took a donation of 7 pounds of food. If the dogs got the same amount of the food, how much did each dog get?	In order to meet his fitness goals, Andrew likes to run 7 miles each week. If he runs 4 miles each day, how many days will it take him to run all 7 miles?

Take a look at the student work in Figures 6.20 and 6.21 and consider how the students describe or draw what is happening in the given word problems. Then look at the teacher commentary that follows the student work and consider what the teachers noticed in the student work.

FIGURE 6.20   **FIGURE 6.21**

STUDENT WORK

This is 7 pounds of dog food. Each dog gets one pound, which I have circled. That leaves three pounds left over.

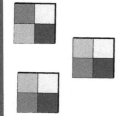

I knew that I couldn't give each dog another whole pound of food, so I had to change what a square means. Each square is now four separate squares. This lets me divide the rest of the three up into quarters.

Andrew ran 7 miles each week so I started with 7 tiles. Then I tried to think of what he did each day.

Since he ran 4 miles each day I made a group of 4 tiles and I had 3 tiles left. Our table talked about that a long time.

We agreed that Andrew did 4 miles on the first day, but on the second day didn't finish all 4 miles.

Jeff said it was $1\frac{3}{7}$ of a day because there was one whole day and then there were 3 out of the 7 days.

Joyce said it was $1\frac{3}{4}$ because he did 3 of the 4 miles that should have happened on the second day.

TEACHER RESPONSE

This is pretty clever. When she chose the square tiles, I was worried about how she could represent the quarters of a pound that I knew were in the answer. Changing one square tile from a unit whole (1 pound) to a referent whole ($\frac{1}{4}$ pound) is a good solution for students who know what they are doing. I will have to circle back to make sure that she can use this representation to come up with an answer. Or I could pair her with someone who has used a different representation but similar strategy ...

What a great conversation this table had about this problem! Jeff's and Joyce's different interpretations ended up being the beginning of a great classroom discussion. The students finally agreed that the denominator of the answer had to be 4 and not 7. Since each one of Andrew's day goals was 4 miles, they agreed that $\frac{3}{4}$ of a day made more sense than $\frac{7}{4}$ days.

VIDEO

Video 6.4

Sharing Dog Food With Color Tiles

Video 6.5

Andrew Running With Color Tiles

The work samples for these problems end with students wondering about the answers they had produced using a discrete model manipulative. Both had left the problem unresolved in their groups, but the conversation also led to better discourse in the classroom. In these problem contexts the manipulative model leaves room for confusion and therefore requires students to engage in some productive struggle. As a matter of fact, the student in Figure 6.21 reported that all of the students at his table were not in agreement. Let's explore the origin of the confusion and how it arises both within the problem context and with the tool the students decided to use.

TRACKING WHOLES IN PARTITIVE DIVISION In the shelter dog problem (Figure 6.20), the unit of the unknown factor (x pounds) matches the unit of the full quantity (7 pounds) and not the divisor, so we can conclude that this is likely a partitive division context: We know the multiplier factor and are looking for the missing measure factor. Both the dividend (7 pounds) and the quotient (x pounds) are colored in the equations below for you to see, while the divisor remains uncolored. As we saw earlier, when the unit (pounds) is distributed to an equal number of sharers (dogs), the problem is a partitive division model. Also, by narrowing in on the question words "How much … ?" we can verify that "how much" measures pounds of dog food, not dogs!

7 pounds of dog food is fair shared by 4 dogs. How much does each dog get?

$$7 \text{ pounds} \div 4 \text{ dogs} = x \text{ pounds}$$
$$7 \div 4 = x$$

The student whose work is shown in Figure 6.20 recognized that 7 pounds of dog food can be represented with seven separate square tiles, and then she gave each dog one full pound of food before grappling with the remainder of 3. Then she let the 4 in the divisor be her guide. If she had to divide this dog food and give it to 4 dogs, she was going to make sure that there would be fourths to give. Note the flexible change in her representation that followed her thinking. The unit whole began as a single square tile. In the second stage of her problem, she changed the unit whole to be four square tiles. Each square tile now represents $\frac{1}{4}$ of a pound of dog food instead of 1 pound. That's a clever strategy and it is one of the benefits of students using a physical model over a visual model. The exchange was seamless and the problem essentially restarted to work only with the remainder.

The unit of the quotient is now in pounds and each square tile represents a quarter pound. The quotient has now become a focus of the problem. In the beginning we called the pound of dog food the unit whole, but we are now referring to the quotient, and the answer we give references how many pounds each dog gets. That unit is not the same as the unit whole. We refer to this new unit as the **referent whole**. For the referent whole in this phase of the problem, one square tile represents $\frac{1}{4}$ of a pound, not a whole pound, which remains the unit whole. But the answer to this problem is neither 7 nor $1\frac{3}{7}$, but $1\frac{3}{4}$: one unit whole (1 pound) and 3 referent wholes (3 of the $\frac{1}{4}$ pounds). To learn more about referent wholes, see Philipp and Hawthorne (2015).

Referent whole: In a problem context, a term used to label a unit that is distinguished from the unit whole originally established in the problem.

Now that you have heard the student's strategy and thought about the difficulties she had arriving at a final quotient, it is valuable to take out your counters or tiles and act out the problem yourself, one step at a time. If you are working with a team of teachers, this would be a good time to try the student's strategy and discuss the challenges and resolutions she made along the way. Video 6.4 narrates this example of student work.

TRACKING WHOLES IN MEASUREMENT DIVISION In the running problem, the unit of the unknown factor (x days) does *not* match the unit of the full quantity (7 miles) nor does it match the divisor, so we can conclude that this is likely a measurement division context: We know the measure factor and are looking for the missing multiplier factor. Both the dividend (7 miles) and the divisor (4 miles) are colored in the equations below for you to see, leaving the quotient (days) uncolored. This helps us understand that the question is asking how the miles run in one day are part of the full week's number of miles in Andrew's fitness goals. The unit of the answer is days, not miles: How many days will it take Andrew to meet his goal of 7 miles in one week? The problem context follows a measurement division model.

> *The total number of miles needed is 7. There is a 4 mile chunk of running each day.*
> *How many full-day chunks of running did Andrew do?*

$$7 \text{ miles} \div 4 \text{ miles} = x \text{ days}$$
$$7 \div 4 = x$$

Measurement division can be explained through repeated subtraction. In this case $7 - 4$ fulfills one day of Andrew's goal. The remainder is 3 miles. Since he cannot fulfill a second day, we can wonder what portion (or fraction) of a second day's progress he has met. As we saw with the shelter dog problem (Figure 6.20), the quotient in this problem has a new referent whole: the number of days it takes Andrew to meet his fitness goal. Framing the problem by returning to the context helps answer the question "How many days?" As Joyce mentions in her explanation in Figure 6.21, Andrew achieves one full day of his goal (1 day, or 4 miles) and three out of the four miles that make up a second day's goal ($\frac{3}{4}$ day, or 3 miles) for a total of $1\frac{3}{4}$ days (7 miles). Now, you might be wondering what $1\frac{3}{4}$ days really means. All of the work we just did happened in the mathematizing sandbox. As you exit the sandbox and revisit the context, you might conclude that the answer of $1\frac{3}{4}$ days doesn't make sense and instead choose to give an answer using the next whole number, 2 days, which is a more appropriate value for the unit "days."

Now work through the running problem on your own, as well as with your team, using square tiles or another representation. Explain how Joyce got her answer. Explain how Jeff might have arrived at his answer. As a team, discuss strategies for helping students work through the change necessary for dealing with the referent unit in the quotient. You can hear our thinking about this problem in Video 6.5.

If $7 \div 4$ is not the expression that immediately came to you for one or both of these problems, remember that you are not alone. As we said previously, measurement division problem situations are often not recognized as "real" division. You may have noted that despite the different problem contexts and the different models of division, both of these problem types have the same division equation to represent them: $7 \div 4 = 1\frac{3}{4}$. This division structure is normally found in fifth grade standards, but most standards do not unpack the complexity of the thinking that underlies this simple division equation. The confusion arises because the answer (quotient) is not a whole number. In other words, when we find the quotient, there will be a remainder, and fifth grade students are only starting to learn about strategies for talking about and representing remainders or partial units in the quotient.

Fraction division can be one of the most difficult topics in the intermediate and middle grades. As Zalman Usiskin (2012) said,

> *Neither of these [skills or properties which explain invert & multiply] conveys the most important understanding of division of fractions to the user of mathematics, who may argue that unless you can recognize situations outside of naked arithmetic that involve the division of fractions, you really do not understand division of fractions.*

Notes on Working With Manipulatives

The flexibility of working with a discrete model like square tiles allows students to rethink and then change the value of each unit. In the dog food problem in Figure 6.20, the square tile "crashed" because it couldn't be partitioned into four equal pieces. The model needed to be adapted to represent a fractional value. The important thing is that students be able to justify the choices they are making and be able to explain their representations. For example, as we saw in the dog food problem, the unit whole can be changed. When the tiles do not show a printed value, it is much easier to assign a value that is relational. Kids and teachers alike enjoy working with fraction tiles, and their precision is helpful, but sometimes the printing on fraction tiles is a drawback. It is sometimes valuable to turn the fraction tiles upside down so that the printed fractions themselves do not show, which we'll see in Chapter 8.

Selecting an appropriate manipulative is a personal decision, one that each student must make. Our job is to make sure that the models students select match their own thinking, not ours. This may require you to listen carefully and for them to communicate their thinking with you so that you can "get in their head." Then you will be able to ask questions that help guide them to make choices. See the list of strategies in Figure 6.22 (introduced in Chapter 2), for a reminder on working with multiple models.

FIGURE 6.22 ENCOURAGING MULTIPLE MODELS IN PROBLEM SOLVING

1. **Choose**: Encourage individual choice of pictorial representations.

2. **Explain**: Ask students to explain what the parts of their pictorial representation mean and explain the relationships between those parts.

3. **Justify**: Challenge students to defend their choices. Challenge students' correct representations just as much as you would ask them to justify incorrect representations.

4. **Model**: Explicitly model new forms of diagrams or manipulatives that you choose to use, explaining your decisions as you demonstrate how you are using the tool. We are *not* suggesting you explicitly teach students to use the tool. Simply, model your own thinking process as you employ a visual, but reinforce to students that you are held to the same standard for justifying your decisions as they are.

5. **Connect:** Ask students to describe how two representations or models relate to each other. Encourage them to identify how each element of the problem appears in each model. Ask them to explain when they might prefer one model or representation over another.

6. **Share:** Ask students to explain a novel visual approach to their peers and discuss how they model their thinking process.

7. **Expect:** Communicate that you expect to see visual diagrams or manipulatives used to explain mathematical ideas.

8. **Crash:** No representation works in every context or situation. Expect any model to fail at some point, and encourage students to change their representation when the model crashes.

KEY IDEAS

Equal Groups division problems are situations where one of the two factors, either the one representing the size of the group (the measure) or the one representing the number of groups (the multiplier), is the unknown element in the problem. These are some of the key ideas we want you to remember and share with your students as you learn about Equal Groups division problems:

1. Equal Groups multiplication and division are related to repeated addition and subtraction, but they aren't the same.

2. *Dividend, divisor,* and *quotient* are useful terms for identifying a number's position in an equation. *Measure factor, multiplier factor,* and either *product* or *quotient* are used to identify the role of quantities in a mathematical story.

3. Because Equal Groups are asymmetric multiplication problems, there are two related division problems, depending on which factor is missing.

4. If the known factor is the multiplier factor (the number of groups), the division is referred to as partitive or fair-share division. Therefore, the missing factor is the measure factor (the size of the group).

5. If the known factor is the measure factor (the size of the group), the division is referred to as measurement or quotitive division. The missing factor is therefore the multiplier factor (the number of groups).

6. Partitive and measurement division exist only in the context of a problem or in the modeling of a problem situation. For example, $36 \div 9$ is neither partitive nor quotitive. The context of a problem situation determines which model it is.

7. There can be a whole number of groups (the multiplier factor is a whole-number value) or a problem can include a partial group when the multiplier is a fraction or decimal value.

8. Group size can be a whole-number value or a fractional value. For some contexts, a group size that is not a whole number may not make sense.

9. The equation that best shows the problem situation might be different from the equation that helps with the computation used to find the solution.

TRY IT OUT!

IDENTIFY THE PROBLEM SITUATION

Decide whether each of the following problems shows a partitive or measurement model of division. Write an equation that represents the situation. Give reasons for your thinking or make a model to demonstrate your decision.

1. There are 7 baskets at the farmers market and all together they hold 28 sweet onions. Each basket holds the same number of sweet onions. How many sweet onions are there in each basket?

2. There are 8 pieces of art in each display area at the school art show. There are 24 pieces of art all together. How many display areas are there at the school art show?

3. The groundskeeper noticed that the 16 trees along the river have a total of 128 eggs in nests about to hatch. There is an equal number of eggs hatching in each tree. How many eggs are in each tree?

4. There are 84 apples in the harvest gift basket. Adara took three and gave them to the teacher next door. If she continued giving away apples three at a time, how many teachers would receive a portion?

5. The cakes from Zemora's bakery are cut in three equal pieces before serving. If Zemora bakes 50 cakes a day, how many servings can she sell each day?

6. Carrie wants to decorate her new wreath with bows. Each bow takes $\frac{1}{4}$ yard of ribbon. The spool of ribbon holds 20 yards. How many bows can she make?

7. James ordered 3 pizzas for 5 friends to share. How much pizza does each person get, given that they choose to eat the same amount?

8. Priella had 10 ounces of prime rib. She cut off 3-ounce portions for each dinner party guest. How many servings could she make?

WRITE THE PROBLEM

For each of the following equations, write a word problem that matches. Include a representation that corresponds to the situation.

1. $15 \div 3 = 5$

2. $15 \div 5 = 3$

3. $138 \div 23 = 6$

4. $138 \div 6 = 23$

5. $6 \div \frac{1}{5} = 30$

6. $\frac{1}{5} \div 6 = \frac{1}{30}$

7. $4 \div 3 = 1\frac{1}{3}$

8. $8 \div 5 = 1\frac{3}{5}$

BRANCH OUT

1. In Chapter 5, we featured the book *The Doorbell Rang* by Pat Hutchins (1986). Revisit the book and compare the division model in that book with the division model seen in *Divide and Ride* by Stuart Murphy (1997).

2. As teachers we frequently divide resources and materials in our classrooms. Make it an active part of your routine to consider whether you are dividing partitively or quotitively. If you are thinking about giving a fair share to each student, that is partitive thinking. If you are thinking about giving each student an exact amount and are trying to figure out how many times you can distribute that amount, you are thinking quotitively. By thinking about this idea frequently, you will be better able to make decisions when balancing the division word problems you give students.

REFLECT

1. Discuss the ways that attributes of manipulatives were used in this chapter to highlight mathematical features. How can you help students use attributes of various manipulatives productively?

2. How does a focus on the partitive and measurement division models change your thinking about how you structure a division unit?

3. If a student creates an inaccurate representation but still generates a correct answer, what should happen next?

4. We did not directly discuss remainders as a separate topic in this book. With your colleagues, revisit some of the problems and consider the role of remainders in problems with both partitive and measurement models of division.

5. Refer to the Multiplication and Division Problem Situations table at the beginning of this chapter (you can download a copy from http://resources.corwin.com/problemsolving3-5). Examine the textbook you use for the grade you teach and read the word problems, looking for Equal Groups problems (division). Classify the word problems you find, making a tally on the table for each example. If you encounter a multistep problem, classify it by the first action that should take place in the problem. If you aren't sure whether it is an Equal Groups problem, save it for later.

NOTES

CHAPTER SEVEN

Multiplicative Comparisons
Another Asymmetric Relationship

Thinking About Multiplicative Comparisons

In Chapters 5 and 6 we thought about Equal Groups situations with a focus on the role of the factors in both multiplication (Chapter 5) and division (Chapter 6). With one factor showing the number of groups (the multiplier factor) and one factor showing the size of the groups (the measure factor), this asymmetric situation can be expressed using both multiplication and division equations. In this chapter we will see that Equal Groups situations are not the only asymmetric multiplication and division problem situations. Multiplicative Comparisons are another asymmetric problem type.

Multiplication and Division Problem Situations

	Resulting Value Unknown	Scale Factor (Times as Many) Unknown	Original Value Unknown	
Multiplicative Comparison	Amelia's dog is 5 times older than Wanda's 3-year-old dog. How old is Amelia's dog? $5 \times 3 = x$ $x \div 5 = 3$	Sydney has \$15 to spend on dog treats. Her best friend has \$5. Sydney has how many times more dollars than her friend has? $x \times 5 = 15$ $5 = 15 \div x$	Devonte has 15 dog toys on the floor in his living room. That is 3 times the number of toys in the dog's toy basket. How many toys are in the toy basket? $3 \times x = 15$ $15 \div 3 = x$	

Note: These representations for the problem situations reflect our understanding based on a number of resources. These include the tables in the Common Core State Standards for mathematics (Common Core Standards Initiative, 2010), the problem situations as described in the Cognitively Guided Instruction research (Carpenter, Hiebert, & Moser, 1981), in Heller and Greeno (1979) and Riley, Greeno, & Heller (1984), and other tools. See the Appendix and companion website for a more detailed summary of the documents that informed our development of this table.

ASYMMETRICAL (NONMATCHING) FACTORS

	Product Unknown	Multiplier (Number of Groups) Unknown	Measure (Group Size) Unknown	
Equal Groups (Ratio/Rate)*	Mayim has 8 vases to decorate the tables at her party. She places 3 flowers in each vase. How many flowers does she need? $8 \times 3 = x$ $x \div 8 = 3$	Mayim has some vases to decorate the tables at her party. She places 3 flowers in each vase. If she uses 24 flowers, how many vases does she have? $x \times 3 = 24$ $x = 24 \div 3$	Mayim places 24 flowers in vases to decorate the tables at her party. If there are 8 vases, how many flowers will be in each vase? $8 \times x = 24$ $24 \div 8 = x$	
	Resulting Value Unknown	Scale Factor (Times as Many) Unknown	Original Value Unknown	
Multiplicative Comparison	Amelia's dog is 5 times older than Wanda's 3-year-old dog. How old is Amelia's dog? $5 \times 3 = x$ $x \div 5 = 3$	Sydney has \$15 to spend on dog treats. Her best friend has \$5. Sydney has how many times more dollars than her friend has? $x \times 5 = 15$ $5 = 15 \div x$	Devonte has 15 dog toys on the floor in his living room. That is 3 times the number of toys in the dog's toy basket. How many toys are in the toy basket? $3 \times x = 15$ $15 \div 3 = x$	

SYMMETRICAL (MATCHING) FACTORS

	Product Unknown	One Dimension Unknown	Both Dimensions Unknown
Area/Array	Mrs. Bradley bought a rubber mat to cover the floor under the balance beam. One side of the mat measured 5 feet and the other side measured 8 feet. How many square feet does the mat measure? $5 \times 8 = x$ $x \div 8 = 5$	The 40 members of the student council lined up on the stage in the gym to take yearbook pictures. The first row started with 8 students and the rest of the rows did the same. How many rows were there? $8 \times x = 40$ $x = 40 \div 8$	Mr. Donato is arranging student work on the wall for the art show. He started with 40 square entries and arranged them into a rectangular arrangement. How many entries long and wide could the arrangement be? $x \times y = 40$ $40 \div x = y$
	Sample Space (Total Outcomes) Unknown	One Factor Unknown	Both Factors Unknown
Combinations** (Fundamental Counting Principle)	Karen makes sandwiches at the diner. She offers 3 kinds of bread and 7 different lunch meats. How many unique sandwiches can she make? $3 \times 7 = x$ $3 = x \div 7$	Evelyn works at the ice cream counter. She says that she can make 21 unique and different ice cream sundaes using just ice cream flavors and toppings. If she has 3 flavors of ice cream, how many kinds of toppings does Evelyn offer? $3 \times x = 21$ $21 \div 3 = x$	Audrey can make 21 different fruit sodas using the machine at the diner. How many different flavorings and sodas could there be? $x \times y = 21$ $x = 21 \div y$

Sandbox Notes

Remember that the focus of exploration for any problem isn't simply to find any workable way to represent the problem but, rather, to try out multiple representations in the search for the one that most accurately represents the problem situation. By paying attention to the quantities and articulating to yourself the work each does—in short, by following the guiding questions—you will not just be solving the problem but also be building an understanding of the operation.

As you have done in previous chapters, ask yourself these questions to focus your thinking:

- *Think about the numbers in each situation. What do they represent? Which are quantities? Which are not? What work do they do?*

- *How can you represent the quantities in the word problems with your manipulatives or pictures?*

- *What number sentence best shows what is happening in each story?*

As you put the problems in Figures 7.1 and 7.2 into your own words, pay special attention to the quantities and the work each does in both problems. You may also take the values out of the picture at first and focus on the relationships, using *some* in place of the quantities. This strategy may help you to zero in even more sharply on their different functions in each problem.

FIGURE 7.1	FIGURE 7.2
Rajesh had 12 grapes for a snack. Latika had 3 more grapes in her snack than Rajesh did. How many grapes did Latika have?	Joyce lives 12 miles from her school. Andrew lives 3 times as far from school as Joyce does. How far away from school does Andrew live?

ENTER THE PROBLEM

FIGURE 7.3 A MODEL FOR MATHEMATIZING WORD PROBLEMS

STUDENTS AND TEACHERS THINK ABOUT THE PROBLEMS

Take a look at the student work in Figures 7.4 and 7.5 and consider how the students describe or draw what is happening in the given word problems. Then read the teacher commentary that follows and consider what the teachers noticed in the student work.

FIGURE 7.4   **FIGURE 7.5**

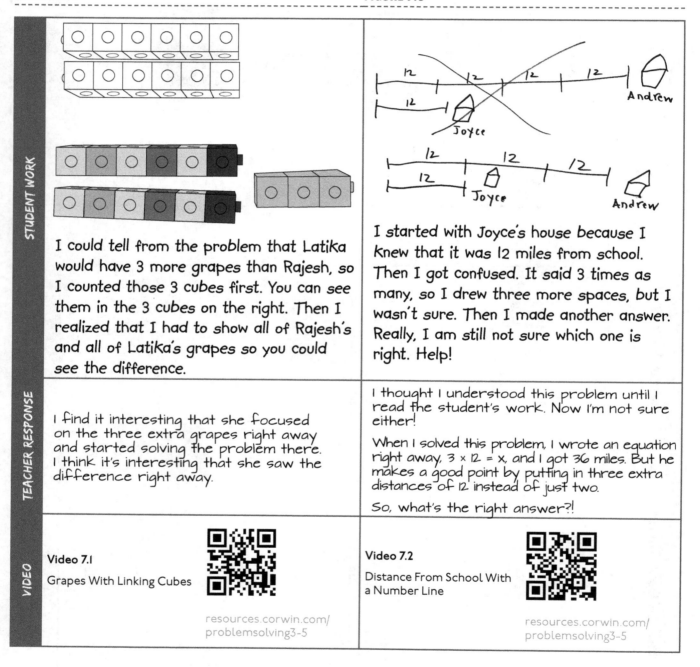

STUDENT WORK

I could tell from the problem that Latika would have 3 more grapes than Rajesh, so I counted those 3 cubes first. You can see them in the 3 cubes on the right. Then I realized that I had to show all of Rajesh's and all of Latika's grapes so you could see the difference.

I started with Joyce's house because I knew that it was 12 miles from school. Then I got confused. It said 3 times as many, so I drew three more spaces, but I wasn't sure. Then I made another answer. Really, I am still not sure which one is right. Help!

TEACHER RESPONSE

I find it interesting that she focused on the three extra grapes right away and started solving the problem there. I think it's interesting that she saw the difference right away.

I thought I understood this problem until I read the student's work. Now I'm not sure either!

When I solved this problem, I wrote an equation right away, 3 × 12 = x, and I got 36 miles. But he makes a good point by putting in three extra distances of 12 instead of just two.

So, what's the right answer?!

VIDEO

Video 7.1

Grapes With Linking Cubes

resources.corwin.com/
problemsolving3-5

Video 7.2

Distance From School With a Number Line

resources.corwin.com/
problemsolving3-5

We frequently ask teachers and students, "Where do you see 3 [or whatever the important number is] in this representation?" This is particularly important when looking at someone else's work, for example, a colleague's work, a student work sample, or a problem such as the ones presented here. If you are working as a team, take a moment to highlight where you see the 3 in each problem. Note in Figure 7.5 and Video 7.2 the student's doubt about whether to add two "distances" of

12 miles or three and the teacher's own doubt in response. Are you having a similar response or do you feel certain of your representation? It is important for us, as teachers, to consider how others may be thinking about the problem because it sheds light on what our students might do and better prepares us to offer strategic guiding questions in these situations.

ADDITIVE VERSUS MULTIPLICATIVE COMPARISON

Let's now look closely at the function of the 3 in the problems in Figures 7.1 and 7.2. The value 3 is the change for both comparisons, but the role of the 3 in each word problem is very different. Latika has 3 more grapes than Rajesh. If each of them happens to get 10 more grapes, she would still have 3 more than he does. The difference between them will always be exactly 3 grapes, as shown in the student's representation in Figure 7.4 with the three extra blocks. You might already recognize this as an Additive Comparison problem. The home-to-school distance problem in Figure 7.5, however, also illustrates a change by 3, but in this case in the form of a **Multiplicative Comparison** problem situation. The story and equation look like this:

$$\text{Joyce's distance} \times 3 = \text{Andrew's distance}$$
$$12 \times 3 = x$$

The 3 in this problem functions as a multiplier (3 times the distance) while the 12 functions as a measure (the distance). Because Multiplicative Comparison problems will by definition have factors that do different work, they are always asymmetric, similar to the way Equal Groups problem situations are. The 3 indicates that traveling to Andrew's house is equivalent to traveling the 12 miles to Joyce's house *three* times. This is often referred to as scaling or a scale factor. This also clarifies the confusion expressed by both the student and the teacher in Figure 7.5. The distance is not three distances *in addition* to the 12 miles as the student drew and then crossed out but, rather, is equivalent to three of Meg's distances.

The student's corrected pictorial representation is accurate, but we could help this student build a strong operation sense by demonstrating the correspondence between the scale factor and the measure factor using objects. The chips in Figure 7.6 show that for every mile that Joyce's house is from the school, Andrew's is three miles away. Of course, this particular problem applies only to the single occurrence of these two individuals' house-to-school distances, but this problem is setting the stage for students' later introduction to ratios in grade 6 by emphasizing the multiplicative relationship.

> Multiplicative Comparison: A problem situation that compares two measures by describing their difference in terms of how many times greater (or less) one is than the other.

> Scaling or scale factor: The factor that describes "times as many" is often referred to as a scale factor, and the action as scaling.

FIGURE 7.6

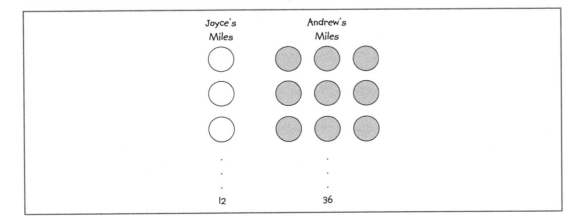

GROWING FASTER

As the model in Figure 7.6 demonstrates, the Multiplicative Comparison is a completely different kind of change than an Additive Comparison. The result of a multiplicative change is more sensitive to the quantities acting on it, which magnifies the impact of the change more than they would in an additive change. For example, for each increase of 1 in the multiplicative change value, the resulting quantity changes by 12. If Andrew lived 4 times as far from school as Joyce did, then the change from 3 to 4 "times" would represent an additional 12 miles between his home and school, not one additional mile. He would live a full 48 miles away, instead of 36 miles away. Expressed as a model using the same form of chip diagram as in Figure 7.6, the model would instead show four chip distances for Andrew for every one chip distance for Joyce (Figure 7.7).

FIGURE 7.7

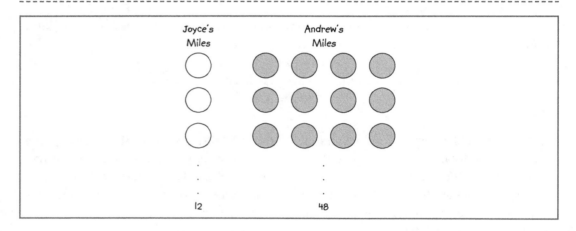

Understanding the difference between these two problems represents a major milestone in students' mathematical development. Many of the students in this grade band are only beginning to make sense of the multiplicative thinking that will characterize their middle school curriculum, and some students may not even achieve strong multiplicative thinking until well into adulthood (Piaget & Inhelder, 1973). This topic is introductory for your students at this grade level, so it is possible that a more concrete approach can provide better access. In most standards, students are only beginning to understand what "times as many" or "times as far" really mean and to be able to represent it in images and in equations. This is an important early understanding for ratio and proportional reasoning in middle school.

Multiplicative Comparison problems can pose a challenge to students. But why? It could be because this problem type is far more challenging than the others, or it could be because students do not have much experience acting out and building representations to make sense of these problem types (Franke, 2018). Fortunately, most fourth-grade standards now ask students to make sense of problems that use the language "times as many" or other variations that are related to comparisons. Our recommendation is that all students have access to problems of this type intermixed with the more easily accessible Equal Groups types. By starting with an early introduction, offering plenty of experiences modeling the problem type, at least starting in fourth grade, you can help students familiarize themselves with Multiplicative Comparison problems. You can also support the development of students' operation sense by actively encouraging the use of multiple representations, providing plenty of experience with posing and solving unfamiliar comparison problems, and looking for opportunities to compare multiplicatively in the classroom environment so that students can become comfortable with this problem type.

Figure 7.8 identifies some situations where your students might encounter Multiplicative Comparison relationships. As before, we have provided some information and examples to get you started. Note also that unlike the multiplier factor in the Equal Groups category of problem situations, a true scale factor in a Multiplicative Comparison is not clearly associated with a unit of measure. (Later in this chapter we will see other multiplicative situations that do not have scale factors.)

FIGURE 7.8 MULTIPLICATIVE COMPARISON SITUATIONS

ORIGINAL VALUE (MEASURE)	SCALE FACTOR (MULTIPLIER)	RESULTING VALUE (PRODUCT)
Joyce's distance from school	3	Andrew's distance from school
Cost of small package of snacks	2	Cost of large package of snacks
Height in feet	12	
A kitten's weight		
		Ounces of soda
	10	

REASONING AROUND 10

As you read the problems in Figures 7.9 and 7.10, think about the manipulative or pictorial models that your students might choose to model these problems. How do these problems promote reasoning around 10?

FIGURE 7.9	FIGURE 7.10
Michiko is buying fresh fish to prepare at her dinner party. The recipe calls for 0.4 pounds per person. She has invited 10 people to the party, so she needs 10 times as much fish. How many pounds of fish does she need to buy?	Kelsey's favorite television baking star recommends that bakers measure out flour in grams instead of using measuring cups. She has a bread recipe from a restaurant that makes 10 loaves, but she wants to make only one loaf. The recipe calls for 3,960 grams of flour, so she needs 10 times less flour than a full recipe. How much flour does she need for one loaf of bread?

One of the most important conceptual understandings students need to have is an understanding of our base 10 number system. As you examine the student work in Figures 7.11 and 7.12, think about how the students demonstrate their understanding of the base 10 system (or not) as they work on these problems. What does the teacher see in their work?

The problems in Figures 7.9 and 7.10 are both Multiplicative Comparison problems and are specifically related to multiplication or division by 10. This is a key concept in grades 3–5 and it is also tied to relative thinking. Relative thinking and place value are at the root of our base 10 system—each place value is 10 times greater than the one that precedes it: 10 is 10 times 1, 100 is 10 times 10, and so on. In fractions, $\frac{1}{100}$ is $\frac{1}{10}$ of $\frac{1}{10}$, and in decimals 0.1 is one-tenth of 1. Understanding this concept is not the same skill as recognizing, identifying, and naming the value of each digit in a number. Students may be able to point to a digit in the tens place and name it correctly. They may be able to tell you that a 5 in the hundreds place has a value of 500. They may even be able to count over and tell which digit is in the thousandths place, but none of these abilities is the same as recognizing the multiplicative relationship between the digits in each place. Simply "adding a zero" or counting the decimal places is not a strategy that develops this multiplicative understanding. Many assessments may include skill-based items related to base 10 understanding and still not reveal whether students have mastery of these relationships.

Notice that the student whose work is shown in Figure 7.11 set out right away to make groups of 0.4, so the value of one serving of fish is 0.4 (4×0.1), even if it is not said explicitly. The student's writing isn't confident, so we aren't quite sure if she understood immediately what to do with the bundles of 0.4. If you approached a student's desk at this point and saw the bundles of 0.4, what would you say? Think about how you might direct the student back to the context to make sense of what they are looking for. What does each of these bundles of 0.4 stand for? How many are there? What is the unit? How do you know that? What unit are you looking for in the answer? Can you think of other questions that can prompt students to revisit the problem context so that they can make sense of the model they have built? This student recognized that the goal was to figure out the number of pounds and was able to wrap up the problem's solution by circling 4 sets of 10 rods. Video 7.3 walks through this student's thought process.

FIGURE 7.11   FIGURE 7.12

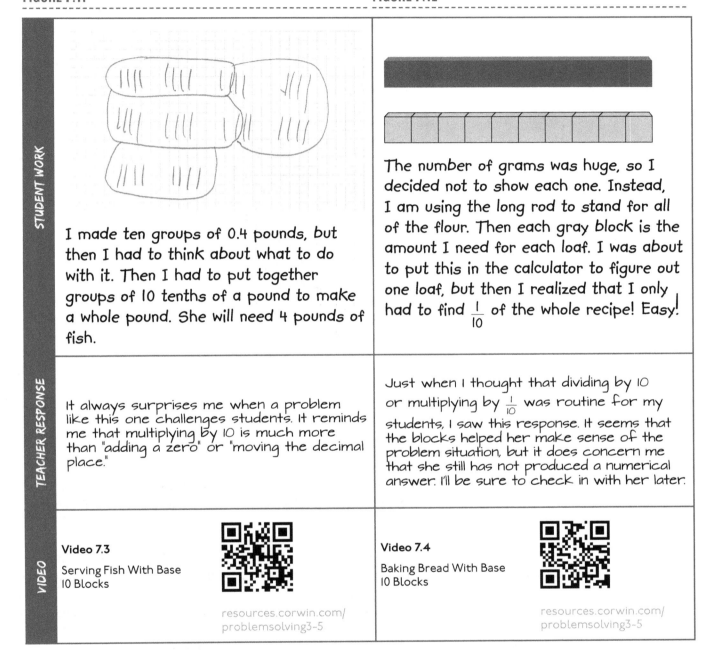

STUDENT WORK

I made ten groups of 0.4 pounds, but then I had to think about what to do with it. Then I had to put together groups of 10 tenths of a pound to make a whole pound. She will need 4 pounds of fish.

The number of grams was huge, so I decided not to show each one. Instead, I am using the long rod to stand for all of the flour. Then each gray block is the amount I need for each loaf. I was about to put this in the calculator to figure out one loaf, but then I realized that I only had to find $\frac{1}{10}$ of the whole recipe! Easy!

TEACHER RESPONSE

It always surprises me when a problem like this one challenges students. It reminds me that multiplying by 10 is much more than "adding a zero" or "moving the decimal place."

Just when I thought that dividing by 10 or multiplying by $\frac{1}{10}$ was routine for my students, I saw this response. It seems that the blocks helped her make sense of the problem situation, but it does concern me that she still has not produced a numerical answer. I'll be sure to check in with her later.

VIDEO

Video 7.3

Serving Fish With Base 10 Blocks

resources.corwin.com/ problemsolving3-5

Video 7.4

Baking Bread With Base 10 Blocks

resources.corwin.com/ problemsolving3-5

The representation in Figure 7.12 shows a student who is starting to make the connection between a known calculation strategy (dividing by 10) and reasoning about a tenth of a quantity. As we see in this student's hesitation, these are not the same skills and understandings. Another interesting feature that emerges in this student's model is the use of 10 separate units (each representing a single loaf) to demonstrate $\frac{1}{10}$ of the greater quantity (a recipe). This is a clear model of "$\frac{1}{10}$ as much" or "10 times less" or "10 times fewer." As a matter of fact, the student doesn't even offer the actual answer (396 grams). As students learn to make sense of multiplicative thinking, having ample experiences with manipulatives to represent the relationships in the base 10 system can continue to reinforce these multiplicative ideas.

MULTIPLICATIVE COMPARISON, MEASUREMENT, AND CONVERSION

Another common context for Multiplicative Comparison is in measurement conversions. Look at the task in Figure 7.13. What are some possible measurement strategies that you would expect students to employ? What answers might they give? What understandings and misconceptions do you anticipate?

FIGURE 7.13

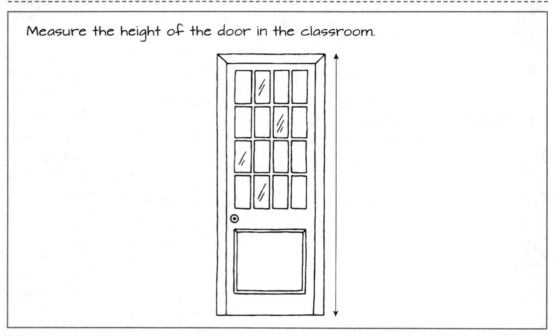

Measure the height of the door in the classroom.

Image Source: Aluna1/iStock.com

Look at the student work in Figures 7.14 and 7.15 and consider how the students describe or draw what is happening in this word problem. Then look at the teacher commentary that follows the student work.

The measurements and written explanations in the two student work samples represent two possible approaches to measurement. The students whose measurement is presented in Figure 7.14 likely used inches as a unit of measure. The teacher acknowledges the students' accuracy and also rightfully identifies that the missing reference to a unit is problematic. In grades 3–5, students are still working to form benchmarks for common units of measure, so it is important to pose follow-up questions about the unit of measure to assess students' understanding.

The student work in Figure 7.15 does specify that the 7 represents a unit of measure, the ruler, but doesn't mention that this corresponds to 12 inches or to one foot. Of course, knowing and using standard units of measure is important: 7 inches is a far cry from 7 feet. The teacher is concerned about how the students measured (and will observe closely next time) but has confidence in the result the students found.

FIGURE 7.14   **FIGURE 7.15**

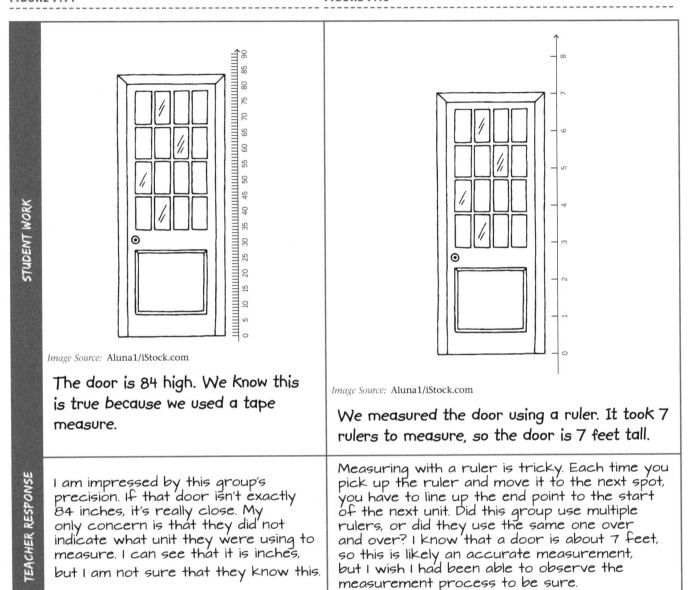

STUDENT WORK

Image Source: Aluna1/iStock.com

The door is 84 high. We know this is true because we used a tape measure.

Image Source: Aluna1/iStock.com

We measured the door using a ruler. It took 7 rulers to measure, so the door is 7 feet tall.

TEACHER RESPONSE

I am impressed by this group's precision. If that door isn't exactly 84 inches, it's really close. My only concern is that they did not indicate what unit they were using to measure. I can see that it is inches, but I am not sure that they know this.

Measuring with a ruler is tricky. Each time you pick up the ruler and move it to the next spot, you have to line up the end point to the start of the next unit. Did this group use multiple rulers, or did they use the same one over and over? I know that a door is about 7 feet, so this is likely an accurate measurement, but I wish I had been able to observe the measurement process to be sure.

Unlike other mathematical skills, measurement *requires* students and teachers to work in the physical world and translate what they see and observe into symbols and other representations in order to communicate their problem context. Measurement is also a critical skill in the creation of mathematical models: Models depend on accurate and appropriate measurements, with full understanding of the units being used. Here is a challenge for us as teachers. What do your measurement lessons look like? What do students measure? Are these data used for any purpose? What do the measurement conversions our students do look like? Conversions between units of measure require multiplicative thinking as students visualize and calculate how many times greater (or less) one unit of measure is than another unit. While conversion between units used to be reserved for middle school, standards movements have changed this trend and grade 4 is often now the first grade to introduce measurement conversion. Initially, conversions are limited to converting from the larger unit to the smaller unit. For example, the students' door measurements in Figures 7.14 and 7.15 are an ideal task to introduce conversion. Ask students: "How many inches are in 7 feet?"

$$7 \text{ feet} \times 12 \text{ inches/foot} = x \text{ inches}$$
$$7 \times 12 = x$$
$$x = 84 \text{ inches}$$

The double number line in Figure 7.16 can also visually demonstrate the relationship between the number of feet and the number of inches. We can even ask students to interpolate how many inches there are in $5\frac{1}{2}$ feet simply by estimating using the number line. Do you think students have enough information to extrapolate how many inches are in 12 feet? 50 feet? If not, what additional understandings do they need to have?

FIGURE 7.16 USING A DOUBLE NUMBER LINE TO ILLUSTRATE MEASUREMENT CONVERSIONS

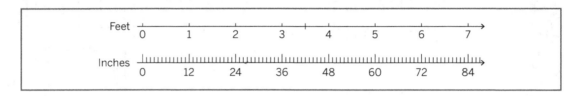

Interestingly, the Common Core State Standards ask fourth graders to convert in only one direction, from the larger unit of measure to the smaller unit. In fifth grade the same standards have students convert in both directions, while still staying within the same measurement system (National Governors Association Center for Best Practices and Council of Chief State School Officers, 2010). Figure 7.17 outlines two sample contexts that illustrate the difference between the units-of-measure conversions students are expected to do in fourth and fifth grades.

FIGURE 7.17 GRADE-LEVEL CONTEXTS FOR UNIT CONVERSIONS

4TH GRADE	5TH GRADE
How many cups are in 3 gallons?	The recipe calls for 192 cups of water. How many gallons is that?
3 gallons × 16 cups/gallon = x cups	192 cups ÷ 16 cups/gallon = x gallons
3 × 16 = x	192 ÷ 16 = x
There are 48 cups in 3 gallons.	192 cups is the same as 12 gallons.
How many centimeters are in 7 meters?	There are 350 centimeters of lace available for the dress. How many meters is that?
7 meters × 100 cm/m = x cm	350 cm ÷ 100 cm/m = x
7 × 100 = x	350 ÷ 100 = x
There are 700 centimeters in 7 meters.	350 cm of lace is the same as 3.5 meters.

As students engage in Multiplicative Comparisons, their patterns of thinking should start to shift from the absolute thinking required for Additive Comparisons (How many more votes did she get than he got?) to the relative thinking of Multiplicative Comparisons (How many times more votes did she get than he got?). The structure of the sentences that distinguish absolute and relative thinking are not that different, but the mathematical thinking is a giant leap forward for students in grades 3–5 and beyond. As we look at Multiplicative Comparison using fractions and decimals, we will continue to explore this transition.

Moving Beyond Whole Numbers

In the example in Figure 7.18, we used an indeterminate quantity of money intentionally because removing quantities from a problem and focusing only on the relationships is often a more productive starting point. Even though the problem doesn't ask students to solve for a specific quantity, some answers would probably include fractions (likely expressed as decimals).

Use the workspace provided to show at least one solution for the problem in Figure 7.18. There is a large space for drawings and images. Don't forget to include verbal descriptions, number lines, or equations.

FIGURE 7.18

Lauren and Kimmie keep the money they earn in their piggy banks. Today they each got $3 for raking leaves in the front yard. They put the money in their respective piggy banks. Whose savings balance grew the most?

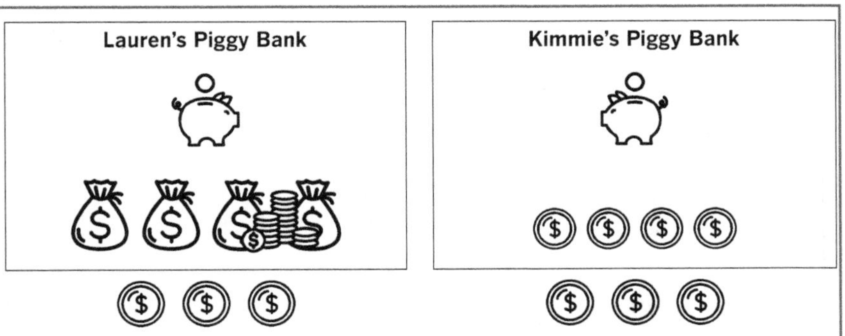

Lauren's Piggy Bank

Kimmie's Piggy Bank

Image Source: nidwlw/iStock.com

ENTER THE PROBLEM

EXPLORE

STUDENTS AND TEACHERS THINK ABOUT THE PROBLEMS

Look at the student work in Figures 7.19 and 7.20 and consider how the students describe or draw what is happening in this word problem. Then look at the teacher commentary that follows the student work.

FIGURE 7.19   **FIGURE 7.20**

	Student Work	Student Work
STUDENT WORK	 Lauren's and Kimmie's balances grew by the same amount. Both have $3 more.	 Kimmie's balance grew more than Lauren's. Kimmie's only had $4 to start with so she almost doubled her money. Because of that it seems like more money. I don't even think that Lauren would notice getting that extra money.
TEACHER RESPONSE	This makes sense to me.	Oh. I didn't think about that! He is comparing the new money to the amount the girls already had. So, in a way, Kimmie's piggy bank grew more. There's a way to show that mathematically, I'm sure.

ABSOLUTE AND RELATIVE CHANGE

Absolute change:
An additive change expressed using either addition or subtraction between values. Example: $6\frac{1}{2}$ is one and a half plus 5. $1\frac{1}{2} + 5 = 6\frac{1}{2}$.

The question raised in Figure 7.18 is a tough one, even for adults. The obvious answer is that their savings balances grew by the same amount, but once children think about it a bit more, they often notice that it seems just a little bit… wrong. Children start to expect that there is something about how much money each girl starts with that matters in some way. It's as if the change is related to the answer. It is! As a matter of fact, we want students to begin making this distinction because it is an early understanding of the difference between **absolute change** and **relative change** (Lamon, 2012). In grades 3–5, students are beginning to explore change as multiplicative after several years of working comfortably within the world of additive change. When multiplication is introduced formally, typically in third grade, it is only the beginning of a long process of learning to engage in thinking and reasoning about multiplicative relationships.

In this example, we know that Kimmie had exactly $4 already in her piggy bank and Lauren had a lot more. Thus, $3 would be less of an increase to Lauren than it would be to Kimmie.

Kimmie has $1\frac{3}{4}$ times as much money as she had before. The important mathematical idea at the upper range of these grade levels is that she has more. If she had $1\frac{1}{2}$ times as much money, it would be more than she started with, yet less than $1\frac{3}{4}$ times. If she had 1 times as much money, she would have the exact same amount. But if she had $\frac{3}{4}$ as much money, she would have less. This is the first time that students encounter this idea. It is a confounding phenomenon that multiplication can make things smaller! Doing these calculations is not the focus of the discussion here, as there are other standards that address the computation. The purpose of this kind of task is to unpack how "times as many" and multiplication by values greater than 1 and less than 1 express a relative change. Ask students to estimate how many times more money Lauren has now than she had before. Look for answers that are close to but more than 1, such as 1.05 or $1\frac{1}{100}$ times as much because the amount in her piggy bank barely increased. If students offer answers like $1\frac{1}{2}$ times or 5 times, you have an opportunity to explore this idea in much more depth with them.

> **Relative change:** A multiplicative change expressed using a ratio (multiplication or division). Example: $7\frac{1}{2}$ is one and a half times 5. $1\frac{1}{2} \times 5 = 7\frac{1}{2}$.

HELPING STUDENTS TRANSITION TO MULTIPLICATIVE THINKING

Look at the two problems in Figures 7.21 and 7.22. What is similar between the two problems and what is different? Use the workspace provided to draw representations of the problems or for verbal descriptions, number lines, or equations. Consider where there is multiplication in these problems.

Vilma and Ken are running the school store. At the beginning of the year they bought supplies and sold them throughout the year. Pencils sold out, so they made a note to buy more next year. At the end of the school year they took an inventory of what was left so that they could decide what to buy for next year. Here is their inventory:

	BOUGHT	SOLD	HOW MANY LEFT
Boxes of Pencils	8	8	0
Boxes of Erasers	12	9	3

FIGURE 7.21

How many boxes of pencils should Vilma and Ken buy for next year? Explain your answers using words, pictures, and numbers.

FIGURE 7.22

Vilma and Ken knew they had sold only 9 boxes of erasers last year. They want to know what portion they sold of the amount they bought. Use fractions to show what portion they sold last year. Show your answers using words, pictures, and numbers.

EXPLORE

Take a look at the student work in Figures 7.23 and 7.24 and consider how the students describe or draw what is happening in the given word problems. Then look at the teacher commentary that follows and consider what the teachers noticed in the student work.

FIGURE 7.23

FIGURE 7.24

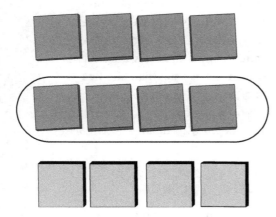

We think they should buy more pencils this year. We know that kids use lots of pencils, AND we ran out last year! Twice as many might be too much, but maybe we can buy $1\frac{1}{2}$ times as many. That's halfway between buying the same amount and twice as much.

We used the squares to help us figure out how many boxes of pencils to buy. 8 boxes is too few, but twice as many, that's 16, is too many. Half of 8 is 4, so we think we could sell 4 more boxes than last year, so we have to buy 8+4=12 boxes.

$1\frac{1}{2}$ (times as many) $\times 8$ (boxes) $= x$ (boxes)

$1\frac{1}{2} \times 8 = 12$

We should buy 12 boxes this year.

Erasers didn't sell very well so we knew that we need to have less this year. We have to figure out how much less. We know it's three boxes less, but the principal wants to know more information than that so we did this.

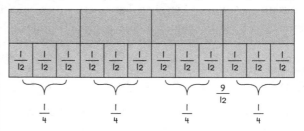

We used $\frac{1}{12}$ tiles to represent the 12 eraser boxes we ordered last year. Each tile is one box of erasers. We sold 9 boxes, which we marked as $\frac{9}{12}$.

Then we noticed that $\frac{9}{12}$ is the same as 3 of the blue tiles and the whole set of 12 is the same as 4 blue tiles. Those tiles each represent $\frac{1}{4}$ of the erasers we bought. We sold three out of four $(\frac{3}{4})$ of the boxes of erasers that we bought.

$\frac{1}{4}$ of the boxes (3 boxes) are still left. We thought our equation was wrong at first because we multiplied and got a smaller number. Today we learned that this is ok.

$\frac{3}{4}$ (as many) $\times 12$ boxes bought = 9 boxes sold

$\frac{3}{4} \times 12 = 9$

TEACHER RESPONSE

The kids in this group reasoned about how many pencils to buy. They recognized that two times might be too many, but they were able to settle on $1\frac{1}{2}$ times as many and make sense of it.

The use of the $\frac{1}{12}$ tiles was insightful because it allowed the students to manipulate a model of the 12 boxes and use them to show $\frac{9}{12}$. I noticed that they recognized that $\frac{9}{12}$ could also be called $\frac{3}{4}$ and at the same time recognized that $\frac{3}{4}$ is also the scale factor. They learned a lot about multiplication today.

VIDEO

Video 7.5

Pencils With Color Tiles

resources.corwin.com/
problemsolving3-5

Video 7.6

Erasers With Fraction Bars

resources.corwin.com/
problemsolving3-5

These problems approach the real-life sorts of problems that students might have the occasion to solve in the context of any kind of activity that involves buying and selling: Keeping track of what is bought and what is sold has broad applicability. It is important to make clear that both of these solutions are Multiplicative Comparisons. You may have noted that an Additive Comparison also works in these situations. However, students may not, as the students here did, naturally think of a multiplicative solution even once they're in the middle school grades. It does, however, remain a goal for all students because multiplicative solutions have the greatest flexibility over the long term.

Can Multiplication Make a Quantity Smaller?

One of the most interesting effects of multiplication—one that frequently appears in the scaling context—is multiplication that results in a smaller product. For example, the problem in Figure 7.22 describes a decrease in the number of erasers needed for the second year. Expressing this additively is done with subtraction or even addition ($12 - 3 = 9$ or $9 + \_\_\_ = 12$), but a multiplicative change can also be shown. Multiplication can be used to express a change to a smaller quantity. In the student work shown in Figure 7.24, it is $\frac{3}{4} \times 12 = 9$. As students work on problems like these, highlight how the context of the situation helps make sense of this surprising outcome. How is it possible that the scale factor $\frac{3}{4}$ transforms the quantity from 12 to 9? Similarly, starting with 12 boxes, what can you multiply by to end up with fewer boxes? Try these examples, even using a calculator. If students struggle to recognize that this is really possible, ask them what these scale factors have in common. (They are less than 1!)

$$\frac{1}{2} \times 6 \qquad \frac{1}{4} \times 20 \qquad \frac{3}{4} \times 15 \qquad \frac{1}{8} \times 16 \qquad \frac{2}{3} \times 9 \qquad \frac{1}{3} \times 18$$

The solution to the pencil box problem in Figure 7.21 correctly interprets $1\frac{1}{2}$ as a scale factor because the context describes the factor as showing how many times more pencils the students might buy. Therefore, the number of square tiles used in the solution also is increased by a factor of $1\frac{1}{2}$. In contrast, most standards treat $1\frac{1}{2} \times 8$ and $8 \times 1\frac{1}{2}$ as if they were equivalent expressions. As we described in detail in Chapter 5, the commutative property is useful in computation but less useful in problem-solving situations. We encourage you to maintain the distinction between the scale factor and the measure factor so that students learn to recognize these roles, not just in routine word problems but also in a real-life context that they wish to mathematize.

Now, let's look deeper at the student solutions and the teacher responses in Figure 7.23. Starting with 8 boxes of pencils (the measure factor), students have to decide how many more pencils to purchase. You may have observed that the students were not asked "how many times more" pencils to purchase but, rather, were asked a general question. But they still responded with "$1\frac{1}{2}$ times as many." As you probably know, this is not a typical response for a fifth grader. Still, because most standards now ask students to answer questions like these multiplicatively, we are providing a model for what that could look like at an appropriate grade level. Although the term *scale factor* looks ahead to the mathematics that students will do in later grades, a similar term is included in Common Core State Standard 5.NF.B.5, which is interpreting multiplication as "scaling" (National Governors Association Center for Best Practices and Council of Chief State School Officers, 2010). If all of this talk of scale is making you think of a key to a map or about the scale of a piece of furniture in a room, or about scale models, you are on the right track because *scale* refers to a measurement that is proportionally related to some other measurement.

Returning to the pencil problem, the student response in Figure 7.23 shows evidence that the students tested several scale factors before settling on $1\frac{1}{2}$. Their reasoning is the important focus of this problem. They concluded that twice as many (×2) was too much and that the same (×1) was too few. Recognizing that $1\frac{1}{2}$ is halfway between the two is the important realization for this grade level. The precise answer ($1\frac{1}{2} \times 8 = 12$) is secondary. You can challenge fifth-grade students to estimate how many times bigger one object is than another. The primary goal is to identify whether a scale factor is less than one, equal to one, or greater than one, so precision is not necessary.

The student solution in Figure 7.24 addresses a more challenging problem because the scale factor was less than 1. While writing this book, we realized that the English language does not have an easy sentence structure to describe a scale factor that is less than 1. It's acceptable to say "How many times greater than 8 is 12?" But the complementary statement is awkward. "How many times less than 12 is 8?" And nothing about this language indicates that a fraction will be the response. In fact, a key-word-based strategy might even call for subtraction! In this case the numbers reveal information but the language does not. As teachers, we need to look for situations that call for expressing less than the starting quantity so that students become accustomed to recognizing the mathematical situations that call for a scale factor less than 1. If you are working with a team of colleagues, take time to brainstorm some real-life situations that call for a scale factor. Think of some situations that scale greater than a starting value and others that can be scaled to a lesser starting value.

Multiplicative Comparisons may seem similar to Additive Comparisons on the surface, but as we go deeper into the topic, we realize that Multiplicative Comparisons are better seen as an introduction to the kinds of thinking students need to do in middle school and beyond. Contexts like the piggy bank problem in Figure 7.18 tap into students' emergent sense that how much you earn depends greatly on how much you already have. Similarly, we might ask students what it would feel like to find $10 on the ground. As soon as they are able to recognize that "it depends," you know they are ready to engage with some relative thinking. After all, the excitement over finding $10 depends on how much money you already have. At this point, we can introduce comparison contexts and lead students to engage in multiplicative thinking.

KEY IDEAS

1   Multiplicative Comparison problems are asymmetric multiplication; the factors do different jobs.

2   One factor represents the original quantity (the measure) and the second factor represents the scale factor ("times as many"). The scale factor can be more than one (for example, three times as many) and give a greater value, or less than one (for example, $\frac{1}{4}$ as much) and give a lesser value.

3   When measuring, students should recognize that the same object can be measured with two different units, thus having the same measurement but with different values. For example, there are 4 times as many cups in this pitcher (12 cups) than there are quarts (3 quarts).

4   Students should recognize that each place value varies from the one next to it by a factor of 10. The value of a digit is either "10 times greater" or "10 times less" than the one next to it.

5   Multiplicative Comparison represents a different kind of mathematical thinking, not just another problem structure.

6   Multiplicative Comparisons are precursors to proportional reasoning.

7   Multiplicative Comparison represents relative thinking. The difference between two values depends on (is relative to) the actual values.

TRY IT OUT!

IDENTIFY THE PROBLEM SITUATION

For each of the numberless word problems that follow, insert quantities and then write two possible answers to the problem. One should show an Additive Comparison and the other a Multiplicative Comparison. There are no right answers to these exercises, so your explanation and reasoning are more important than the actual answer. This set of exercises is best done with a group.

SAMPLE:

Cara has a lot of cats. She visited the shelter one day and fell in love with one of the cats. Now she has more cats!

a   Additive Comparison: *Cara had 3 cats. Now she has 1 more cat and a total of 4 cats.*

b   Multiplicative Comparison: *Cara used to have three cats. Now she has $1\frac{1}{3}$ of the number of cats she had before! Cara loves her 4 cats!*

(continued)

(continued)

1   Abdel made lemonade for the picnic, but it was too sweet, so the next time he made it he added more lemon juice. Now it is more lemony!

  a   Additive Comparison:

  b   Multiplicative Comparison:

2   Lindsay bought a new house. It was bigger than her studio apartment. She now has more square feet.

  a   Additive Comparison:

  b   Multiplicative Comparison:

3   Sharon saved for a new pair of skates, but she lost some of her money. Now she has less money.

  a   Additive Comparison:

  b   Multiplicative Comparison:

4   Tomás had some baseball cards, but he dropped some of them in the rain! Now he has fewer cards.

  a   Additive Comparison:

  b   Multiplicative Comparison:

5   Khaleda downloaded some songs from a new band. Now she has more songs.

  a   Additive Comparison:

  b   Multiplicative Comparison:

WRITE THE PROBLEM

For each of the expressions that follow, write a word problem that matches, explaining whether the scale factor will create a product greater or less than the measure factor. For added experience, include a representation that corresponds to the situation.

1   $\frac{3}{5} \times 20$

2   $\frac{1}{4} \times 12$

3   2×6

4   $1\frac{1}{3} \times 6$

5   $2\frac{1}{2} \times 10$

6   $\frac{5}{6} \times 30$

BRANCH OUT

Building off of children's literature is one of the best ways to encourage students to pose mathematical problems. The book suggested here may have a more direct connection to the mathematics than other books, but we encourage you to look in all of the books you read to students for opportunities to compare.

Introduced in Chapter 4, the book *Actual Size* (Jenkins, 2011) shares real-size images of portions of animals, so that students can make comparisons. The language "The squid eye is bigger than my eye" is appropriate for primary comparisons, but the next question to pose is "How much bigger?" Now students can ask "How many times bigger?" and use rulers and other measuring devices to make comparisons. Recall that the goal at these grade levels is to recognize that when the comparison is less than one times as big, the object is smaller, and that when the scale factor is more than one, the object is larger. Encourage students to make estimations of the scale factor. Precision will come in later grades.

REFLECT

1   The transition from thinking about change as additive to considering change as multiplicative is a challenging but important one for students. What are some ways you can incorporate discussions about multiplicative change into daily routines?

2   Standards have moved some aspects of middle school mathematics into grades 3–5, and Multiplicative Comparison is one of these standards. This likely offers some challenges to teachers accustomed to teaching a certain set of content. What are some ways you are adapting to these changes?

3. Using a copy of the Multiplication and Division Problem Situations table at the beginning of this chapter (you can also download a copy from http://resources.corwin .com/problemsolving3-5), examine the textbook you use for the grade you teach and read the word problems. Look for examples of Multiplicative Comparison problems. As you classify the word problems you find, make a tally on the table for each type. You might even decide to make note of the scale factor and the measure factor. If you encounter a multistep problem, classify it by the first action that should take place in the problem. If you aren't sure if it is a Multiplicative Comparison problem, consider what else it might be.

CHAPTER EIGHT

Area and Array
Two Factors, Same Job

Thinking About Area and Array Situations

In previous chapters, we looked at a variety of asymmetric multiplication situations, all containing factors that do different work in the problems. In this final multiplication and division chapter, we will look at symmetric situations, referred to as Area and Array problem situations, in which the roles of the factors are interchangeable.

Multiplication and Division Problem Situations

	Product Unknown	One Dimension Unknown	Both Dimensions Unknown
Area/Array	Mrs. Bradley bought a rubber mat to cover the floor under the balance beam. One side of the mat measured 5 feet and the other side measured 8 feet. How many square feet does the mat measure? $5 \times 8 = x$ $x \div 8 = 5$	The 40 members of the student council lined up on the stage in the gym to take yearbook pictures. The first row started with 8 students and the rest of the rows did the same. How many rows were there? $8 \times x = 40$ $x = 40 \div 8$	Mr. Donato is arranging student work on the wall for the art show. He started with 40 square entries and arranged them into a rectangular arrangement. How many entries long and wide could the arrangement be? $x \times y = 40$ $40 \div x = y$
	Sample Space (Total Outcomes) Unknown	**One Factor Unknown**	**Both Factors Unknown**
Combinations** (Fundamental Counting Principle)	Karen makes sandwiches at the diner. She offers 3 kinds of bread and 7 different lunch meats. How many unique sandwiches can she make? $3 \times 7 = x$ $3 = x \div 7$	Evelyn works at the ice cream counter. She says that she can make 21 unique and different ice cream sundaes using just ice cream flavors and toppings. If she has 3 flavors of ice cream, how many kinds of toppings does Evelyn offer? $3 \times x = 21$ $21 \div 3 = x$	Audrey can make 21 different fruit sodas using the machine at the diner. How many different flavorings and sodas could there be? $x \times y = 21$ $x = 21 \div y$

**Combinations are a category addressed in middle school mathematics standards. They are introduced briefly in Chapter 8 for illustration purposes only and will be developed more extensively in the grades 6–8 volume of this series.

Note: These representations for the problem situations reflect our understanding based on a number of resources. These include the tables in the Common Core State Standards for mathematics (Common Core Standards Initiative, 2010), the problem situations as described in the Cognitively Guided Instruction research (Carpenter, Hiebert, & Moser, 1981), in Heller and Greeno (1979) and Riley, Greeno, & Heller (1984), and other tools. See the Appendix and companion website for a more detailed summary of the documents that informed our development of this table.

ASYMMETRICAL (NONMATCHING) FACTORS

	Product Unknown	Multiplier (Number of Groups) Unknown	Measure (Group Size) Unknown	
Equal Groups (Ratio/Rate)*	Mayim has 8 vases to decorate the tables at her party. She places 3 flowers in each vase. How many flowers does she need? $8 \times 3 = x$ $x \div 8 = 3$	Mayim has some vases to decorate the tables at her party. She places 3 flowers in each vase. If she uses 24 flowers, how many vases does she have? $x \times 3 = 24$ $x = 24 \div 3$	Mayim places 24 flowers in vases to decorate the tables at her party. If there are 8 vases, how many flowers will be in each vase? $8 \times x = 24$ $24 \div 8 = x$	
	Resulting Value Unknown	**Scale Factor (Times as Many) Unknown**	**Original Value Unknown**	
Multiplicative Comparison	Amelia's dog is 5 times older than Wanda's 3-year-old dog. How old is Amelia's dog? $5 \times 3 = x$ $x \div 5 = 3$	Sydney has $15 to spend on dog treats. Her best friend has $5. Sydney has how many times more dollars than her friend has? $x \times 5 = 15$ $5 = 15 \div x$	Devonte has 15 dog toys on the floor in his living room. That is 3 times the number of toys in the dog's toy basket. How many toys are in the toy basket? $3 \times x = 15$ $15 \div 3 = x$	

SYMMETRICAL (MATCHING) FACTORS

	Product Unknown	One Dimension Unknown	Both Dimensions Unknown
Area/Array	Mrs. Bradley bought a rubber mat to cover the floor under the balance beam. One side of the mat measured 5 feet and the other side measured 8 feet. How many square feet does the mat measure? $5 \times 8 = x$ $x \div 8 = 5$	The 40 members of the student council lined up on the stage in the gym to take yearbook pictures. The first row started with 8 students and the rest of the rows did the same. How many rows were there? $8 \times x = 40$ $x = 40 \div 8$	Mr. Donato is arranging student work on the wall for the art show. He started with 40 square entries and arranged them into a rectangular arrangement. How many entries long and wide could the arrangement be? $x \times y = 40$ $40 \div x = y$
	Sample Space (Total Outcomes) Unknown	**One Factor Unknown**	**Both Factors Unknown**
Combinations** (Fundamental Counting Principle)	Karen makes sandwiches at the diner. She offers 3 kinds of bread and 7 different lunch meats. How many unique sandwiches can she make? $3 \times 7 = x$ $3 = x \div 7$	Evelyn works at the ice cream counter. She says that she can make 21 unique and different ice cream sundaes using just ice cream flavors and toppings. If she has 3 flavors of ice cream, how many kinds of toppings does Evelyn offer? $3 \times x = 21$ $21 \div 3 = x$	Audrey can make 21 different fruit sodas using the machine at the diner. How many different flavorings and sodas could there be? $x \times y = 21$ $x = 21 \div y$

online resources Full chart available for download at **http://resources.corwin.com/problemsolving3-5**

Sandbox Notes

The two routine word problems in Figures 8.1 and 8.2 seem straightforward at first glance, particularly if $3 \times 12 = 36$ is a known fact. But let's see what your sandbox exploration can uncover. Keeping in mind the guiding questions that follow, try out a variety of representations: number lines, verbal descriptions, equations, as well as pictorial representations.

- *Think about the numbers in each situation. What do they represent? Which are quantities? Which are not? What work do they do?*

- *How can you represent the quantities in the word problems with your manipulatives or pictures?*

- *What number sentence best shows what is happening in each story?*

The two problems in Figures 8.1 and 8.2, like all of the problems we've used to introduce the chapters, contain the same numbers, but they are used in different contexts. As you have before, put the problems in your own words. Look closely at the two problems. What is similar between the two problems? What is different?

FIGURE 8.1

FIGURE 8.2

Bradley bought a new rug for the hallway in his house. One side measured 3 feet, but he wasn't sure what the other side measured because it was rolled up. The label said that it was a 36 ft² rug. How long is the rug?	Daniel bought a 36-pack of water bottles to give away at the school relay race. If each racer gets 3 bottles, how many people does this pack of water bottles serve?

ENTER THE PROBLEM

FIGURE 8.3 A MODEL FOR MATHEMATIZING WORD PROBLEMS

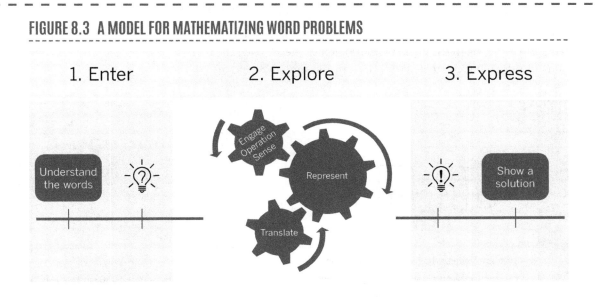

STUDENTS AND TEACHERS THINK ABOUT THE PROBLEMS

Look at the student work in Figures 8.4 and 8.5 and consider how the students describe or draw what is happening in the given word problems. Then look at the teacher commentary that follows and consider what the teachers noticed in the student work.

FIGURE 8.4   **FIGURE 8.5**

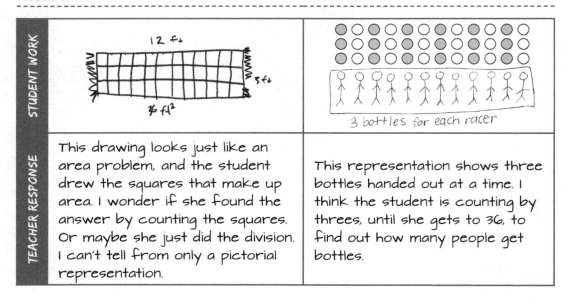

STUDENT WORK	12 ft / 3 ft / 36 ft²	3 bottles for each racer
TEACHER RESPONSE	This drawing looks just like an area problem, and the student drew the squares that make up area. I wonder if she found the answer by counting the squares. Or maybe she just did the division. I can't tell from only a pictorial representation.	This representation shows three bottles handed out at a time. I think the student is counting by threes, until she gets to 36, to find out how many people get bottles.

A comparison of these two problems may also seem straightforward initially, but let's dig deeper and unpack the complexities, looking first at Figure 8.5. The teacher's speculation that the student found the answer by "counting by threes" points to the strategy of repeated subtraction. Repeated subtraction, because it can occur when there is a multiplier factor and a measure factor, is one sign the problem is an Equal Groups problem situation. It can be represented this way:

$$x \text{ (giveaways)} = 36 \text{ (bottles)} \div 3 \text{ (bottles/giveaway)}$$
$$x = 36 \div 3$$

Figure 8.4, by contrast, shows a very different problem situation marked by a different relationship between the factors. Whereas an Equal Groups problem contains factors that play two different roles and, consequently, are not interchangeable, the **Area/Array** problem situation describes a different relationship. In the rug example (Figure 8.1), there are length and width dimensions, and although you might call 3 feet the width and 12 feet the length, this is not a rule: the two dimensions are interchangeable if we rotate the rug, or even if we do not rotate the rug.

Area/Array: A problem situation that describes a symmetric problem context. The factors are interchangeable.

SYMMETRIC VERSUS ASYMMETRIC MULTIPLICATION

When the factors in a problem situation do the same work, the multiplication is called *symmetric* (Kouba & Franklin, 1993). Area problems are symmetric, as are most array-like problem situations. Think about a situation that involves arranging cans on a shelf. You might count how many cans wide they are placed on the shelf and then count the depth of cans. You likely know that you can find the number of cans (the product) by using multiplication in this symmetric situation.

In contrast, Equal Groups problems are referred to as *asymmetric*. Because the factors have different roles, asymmetric problem situations represent contexts that generate partitive and measurement models of division. Symmetric situations cannot be partitive nor quotitive because the concepts of fair share and repeated subtraction are nonsensical in an Area/Array problem. Consider again the rug context in Figure 8.1. It does not make sense to fair share the 36 square feet of the rug with the 3 feet shared from the side. What would that look like? Similarly, if we consider repeatedly subtracting 3 feet from the rug until we exhaust the whole 36 square feet, we'd also find that this does not make sense in a real-world context.

It's not surprising that the teacher comments in Figure 8.4 indicate some uncertainty about how the student used the model to calculate the answer. Yes, the student likely counted the squares of area, but unlike the Equal Groups bottle giveaway problem in Figure 8.2, the rug model and problem situation don't have a counting strategy embedded in them that can be acted out. Let's look more closely at why and how that affects students' ability to model these problem situations.

One researcher gave a group of fifth graders the task illustrated in Figure 8.6 and asked, "What would you get if you multiplied 4 by 3? You would get 12, but 12 what?" (Thompson, 2010, p. 37).

FIGURE 8.6 A SEEMINGLY NONSENSICAL SITUATION

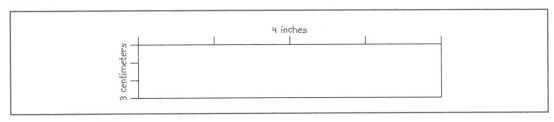

Source: Thompson (2010).

Students worked to make sense of this seemingly nonsensical task, and one student finally suggested that it would have to be 12 rectangular units that measure 1 cm by 1 inch. This could be true, and in a useful context would be an example of an Area/Array problem. It is not, however, a standard unit of area, but it does represent how units of area exist because they are the product of two separate measurements. Because of this invented context, the class came to recognize that Area (and other symmetric) problem situations have the following features:

- A unit of area is created when two like units are combined by multiplication. Area is not a single unit of measure, but a composition of two units related by multiplication (for example, inches times inches, or square inches).

- The product of any two symmetric factors creates a new kind of quantity and a new kind of unit that is different from the two units that produced it. Here are a few additional examples:

  ○ Length (feet) × width (feet) = area (square feet)

  ○ Row × column = cell

  ○ Choice of meat × choice of cheese = number of sandwich types

  ○ Pants options × shirt options = number of possible outfits

This may not seem to be a meaningful distinction for students in grades 3–5 to make, but in terms of understanding the context of word problems and representing them with meaningful models, it is important. The rug problem in Figure 8.1 might have been easy for you to solve without models, especially if you already knew that $3 \times 12 = 36$ and only had to recall the factor to find the missing measurement of the rug. In the tradition of cognitively guided instruction (CGI) projects, this is called a Number Facts strategy because you find the solution based on the computation facts you know (Carpenter, Fennema, Franke, Levi, & Empson, 2014). This is in contrast to the Direct Modeling strategy we have been exploring throughout the book. Educators who use the CGI resources are quite familiar with the problem types and the importance of students creating models of problems.

If the factors and the product in a problem situation do not represent a known fact, the student needs to rely on a modeling strategy. Remember, a meaningful model is one that directly represents the problem situation. Modeling an Area/Array problem situation is, in a sense, modeling the creation of something new. A good example is the student solution in Figure 8.4. The grid the student superimposed on the rug produced squares that can be counted either one by one, or even by using repeated addition. The grid now becomes a tool (or a mathematical structure) to make an Area/Array problem situation resemble an Equal Groups problem. Equal Groups problems are active, so it is easier to act out their solution. It does not, however, change the problem into an Equal Groups problem. We will look at the relationship between modeling strategies and problem types in more detail later in the chapter, but for now take a look at Figure 8.7. It summarizes the key differences between symmetric and asymmetric multiplication.

FIGURE 8.7 ASYMMETRIC VERSUS SYMMETRIC MULTIPLICATION

ASYMMETRIC MULTIPLICATION	SYMMETRIC MULTIPLICATION
The two factors do different work. Only one carries a unit of measure. multiplier factor × measure factor	The two factors have similar, or the same, units. inches × inches
The unit of the product matches the unit of the measure factor. 3 bags × 6 cookies (per bag) = 18 cookies	The unit of the product is a new unit. 3 rows × 15 columns = 45 cells
The problem context is semantically not commutative—the factor roles cannot be exchanged and retain the same meaning in the problem situation. 6 (litters) × 3 (kittens) = 18 kittens is not the same as 3 (litters) × 6 (kittens) = 18 kittens	Factors are essentially commutative and interchangeable. If the length and the width of a shape are swapped, no meaning is lost in the problem context. 4 (meters) × 6 (meters) = 24 square meters is only a rotation different from 6 (meters) × 4 (meters) = 24 square meters
Asymmetric situations can be directly modeled by acting them out, both in multiplication and in division.	Symmetric situations cannot be directly modeled. They require either a known fact or the application of a mathematical structure to find a solution. (This does not include using a calculator because it is a tool for computation, not for problem solving.)

ANOTHER SYMMETRIC PROBLEM SITUATION: THE FUNDAMENTAL COUNTING PRINCIPLE

A well-known sandwich shop chain once printed a claim on the side of their drink cups that there were 37 million possible sandwich combinations, using the ingredients usually found at their stores. How do they get such a huge number?! They used a principle called the Fundamental Counting Principle, or the Counting Principle for short, to calculate that value. Typically, this is part of the study of probability, which is reserved for middle school standards and beyond. Intermediate teachers usually don't teach this concept, but because it is an important example of symmetric multiplication, we will address it here briefly.

The primary use of the Fundamental Counting Principle is to figure out the sample space (a set of possible outcomes). For example, with three shirts and two pants, we could make six possible outfits. It takes time for some students to recognize that each of the outfits is unique. More important, the number of outcomes grows surprisingly quickly as the number of options increases. Here is a simplified example that encourages us to think about the sandwich shop problem:

- 5 bread choices

- 6 meat choices

- 4 kinds of cheese

- 2 (lettuce or no lettuce)

- 2 (tomato or no tomato)

- 2 (mayo or no mayo)

- 2 (mustard or no mustard)

- (You know there are many more options that are not listed here!)
  $5 \times 6 \times 4 \times 2 \times 2 \times 2 \times 2 = 1,920$

For just these few choices, 1,920 unique sandwiches could be created! You can see how the number of possible unique sandwiches grew so quickly with each choice added to the list. Even a simple choice like "mayo/no mayo" doubles the possible outcomes! That's how the number of options for a sandwich can grow to 37 million possible outcomes for this sandwich chain! This variety of multiplication is one of the ways that students can come to terms with how fast multiplication can change a value, either getting very large (or very small) very quickly. One of the most common ways to represent the Fundamental Counting Principle is by using the tree diagram (Figure 8.8).

FIGURE 8.8 THE FUNDAMENTAL COUNTING PRINCIPLE REPRESENTED BY A TREE DIAGRAM

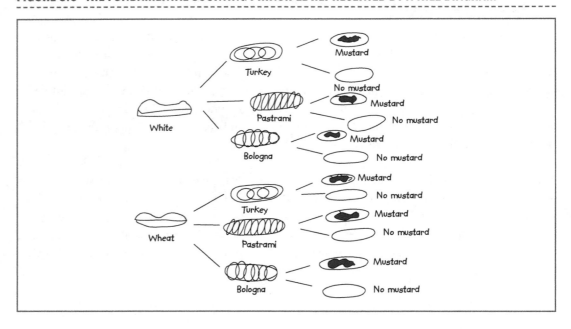

As with other varieties of symmetric multiplication, each of the factors does the same work in the problem. In this case, each factor is an item on a sandwich:

$$2\,(\text{bread types}) \times 3\,(\text{meat types}) \times 2\,(\text{mustard or no mustard}) = 12\,\text{sandwich options}$$

The product of these three factors results in a new kind of unit. In this case we call it a "sub."

Modeling Arrays: Situations or Computation?

Look at the problem in Figure 8.9. Think about how you might respond to this question before you look at the student work that follows.

FIGURE 8.9

Cassandra bought 12 cans of cat food on sale at the store. To put the cans on her shelf, she arranged them in an array so that 6 cans were showing at the front and the cans made 2 rows on the shelf, as shown in the picture below.

Is this an Equal Groups problem situation or an Area/Array problem situation?

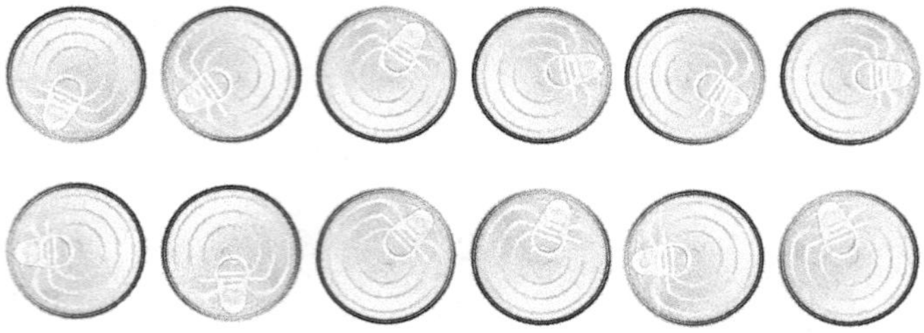

Image Source: Etiennevoss/iStock.com

Look at the student work in Figures 8.10 and 8.11 and consider how the students describe and draw a model of the given situation. Then look at the teacher commentary that follows and consider what the teachers noticed in the student work.

FIGURE 8.10   **FIGURE 8.11**

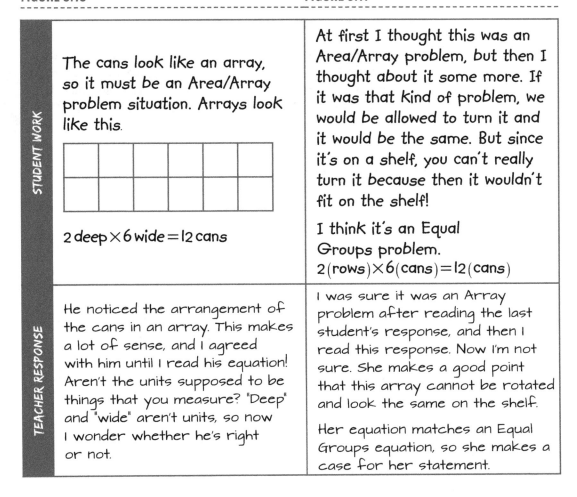

STUDENT WORK	The cans look like an array, so it must be an Area/Array problem situation. Arrays look like this. 2 deep × 6 wide = 12 cans	At first I thought this was an Area/Array problem, but then I thought about it some more. If it was that kind of problem, we would be allowed to turn it and it would be the same. But since it's on a shelf, you can't really turn it because then it wouldn't fit on the shelf! I think it's an Equal Groups problem. 2 (rows) × 6 (cans) = 12 (cans)
TEACHER RESPONSE	He noticed the arrangement of the cans in an array. This makes a lot of sense, and I agreed with him until I read his equation! Aren't the units supposed to be things that you measure? "Deep" and "wide" aren't units, so now I wonder whether he's right or not.	I was sure it was an Array problem after reading the last student's response, and then I read this response. Now I'm not sure. She makes a good point that this array cannot be rotated and look the same on the shelf. Her equation matches an Equal Groups equation, so she makes a case for her statement.

So, is this an Area/Array problem or an Equal Groups problem? And how does the answer to that question affect the students' ability to make a meaningful model? In this problem, the constraint of the shelf's shape (wide and not very deep) pushes this problem toward the Equal Groups side because the two factors are not interchangeable in the real-life context of a shallow shelf. While many resources may refer to anything arranged in columns and rows as an Area/Array problem situation, we would argue that at times the context plays a greater role in dictating whether a problem context is symmetric or asymmetric. If the context were different—say, the cat food cans were just sitting on a big table and arranged into an array—then it would be an Area/Array problem situation, in that the cans could be rearranged, for example, into six rows of two cans. But the problem of arranging those same cat food cans on the shelf, where they are forced into two rows, changes the nature of the problem. Now we have twelve cans that need to be equally distributed into two rows. In this case, we have an Equal Groups problem that is easily modeled into a structure that looks like an array.

ARRAYS AS A MATHEMATICAL STRUCTURE

Arrays are a problem type, and they are also used as a computation tool, often introduced in curriculum materials in the intermediate grades to help students make sense of division or of missing-factor multiplication. Here is an example of what we might see:

Use an array to find the missing factor. $6 \times \underline{\hspace{1cm}} = 132$

Initially students create arrays when they know the two factors and are missing the product, or the total number of cells in the array. To solve missing-factor problems, students are given grid paper and are asked to represent the problem and find the missing factor. How do students find the missing factor? Take a moment to try it yourself using this portion of grid paper.

FIGURE 8.12

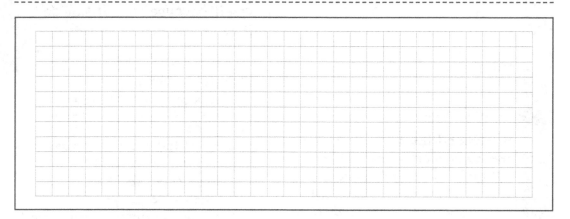

Students are often encouraged to mark landmark numbers or numbers for which they know a multiplication fact. In the example in Figure 8.13, the grid is marked off in sections of 10 cells to make $6 \times 10 = 60$, two times.

FIGURE 8.13

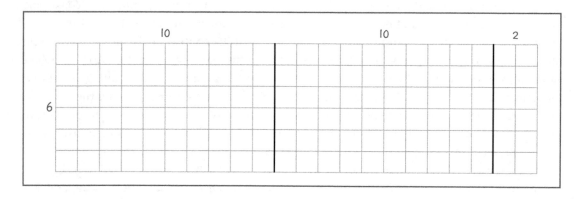

The expectation is that students will eventually abandon the grid lines and employ an ungridded representation of the major landmark facts, as in Figure 8.14.

FIGURE 8.14

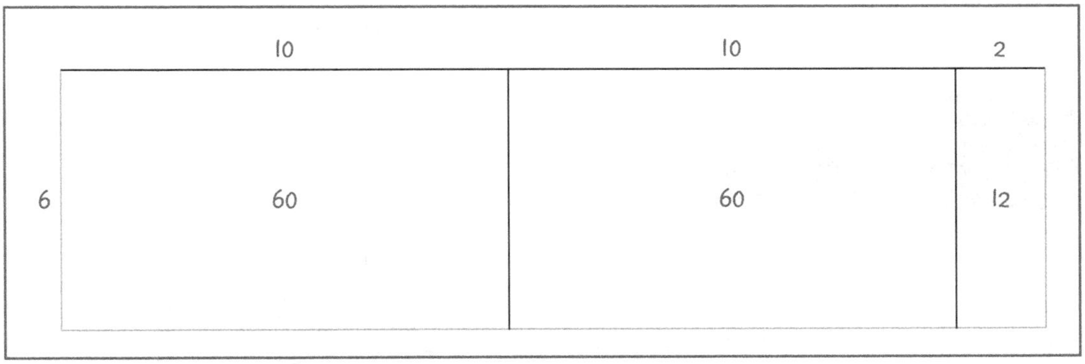

The grid paper in Figure 8.13 is a mathematical structure, much like the one used in the rug problem solution in Figure 8.4. The fact that there are countable squares does not necessarily make this an Equal Groups problem situation. As a matter of fact, this exercise is free of any kind of context from the beginning—the grid is only a tool used for learning efficient computation. We can't assign any problem type to it because it has no context.

Models of and Models for Thinking

The use of arrays as a strategy for computing division or missing-factor problems has great value, but challenges may arise when arrays become a default strategy for modeling *all* division and multiplication problems. As we saw in Figure 8.4, an array can be used to give structure to a problem so that the values can be counted or computed like an Equal Groups problem. The key for us as teachers, however, is not to let the helpfulness of arrays interfere with students building operation sense via models that most closely represent the particular problem situations.

Consider what happens when a student is encouraged to apply what she knows about arrays as a way to explore a solution to an Equal Groups problem (Figure 8.15). In the work samples in Figures 8.16 and 8.17, we see the work of only one student and her productive struggle as she tries to create a working model of a routine word problem. These student work samples are structured differently than previous examples. The teacher's comments on the first sample engage the learner to consider a new way to structure the problem. We then revisit the same student's work to see how she incorporated the teacher's suggestions.

FIGURE 8.15

Kate got 3 birthday cards. Each card had $2 in it. How much money does she have?

FIGURE 8.16   **FIGURE 8.17**

	First Attempt	After Implementing Teacher's Suggestion
STUDENT WORK	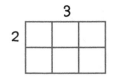 $3\left(\text{cards}\right) \times 2\left(\text{dollars}\right) = $???? This doesn't make any sense. I know the answer is 6, but I only see 5! 3 cards and 2 dollars. But that doesn't make sense... *Image Source:* IrynaDanyliuk/iStock.com	 Now I have 6 things! $3\left(\text{cards}\right) \times 2\left(\text{dollars per card}\right)$ $= 6\left(\text{dollars}\right)$ *Image Source:* IrynaDanyliuk/iStock.com
TEACHER RESPONSE	It's interesting that this student started out with exactly what the problem says–3 cards and 2 dollars–but then realized that she couldn't come up with an answer using that representation. I thought a lot about why that representation didn't work and realized that she may not recognize that 3 is the multiplier factor and 2 is the measure factor. She is treating both factors as measures. I wonder if an array might help her make sense of the problem. I went back to her table and asked her to try out that structure.	I appreciate that she gave up on the first model and persevered. Once she tried the array, I think she recognized right away why she had 6 dollars and not 5! I am not convinced that she will recognize the next Equal Groups problem, but with more practice we are on the right track. The array was helpful in making the connection.

Models of thinking: When a student's model of a problem situation describes how the student interprets and solves a specific task.

Models for thinking: Models that emerge as a student's model for understanding a mathematical idea is no longer tied to a specific problem or task and becomes a tool for reasoning about a new mathematical task.

Dutch researcher Koeno Gravemeijer makes an interesting distinction between models *of* thinking and models *for* thinking in relation to models that students create while mathematizing (Gravemeijer, 1999). A **model of thinking** is a representation students produce to reflect their ideas. Most likely this is an image taken either at the beginning or at the end of the solution process. We like to think of it as a presentation of a mathematical idea.

The **model for thinking** becomes a tool, a working "holder" and "displayer" of thoughts for students as they puzzle through the mathematics. The tool becomes part of the thinking process as it is manipulated to explore an idea, or to reset and start a new strategy. The tool becomes a tool for mathematizing.

The change in the student's thinking about the problem in Figure 8.15, through the use of the array, is a good example of what happens when a model becomes a tool *for* thinking. The card and dollar images represent the units of the problem. In the first attempt to represent the problem (Figure 8.16), the student represents both factors as measures and her solution stalls. She could very easily have given a solution of 6 dollars and moved on because $2 \times 3 = 6$ is likely a known fact for her but, instead, she persisted with creating a different model following the teacher's suggestion. The array (Figure 8.17) prompted an ah-ha moment about the nature of the problem context and she was able to revise her original model to reflect the action in the word problem. Presenting the dollars as a measure factor and using the cards in more of a "container" or "grouping" role, the model now shows an Equal Groups relationship that the student can not only solve but also make sense of. This simple example of the array acting as a model *for* thinking reminds us to continually encourage students to use models as a way of thinking about and wrestling with mathematical ideas, with the end goal being meaningful models that most closely match a problem situation. Creating meaningful models takes skill, practice, and experience to achieve mastery.

Moving Beyond Whole Numbers

This chapter explores the Area/Array problem situation as well as the mathematical structure called an array that is used to model any kind of problem situation and facilitate computation. In this section, as we move into problems that include fractional and decimal factors, we see that the Area/Array problem situation poses challenges for students.

Before we explore these challenges, take the two Area/Array problems in Figures 8.18 and 8.19 into the mathematizing sandbox by trying out different concrete and pictorial models. As you restate the problems and then engage in exploration, think about what is similar between the two problems and what is different.

FIGURE 8.18

FIGURE 8.19

Genni works at the local hardware store and she is in charge of the flooring department. She noticed a $4\frac{1}{2}$-foot tall roll of carpet in the SALE section one day that was marked 36 square feet. Carpet is sold by the foot, so she needed to figure out how long the rolled-up carpet was so that she could price it. How long is the carpet?	Liz works in the lumber department of the local hardware store. She is preparing an order of lumber for a family repairing a fence. The family needs 36 linear feet of lumber. It needs to be cut into $4\frac{1}{2}$-foot long boards. How many boards will she need to cut?

ENTER THE PROBLEM

EXPLORE

STUDENTS AND TEACHERS THINK ABOUT THE PROBLEMS

Look at the student work in Figures 8.20 and 8.21 and consider how the students describe or draw what is happening in the given word problems. Then look at the teacher commentary that follows and consider what the teachers noticed in the student work.

FIGURE 8.20   **FIGURE 8.21**

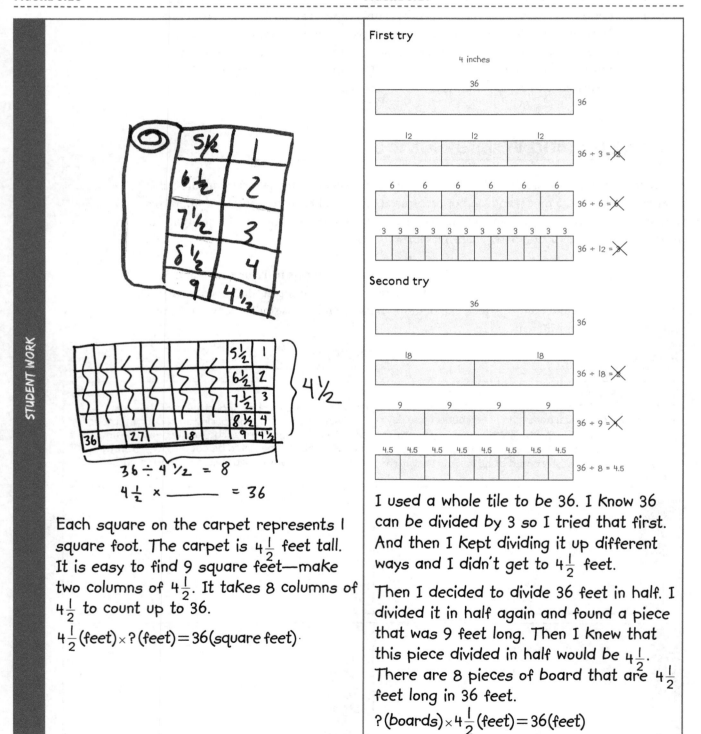

STUDENT WORK

$36 \div 4\frac{1}{2} = 8$

$4\frac{1}{2} \times \underline{\hspace{1cm}} = 36$

Each square on the carpet represents 1 square foot. The carpet is $4\frac{1}{2}$ feet tall. It is easy to find 9 square feet—make two columns of $4\frac{1}{2}$. It takes 8 columns of $4\frac{1}{2}$ to count up to 36.

$4\frac{1}{2}$ (feet) × ? (feet) = 36 (square feet).

First try

4 inches

36 | 36

12 | 12 | 12   36 ÷ 3 = ✗

6 6 6 6 6 6   36 ÷ 6 = ✗

3 3 3 3 3 3 3 3 3 3 3 3   36 ÷ 12 = ✗

Second try

36 | 36

18 | 18   36 ÷ 18 = ✗

9 9 9 9   36 ÷ 9 = ✗

4.5 4.5 4.5 4.5 4.5 4.5 4.5 4.5   36 ÷ 8 = 4.5

I used a whole tile to be 36. I know 36 can be divided by 3 so I tried that first. And then I kept dividing it up different ways and I didn't get to $4\frac{1}{2}$ feet.

Then I decided to divide 36 feet in half. I divided it in half again and found a piece that was 9 feet long. Then I knew that this piece divided in half would be $4\frac{1}{2}$. There are 8 pieces of board that are $4\frac{1}{2}$ feet long in 36 feet.

? (boards) × $4\frac{1}{2}$ (feet) = 36 (feet)

TEACHER RESPONSE

At first I thought this was a carpet with a square pattern on it, but then I realized that he is just using a grid to visualize area. That's pretty interesting, especially the $\frac{1}{2}$ square foot part.

Looking at the table below his carpet picture, I can see that another student might have figured out all of the missing values and filled them in, and part of me wishes he had done that too so that we could see it. But writing only the multiples of 9 along the length is probably easier and more efficient.

I'll be honest, when I first saw the fraction tiles I had no idea how she would get an answer! But once I read her explanation, it started to make more sense! Essentially this is trial and error, but the fraction tiles are used to test her guesses. The first guess was to partition 36 by 3 and then by 2 to see if that worked, I can see that because the first smaller tiles are $\frac{1}{3}$ of the whole and the next are half of that size.

In her second try, she tried to partition by 2. At this point I was starting to wonder if there actually WAS an answer in the tiles! But then when she divided by 2 again, I saw what she saw—half of 9 is $4\frac{1}{2}$. Each tile is $\frac{1}{8}$ of 36.

Wow! It is kind of hard to find the missing factor this way. I wonder if it would have been harder or easier to cut off a $4\frac{1}{2}$ foot piece of lumber one at a time instead of doing it this way. I'll have to pair her with Josh, who solved it using repeated subtraction, and see how they communicate their understandings.

VIDEO

Video 8.1

Carpet Length With a Grid Diagram

resources.corwin.com/ problemsolving3–5

Video 8.2

Fence Boards With Fraction Tiles

resources.corwin.com/ problemsolving3–5

As you hear in Video 8.1, the student whose work is presented in Figure 8.20 recognized that finding the missing dimension of the rolled-up rug is not easy to do. By superimposing a grid on the carpet, he shows that he recognizes that this is an area problem and that he needs to find the missing dimension, in this case, length. But without seeing the entire gridded area, there is no readily apparent solution. The strategy of mentally unrolling the carpet and continuing the visual grid along the whole length of the carpet is helpful. But this also requires some form of guess and check. For example, he counts up to $4\frac{1}{2}$, starts a new row and continues counting the units up to 9. How many of these rows are needed to make up a total of 36 square feet? If you think this sounds a bit like a measurement division (an Equal Groups–type) operation—because the grid counts off $4\frac{1}{2}$ units at a time—you're correct. But because this is an Area/Array problem situation, it is yet another example of drawing on a modeling strategy that matches a different problem situation. The grid is a strategy that is used to find a solution when the context itself does not yield an obvious strategy. In this case, a gridded Area/Array problem is solved using an Equal Groups–like strategy.

Now, reread the lumber problem in Figure 8.19. Did you decide whether it is symmetric or asymmetric? What reasons do you give for your decision? Because the lumber is cut off in specific measures, this situation is most likely a measurement division situation and therefore has to be asymmetric. The student solution in Figure 8.21 and Video 8.2 is an interesting exemplar because—like the strategy proposed in Figure 8.20—it also is a form of a guess-and-check strategy. Using the fraction tiles as a model for thinking about 36 feet of lumber, the student tries first to partition by 3 to see if she can arrive at the board length of $4\frac{1}{2}$ feet. When that path is not fruitful, she starts over again and tries to divide by 2, which eventually leads to a successful solution.

WHEN MODELS MATCH AND WHEN THEY DON'T

In Figure 8.21 the student chose a partitive strategy to find the number of boards that need to be cut. Each of her partitions is trying a new value for the multiplier factor, trying to find the right measure factor. Imagine how this solution might have unfolded differently if the student recognized that the problem context was actually more quotitive in nature. She might have started with lengths of $4\frac{1}{2}$ feet and subtracted them repeatedly to arrive at a solution of 8 boards. Her model did not match the problem situation, and it caused her to guess and check extensively. The teacher wondered how she and Josh, a student who did solve a similar problem quotitively, might put their heads together and find commonalities in their thinking. This is a good opportunity for you to stop and discuss strategy and model selection with your team. What is the value of recognizing when there is a mismatch between the problem situation type and a student's model? What might you say to this student to guide her thinking yet still honor it? How can we productively negotiate a mismatch like this in the classroom environment?

In this book we have presented word problems that are somewhat real life and reasonable, even if some may be odd occurrences, like the carpet remnant on sale at the hardware store. In truth it is unusual in real life to have a missing factor in a symmetric problem context, so it is challenging to come up with reasonable word problems. Many textbooks or other resources are filled with unlikely situations that include references to objects aligned in rows and columns, or areas, or arrays. Sometimes these problems feel more like Equal Groups problem situations even though the text labels the problems "array" or "area." But most problems presented in textbooks typically are of the Equal Groups type and are therefore much more familiar. Despite that, students may still incorrectly match a model to a problem and therefore struggle to find a workable solution. Keep this in mind as you work with students.

REPRESENTING FRACTION AND DECIMAL DIVISION

Look at the problem in Figure 8.22. What kinds of representations would work well in modeling this problem situation? A linear model? An area model? A discrete model?

FIGURE 8.22

MaryAnn needed 0.75 square feet of fancy paper to decorate her jewelry box. The package of fancy papers said that the width of a sheet of paper was 0.5 feet long. How long a piece will she need to cut?

Look at the student work in Figures 8.23 and 8.24 and consider how the students describe or draw what is happening in the given word problem. For this problem we are sharing two work samples instead of including teacher responses. The goal is to explore more models in depth in order to offer readers even more examples of strategies to use for modeling decimal and fraction multiplication and division problem situations.

FIGURE 8.23   FIGURE 8.24

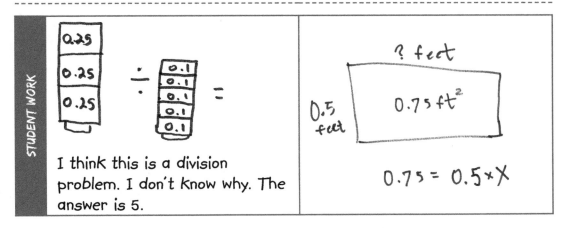

STUDENT WORK

I think this is a division problem. I don't know why. The answer is 5.

Let's first consider which problem situation is represented by the context. The problem in Figure 8.22 is symmetric and it is an Area/Array problem situation. Both sides of the fancy paper piece are measured in feet and the product is a different unit (square feet). The context also has symmetric properties: Fancy papers, which are used in scrapbooking and craft projects, come in sheets that can be rotated and used from any direction. This makes us fairly sure that the problem situation is of the Area/Array type. The student in Figure 8.24 created a reasonably accurate model of the problem context, even leaving the missing dimension represented by a question mark because this is a missing-factor situation. Consider the reasons why the student followed the picture with this equation: $0.75 = 0.5 \times x$. Remember that an equation generated in the mathematizing sandbox is based on the problem and reflects the student's understanding and the pictorial or concrete representation produced. It is not necessarily the equation you might use to compute an answer.

The rectangular model in Figure 8.24 that actually looks like a piece of fancy paper is a far more effective model for visualizing the problem situation than the linear interpretation given in Figure 8.23. It is important for students to learn to use manipulative tools, but it is also important that they use them strategically. In the case of the fancy paper problem, the linear model using fraction bars showing 0.75 and 0.5 does not reflect the meaning of the problem situation. It is true that some students can easily use a representation like this fraction bar representation to make a calculation model: The mismatch of an area problem context and a linear modeling tool may not interfere with their understanding of the problem situation. In other words, some students are able to jump right away to the calculation tool, while holding the operational understanding in their heads. But such mismatched models can create a challenge for other students. The area model in Figure 8.24 gives us more confidence that the student understands the problem context. Figure 8.25 shows another solution strategy for this problem that uses an overlay of a grid to lend mathematical structure.

FIGURE 8.25

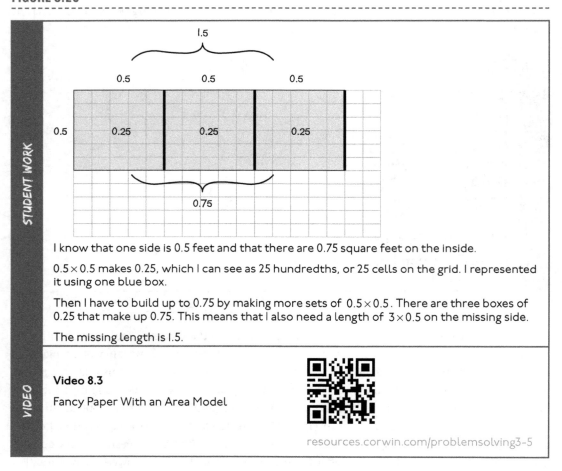

STUDENT WORK

I know that one side is 0.5 feet and that there are 0.75 square feet on the inside.

0.5×0.5 makes 0.25, which I can see as 25 hundredths, or 25 cells on the grid. I represented it using one blue box.

Then I have to build up to 0.75 by making more sets of 0.5×0.5. There are three boxes of 0.25 that make up 0.75. This means that I also need a length of 3×0.5 on the missing side.

The missing length is 1.5.

VIDEO

Video 8.3

Fancy Paper With an Area Model

resources.corwin.com/problemsolving3-5

Does this seem like a complicated way to solve this problem? Yes, it is challenging to model, which is why most teachers will try to "simplify" it and ask students to solve it as the division problem: $0.75 \div 0.5 = 1.5$. This is far more efficient if our goal is to get the answer! Experience tells us, however, that students are not always able to replicate the teacher's thinking and recognize the efficient way to solve a new problem in this way. That is why it is important to focus more on student understanding and less on getting answers. This model, while inefficient, represents just the kind of thinking students need to engage in. Getting the answer one time does not make a student a problem solver! In the end, combining the model and the equation that best match the problem situation can help students make the most progress toward finding and modeling an effective solution for any problem.

KEY IDEAS

1. Symmetric situations are commutative in context. It does not change the meaning of the problem, for example, to rotate a rug 90 degrees and "reverse" the length and width.

2. Symmetric situations are hard to act out because the factors do not suggest any actions.

3. Students can make sense of symmetric situations by adding structure like a grid, a table, or a diagram to organize the information in the problem.

4. The unit of the product in a symmetric situation is different from the unit in the factors. Inches times inches yields square inches. Multiple articles of clothing make outfits.

5. An array is both a type of problem situation and a mathematical structure that can be superimposed on a problem to organize it. The Area/Array problem situation is symmetric. The mathematical structure array can be either symmetric or asymmetric depending on the context.

TRY IT OUT!

IDENTIFY THE PROBLEM SITUATION

Choose three or four of the exercises below that are most relevant to your grade level. For each exercise,

*   Identify the units of both factors and the product.

*   Decide whether the problem situation represents an asymmetric or a symmetric situation.

*   State what is unknown in the problem. If it is asymmetric and a factor is unknown, tell whether it is the multiplier factor or the measure factor.

In some cases, you may not agree with a colleague. If this happens, make your case and discuss your reasoning.

1. The floor of the classroom is covered with ceramic tiles. The side of each tile is one foot long. There are 10 tiles along the front wall and 12 tiles down the side wall. What is the area of the classroom floor?

2. The store salesperson packed up three soap samples for each customer who visited the store for the Grand Opening. When she finished, she noticed that she had emptied a box of 75 samples. How many customers got samples?

(continued)

(continued)

3. Our class gathered temperature data for a month. We measured the temperature outside our own classroom every day. We also looked up the high temperature in 20 other cities around the world each day and recorded that data. We decided to show our data in a spreadsheet. How many pieces of data are on our spreadsheet?

4. There are 6 different parking lots at my favorite mall. After the mall closed, there were still 2 cars in each parking lot. How many cars were still at the mall?

5. The parking lot next to my favorite store has 8 rows of parking spaces. There are 15 parking spaces in each row. How many parking spots does this lot have?

6. The local movie theater has a sign that says the maximum capacity of the theater is 770 people. I counted across the front row and saw that there were 22 seats. How many rows of seats are there?

7. My local pet store has 4 tanks of fancy tropical fish on display and each had the same number of fish in it. The woman working at the store said that they had only 32 fancy tropical fish to sell this week. How many fish are in each tank?

8. My family volunteers for the community's charity pancake breakfast every year. This year I get to make the pancake batter. On the table were 8 dozen eggs. The recipe calls for a half dozen eggs. How many recipes am I able to make?

9. Cats should drink 0.45 liters of water every 3 days. How much should a cat drink each day?

WRITE THE PROBLEM

For each of the following equations, write a word problem that matches. Include a representation that corresponds to the situation.

1. $2 \times 3 = 6$ (symmetric)

2. $2 \times 3 = 6$ (asymmetric)

3. $5 \times 19 = 95$ (symmetric)

4. $5 \times 19 = 95$ (asymmetric)

5. $1.5 \times 8 = 12$ (symmetric)

6. $1.5 \times 8 = 12$ (asymmetric)

7. $2\frac{2}{3} \times 4\frac{1}{2} = 12$ (symmetric)

8. $2\frac{2}{3} \times 4\frac{1}{2} = 12$ (asymmetric)

BRANCH OUT

1. The book *Sundae Scoop* by Stuart Murphy (2003) is a fun way to explore combinations. Ask students to predict how many sundae combinations they can make using only the choices given in the book. Then expand the list and see what happens as the options also expand.

2. To use arrays as a tool for learning and gaining fluency with multiplication facts, use the card sort activity in the *Fluency Without Fear* document from YouCubed (Boaler, 2015). Students match grid arrays to arrays of objects to dot patterns to equations on their way to making sense of their multiplication facts. The document may be downloaded from https://www.youcubed.org/evidence/fluency-without-fear/.

REFLECT

1. In this chapter we discussed the difference between models *of* thinking and models *for* thinking. When a manipulative or model becomes more than just an expression of an answer but, instead, becomes a tool for more reasoning and learning, it becomes an invaluable tool in the classroom. Describe when have you seen this in a classroom.

2. Some curricular resources automatically classify any problem that indicates rows and columns as symmetric. Think of examples of rows and columns that are more asymmetric in nature than symmetric. How can you identify these problem contexts? What difference does it make when modeling the problem context?

3. Arrays are both a symmetric problem type and a mathematical structure. Describe some of the ways that arrays do both jobs.

CHAPTER NINE

Changing How You Teach Word Problems

Think back to the new teacher's classroom we visited at the beginning of this book. She asked her students to solve two word problems:

> Mrs. King has 25 books to give to 8 students for summer reading. If each student gets the same number of books, how many will she have left?

> Richard measured and packed enough flour to make brownies and a cake during the week at a cabin. He is baking the brownies first and the cake later. He has 5 cups of flour. The brownie recipe calls for $1\frac{1}{2}$ cups of flour, and whatever is left he will use for the cake. How much flour is left to use for the cake recipe?

This teacher realized that her students were misled in the first problem by the word *left*, treating it as a key word and thinking that subtraction was the right approach to the problem. Knowing what you know now, what guidance would you give this new teacher if she were your colleague?

Getting Into the Mathematizing Sandbox

Problem-solving protocols are not a new idea. Certainly you have seen models for problem solving in your mathematics textbook, and many books have been written on this subject. Perhaps the most influential problem-solving protocol was written in 1945 by Pólya. His general plan included four steps: Understand, Devise a Plan, Carry Out a Plan, and Look Back. If this protocol were enough to resolve all difficulties with problem solving, there would be no need for this book or any other book on problem solving. Of course, the issue is far from being resolved. We offer in this book a model that targets the space somewhere between Understand and Devise a Plan with the belief that there is a need to explore more deeply what it means to "Understand" a problem mathematically.

The mathematizing sandbox model emphasizes the power and importance of play and interaction with mathematical tools and ideas. Problem solving doesn't ride on a train and barrel through to the end of the track. Sometimes it needs to meander and rest and sit idle to allow thoughts to coalesce into working theories. We chose the metaphor of a sandbox with intention. What do we do in a sandbox? We play, construct, take down, and reconstruct. We get our hands dirty as we pick up new tools and move things around. We shake off the old and use the grains to form new ideas. When we emerge from the sandbox, we take nothing tangible away. But the play has done its work forming ideas in the child's mind. That is the takeaway. When we are young, we don't solve problems so that we can find the answer. We solve problems so that we learn to solve bigger and more important problems. This is how real problem solving works. Figure 9.1 reviews the steps in the mathematizing sandbox model, giving you a chance to think about it again after having applied it multiple times in your own work on the problems in the book.

FIGURE 9.1 A MODEL FOR MATHEMATIZING WORD PROBLEMS

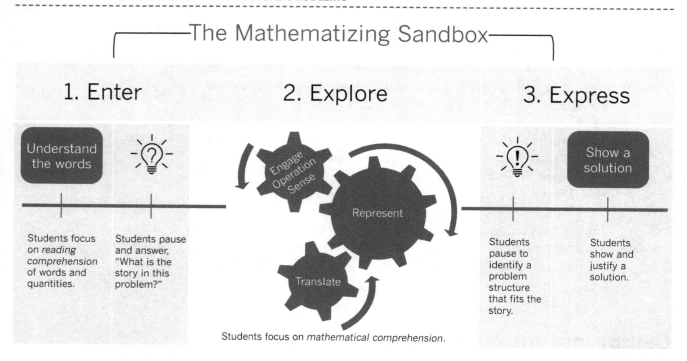

The Mathematizing Sandbox

1. Enter   2. Explore   3. Express

Understand the words

Students focus on *reading comprehension* of words and quantities.

Students pause and answer, "What is the story in this problem?"

Engage Operation Sense

Represent

Translate

Students focus on *mathematical comprehension*.

Students pause to identify a problem structure that fits the story.

Show a solution

Students show and justify a solution.

ENTER:	In this problem-solving model we acknowledge the importance of language and literacy strategies in making sense of the words that frame a problem situation: Understanding what is happening in the problem is a ticket into the sandbox. If the problem is one that the students have identified and posed themselves, this is less of a concern. But for a traditional word problem, it is important to help students decipher the language used in order to understand the context.
	Teachers tell us, and we know from our own work with students, that rushing into a problem often results in "number plucking and plugging" (SanGiovanni & Milou, 2018), a haphazard application of operations that involves little sense making. Here we stop to tell the story in our own words. What is happening? Between each set of word problems and the workspace given to you to write down your own solutions, we stepped in and included questions that helped to guide your thinking or to give you an idea to focus on as you did your own work. In this respect, we intended to model the Pause step of this model.

Chapter Nine. Changing How You Teach Word Problems

175

EXPLORE:	The three parts of Explore are the core content of this book, the place where operation sense is built. Each problem exploration included multiple representations and deliberately made connections (translations) between each of those representations. Sometimes, like in Chapter 6, the same problem was explored using five or more representations, all in the interest of revealing more details about the relationships in the problem and figuring out the right operation to use to find a solution. Sometimes we encountered many solutions in the sandbox, but that was not the primary goal. Our goal was to learn more about the problem, the problem situation, and how to use multiple representations to understand the work of the operation in the problem.
	The pause on the way out of the sandbox gave us the opportunity to generalize what was learned during exploration. For students, we recommend that they spend time deciding which problem situation applies, what element is missing, and then how they will calculate an answer.
EXPRESS:	Finally. Students can compute an answer. That's a long process just to get to the answer, right? Yes. That is intentional. As the teacher, you decide what you would like to see your students express. What evidence from their sandbox work is important to you? Do you want to see an equation? A drawing? Just an answer? We decided not to make that decision for you because you know your students best and you know the contexts in which they will need to show their solutions.

Eight Shifts in Instruction for Building Students' Problem-Solving Skills

In this book we've presented an approach to problem solving that comes from a sense-making point of view. Recognizing that calculation and computation skills are important for student success, we also realize that computation alone is not very effective for preparing students to make sense of word problems or to pose and solve real-world problems. In the discussion that follows, we suggest eight changes that you can make in your teaching practice that will help build strong problem solvers in your classroom.

DO WORD PROBLEMS FOR SENSE-MAKING

Word problems are typically organized in textbooks to give students the opportunity to practice a computation strategy. Instead, we used word problems as a tool throughout the book to highlight the problem situations and many of their variations. Through this very familiar tool, you have had the opportunity to explore common solution approaches, some of which are precisely efficient and others of which are inefficient. But unpacking word problems is not the goal of this book. Building operation sense is. The problem situations that we explored are present in any everyday situation that you and your students wish to mathematize. Do your students want to gather data on waste in the cafeteria in order to start a recycling program? Their discussions won't be about "plus" or "minus." Instead they will talk about comparisons, measurements, and the different kinds of trash (parts and a whole). They focus their problem-solving discussion on the actions they wish to accomplish. The problem situations and the ideas behind them give them tools to DO. That is operation sense. Tools for calculation, like plus and minus, will follow the need for them.

Shift #1: Use word problems to help students learn to recognize the properties of the problem situations that represent a wide range of contexts. Word problems are not just tools for practicing computation.

TREAT CONTEXT AND COMPUTATION SEPARATELY

Separating context from computation is a consistent theme throughout the book. Chapter 2 focused on the power of concrete and visual representations to show the action in a problem situation. We even saw the inefficient computation of adding up by sevens take center stage simply because the strategy matches a football game context! Chapter 5 asked whether the commutative property of multiplication always is as practical in real-life problem solving as we've thought. Sure, the numbers always produce the same final product, but kids know that in an Equal Groups problem situation 2 × 30 is not the same as 30 × 2! By separating and naming the factors in this type of problem situation, we acknowledge the critical importance of meaning and context and separate them from computation. Focusing on context has its own challenges, and they are not insignificant. It is our goal to raise your awareness of the many ways you can subtly but directly make instructional changes in order to hone students' focus on what is happening in a problem, any contextual problem. To be clear, computational skills are critically important, but that's not what this book set out to address.

Shift #2: Focus instruction on finding and explaining the meaning of a problem situation. Figuring out how to calculate an answer comes second.

CREATE MORE AND VARIED REPRESENTATIONS

Representations of mathematical ideas take many forms. In Chapter 1 we outlined five different modes of representation and the ways each mode can help describe what is happening in a problem situation (Figure 9.2) And throughout the book we urged you to try out multiple representations in your own explorations of the problems presented. In Chapter 3 we saw, for example, how a concrete model composed of two-color counters to represent two varieties of juice could be translated into a representation of the same problem using a formal symbolic equation. The power of mathematics is in its capacity to capture and manipulate abstract thoughts and ideas. Students need plenty of experience describing and connecting real-life contexts to the symbolic representations before they can deal wholly within the abstract. Multiple, and connected, representations add shading and nuance to students' understandings, which leads to greater mathematizing power.

Shift #3: Match multiple representations to the details of a problem context. Translating between representations strengthens this understanding.

Chapter Nine. Changing How You Teach Word Problems

177

FIGURE 9.2 FIVE REPRESENTATIONS: A TRANSLATION MODEL

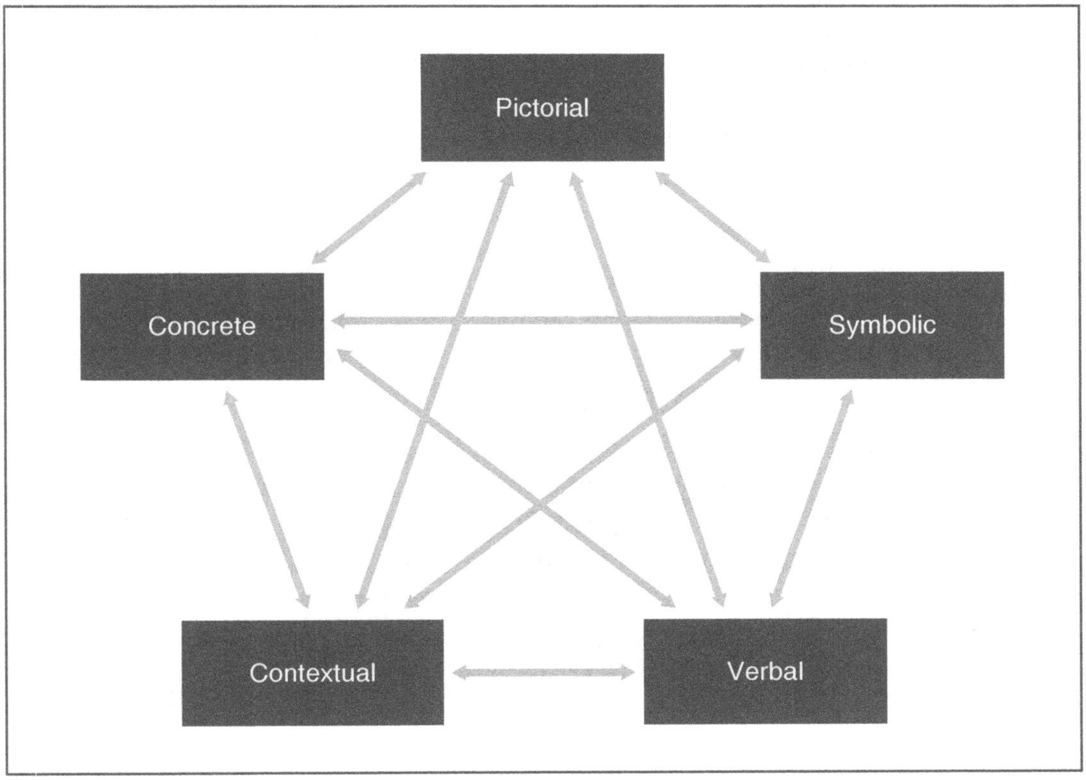

Source: Adapted from Lesh, Post, and Behr (1987).

EXPLORE ALL THE WORK OPERATIONS CAN DO

Each person has an intuitive mental model for each of the operations (+, −, ×, ÷). Sometimes students' mental models are limited to only one or two of the "jobs" that an operation can do. We saw in Chapter 3 that addition can do more than just add things together. It can also describe the relationships among the parts and the whole of a set. In Chapter 6 we dug deeper into the work that division can do and found that division can divvy up a fair share for everyone, but it can also distribute equal shares when you don't know how many sharers there are. This latter model of division often surprises learners. Using the chapter-opening problem situation tables as a guide, this book exposes some of the lesser known work that the operations can do.

Shift #4: Focus student attention on the action or relationships in a problem situation. When students know what they need an operator to do, they are better able to make a good choice.

ADD OPERATION SENSE ROUTINES TO THE SCHOOL DAY

Operation sense is part of the sense-making stage of any problem-solving protocol you might already use. It includes the ability to mathematize a problem situation, to create multiple representations of the actions or relationships in the problem situation, and to assign an appropriate operation to find a solution. A student with a strong operation sense

- Understands and uses a wide variety of models of operations beyond the basic and intuitive models of operations

- Uses appropriate representations of actions or relationships strategically

- Applies their understanding of operations to any quantity, regardless of the class of number

- Can mathematize a situation, translating a contextual understanding into a variety of other mathematical representations

In this book we have explored a wide variety of informal models and commercially available manipulatives, most of which are likely already available in your school or have digital or print alternatives. None of these is appropriate all the time, but part of operation sense is selecting the right tool for the job and using it to make sense of a problem situation.

Shift #5: Operation sense routines might include problem posing, numberless word problems, and acting out problems.

OFFER STUDENTS EXPERIENCES WITH A VARIETY OF PROBLEM SITUATIONS

When focused on context-based instruction, the value or form of the numbers in the problem should not matter. But in some ways they do matter. For example, it matters which quantities are known and unknown, and students need practice with unknown elements in different parts of the problem. Changing number categories, from whole numbers to fractions, for example, is like putting a wrench in the gears of a machine: It can cause a multitude of problems (Figure 9.3). As students experience new number categories, let them wrestle with problem contexts that arise, and observe carefully both the roadblocks they hit and the creative solutions they find. This productive struggle will improve their capacity to solve problems and your capacity to challenge and support them. Remember that students' ability to pose and solve word problems reflecting all of the different problem situations is based on experience. If they never solve multiplicative comparisons using fractions, they will never be comfortable with this structure. Experience matters.

Shift #6: Anticipate that the introduction of a new category of numbers will require a review of the problem situation variations, but don't back away from the challenge.

Chapter Nine. Changing How You Teach Word Problems

179

FIGURE 9.3 THE CHALLENGE OF NEW NUMBER CATEGORIES LEADS TO GROWTH

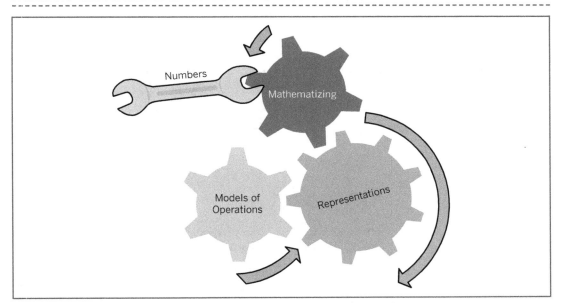

LISTEN TO STUDENTS AND BE CURIOUS

We used dozens of work samples throughout this book to illustrate some of the ways that students might grapple with a focus on context in a problem. Sometimes these examples were chosen specifically to feature the teacher's response to the student work. Often this is because the teacher made an insightful observation about the student's work, one that helps the reader make sense of the new information. Throughout the book we worked to use qualified, non-evaluative language, recognizing that we can only interpret the student work based on the evidence before us. This is also true for you in the classroom. Even when you know your students well, continue to ask for clarification and evidence in your assessment procedures.

Shift #7: Don't assume you know what students are thinking. Be curious! Ask questions!

MAKE TIME FOR MATHEMATIZING IN THE SANDBOX

The mathematizing sandbox is a state of mind more than it is a place to go. The sandbox shows that your priority is exploration and learning. Failed models are expected, but replacement ideas are also expected. For this reason, we would never grade work done in the sandbox. Of course, this means that time will need to be carved out for students to engage in this thinking time. To make the time, do fewer problems. Do more problems in response to questions or concerns your students have posed and fewer randomly assigned problems.

Shift #8: Take time for students to explore and learn to problem solve.

Guidance for Moving Forward: FAQs

Should my students have to memorize the kinds of problems in the tables and their definitions?

We consider it inappropriate to ask students to memorize the problem situation tables and to sort problems into those categories for the sole purpose of categorizing and sorting. Instead, you can use the language in the problems and let students create class anchor charts that describe the characteristics of the problem types that your class encounters. Post examples so that they can remember what the problems look like and what approaches are helpful for problems like the one they are solving. The goal is familiarity with the patterns revealed by the questions throughout the book. These questions are summarized in Figure 9.5.

How do I find more high-quality problems of different types?

The most valuable resource you have might be your textbook and your creativity! Textbook publishers have become much more intentional since 2010 in the word problem types that they include in chapter exercises. Read the problems available to you, classify them according to the problem situation tables, and plan your lesson with supports for each problem situation. Often, minor variations in the given problems will greatly extend their range. You can change which term is unknown or adapt the numbers to suit your current unit of study, for example. Overall, choose problems carefully so that students have exposure to different problem situations over time. If you find the textbook doesn't offer enough variety, other resources are available. One of our favorite sources for word problems is Greg Tang. He has included a word problem generator on his website that will generate lists of problems, and you have the opportunity to select the problem type and which element is unknown (Tang, n.d.): https://gregtangmath.com/wordproblems.

What about those kids who are always racing to finish?

Sometimes the same students who race to finish their work are able to come up with a correct answer. Other times, they are not. If we remember that the goal is to teach a long-term strategy for problem solving rather than a short-term goal of finding an answer, it is easier to be firm in your expectations. Make it clear what you are looking for in their work. Share student representations and discuss them in class. Challenge students to do problems where the values are all unknown so that the focus is squarely on the problem situation. If there are still some students who dive in and race to get an answer, intervene much as you would with a student who is running in the hallways. After all, it is faster to run down the hall of the school, but we ask kids to walk because we know that it is much easier for someone to get hurt when they run. No one will get hurt if students race through the sandbox, but there is still truth to the analogy!

Do I have to do the full mathematizing sandbox for every word problem?

No. It is important to follow the entire process at first so that students develop new thought patterns about problem solving. You want them to understand the operations better at first and you want them to learn to use a wide variety of manipulatives and representations. Lessons in the sandbox intentionally focus on building students' operation sense and making strong connections between the problem situation and its representations, but we know it isn't possible to follow the entire process each and every time.

Chapter Nine. Changing How You Teach Word Problems

181

I have not used concrete representations very much. How do I start? What should I look out for?

Before asking your students to use manipulatives to represent problem situations, provide time to explore the materials. Even a few minutes gives learners an opportunity to see how the pieces fit together, build a tower or other structure, and begin to see what the materials might do.

Take time to learn about a variety of materials; you do not have to start with many different manipulatives all at the same time. We suggested throughout the book which materials we prefer for which situations. Your students may have different preferences, but our suggestions can help you begin. As students become comfortable with the materials, keep them easily available—on their tables or on accessible shelves. Remember to respect your students' choice of manipulative models; what makes sense to us might not be most helpful to them.

In Chapter 2, we provided a list of suggestions for using concrete materials to represent problem situations. We include it again in Figure 9.4 to provide ideas for encouraging productive use of these powerful tools.

FIGURE 9.4 ENCOURAGING MULTIPLE MODELS IN PROBLEM SOLVING

1. **Choose:** Encourage individual choice of physical and pictorial representations.

2. **Explain:** Ask students to explain what the parts of their pictorial representation mean and to explain the relationships between those parts.

3. **Justify:** Challenge students to defend their choices. Challenge students' correct representations just as much as you would ask them to justify incorrect representations.

4. **Model:** Explicitly model new forms of diagrams or manipulatives that you choose to use, explaining your decisions as you demonstrate how you are using the tool. We are *not* suggesting you explicitly teach students to use the tool. Simply model your own thinking process as you employ a visual, but reinforce to students that you are held to the same standard for justifying your decisions as they are.

5. **Connect:** Ask students to describe how two representations or models relate to each other. Encourage them to identify how each element of the problem appears in each model. Ask them to explain when they might prefer one model or representation over another.

6. **Share:** Ask students to explain a novel visual approach to their peers and discuss how they model their thinking process.

7. **Expect:** Communicate that you expect to see visual diagrams or manipulatives used to explain mathematical ideas.

8. **Crash:** No representation works in every context or situation. Expect any model to fail at some point, and encourage students to change their representation when the model crashes.

How do I help my students see the structure in the word problems?

The questions you ask while students are exploring are critically important. You have seen some of these questions while reading, especially where we gave problem pairs for you to explore. Figure 9.5 includes a list of questions you can use to support your students in this process. It includes the questions we have used to prompt you throughout this book as well as more specific questions you might use in classroom conversation.

FIGURE 9.5   QUESTIONS TO SUPPORT YOUR STUDENTS IN THE MATHEMATIZING SANDBOX

General Questions for Entering Problem Situations

- *Think about the quantities in each situation. What do they represent? What work do they do?*

- *How is each quantity related to the other quantities in the problem?*

- *How can you represent the quantities in the word problems with your manipulatives or pictures?*

- *What number sentence best shows what is happening in each story?*

Addition/Subtraction Questions for Exploring Problem Situations

- *Are these problems about action or relationships?*

- *If you see action, what is the change?*

- *If you see relationships, how would you describe the relationships? Are they about groups or about comparing?*

- *Where are the quantities in the word problems represented in your manipulatives or pictures?*

- *How is the operation in your number sentence represented in your physical or visual model?*

Multiplication/Division Questions for Exploring Problem Situations

- *Think about the factors in each situation. What do they represent? What work do they do?*

- *Look at the units in the factors and product in the problem. Do the factors have the same unit or do the factors have two different units?*

- *If the factors have the same unit, do they create a new unit?*

- *If the factors have two different units, what are the containers or groups? What is in each container or group?*

- *Where are the quantities in the word problems represented in your manipulatives or pictures?*

- *How is the operation in your number sentence represented in your physical or visual model?*

The mathematics we teach students in school is about more than getting ready for the test at the end of a unit or the end of the year. It is about seeing our world mathematically and using the math we know to mathematize, to solve problems in our jobs, our careers, and in our everyday lives. Jon Scieszka humorously calls this tendency *the math curse* (Scieszka & Smith, 1995). But we don't see it as a curse. We see it as a super power, which, like literacy, should be available to all!

We hope we have inspired you to see word problems differently, as a tool for developing operation sense rather than only as a vehicle for practicing a procedure. The operation sense that students develop while diving into word problems and other problem situations empowers them to recognize mathematical relationships in their own environment. This power allows them to make their own choices about what is worthy of being mathematized. In this way operation sense is a key component of a sense-making approach to mathematics and of a social justice–inspired mathematics program. Kids learn that they can mathematize any situation they encounter. Feel free to change our problems to suit your students' needs and interests and then ask them what problems they want to mathematize and solve.

APPENDIX:

Situation Tables

Note: These representations for the problem situations reflect our understanding based on a number of resources. These include the tables in the Common Core State Standards for mathematics (Common Core Standards Initiative, 2010), the problem situations as described in the Cognitively Guided Instruction research (Carpenter, Hiebert, & Moser, 1981), in Heller and Greeno (1979) and Riley, Greeno, & Heller (1984), and other tools. See the list below for a more detailed summary of the documents that informed our development of these tables.

References

Carpenter, T. P., Hiebert, J., & Moser, J. M. (1981). Problem structure and first-grade children's initial solution processes for simple addition and subtraction problems. *Journal for Research in Mathematics Education*, 27–39.

Heller, J. I., & Greeno, J. G. (1979). Information processing analyses of mathematical problem solving. In R. Lesh, M. Mierkiewicz, & M. Kantowski (Eds.), *Applied mathematical problem solving* (pp. 181–206). Columbus, OH: The Ohio State University. Retrieved from ERIC database (ED 180 816).

National Governors Association Center for Best Practices and Council of Chief State School Officers. (2010). *Common Core State Standards for Mathematics*. Washington, DC: Author.

Riley, M. S., Greeno, J. G., & Heller, J. I. (1984). Development of children's ability in arithmetic. In *Development of Children's Problem-Solving Ability in Arithmetic. No. LRDC-1984/37.* (pp. 153–196). Pittsburgh University, PA: Learning Research and Development Center, National Institute of Education.

Addition and Subtraction Problem Situations

	Result Unknown	Change Addend Unknown	Start Addend Unknown	
Add-To	Paulo counted out 75 crayons and put them in the basket. Then he found 23 more crayons under the table. He added them to the basket. How many crayons are now in the basket? $75 + 23 = x$ $23 = x - 75$	Paulo counted out 75 crayons and put them in the basket. Then he found some more crayons under the table. He added them to the basket and now there are 98 crayons in the basket. How many crayons were under the table? $75 + x = 98$ $x = 98 - 75$	Paulo was organizing the crayons at his table. He found 23 crayons under the table and added them to the basket. When he counted, there were 98 crayons in the basket. How many crayons were in the basket before Paulo looked under the table for crayons? $x + 23 = 98$ $98 - 23 = x$	
Take-From	There are 26 students in Mrs. Amadi's class. After lunch, 15 left to get ready to play in the band at the assembly. How many students are not in the band? $26 - 15 = x$ $26 = 15 + x$	There are 26 students in Mrs. Amadi's class. After the band students left the classroom for the assembly, there were 11 students still in the classroom. How many students are in the band? $26 - x = 11$ $x + 11 = 26$	After lunch, 15 band students left Mrs. Amadi's class to get ready to play in the assembly. There were 11 students still in the classroom. How many students are in Mrs. Amadi's class? $x - 15 = 11$ $15 + 11 = x$	

	Total Unknown	One Part Unknown		Both Parts Unknown
Part-Part-Whole	The 4th grade held a vote to decide where to go for the annual field trip. 32 students voted to go to the ice skating rink. 63 voted to go to the local park. How many students are in the 4th grade? $32 + 63 = x$ $x - 63 = 32$	The 4th grade held a vote to decide where the 95 students in the grade should go for their annual field trip. 32 students voted to go to the ice skating rink. The rest chose the local park. How many voted to go to the park? $32 + x = 95$ $x = 95 - 32$		The 4th grade held a vote to decide where the 95 students in the grade should go for their annual field trip. Some students voted to go to the ice skating rink and others voted to go to the local park. What are some possible combinations of votes? $x + y = 95$ $95 - x = y$
	Difference Unknown	**Greater Quantity Unknown**	**Lesser Quantity Unknown**	
Additive Comparison	Jessie and Roberto both collect baseball cards. Roberto has 53 cards and Jessie has 71 cards. How many fewer cards does Roberto have than Jessie? $53 + x = 71$ $71 - 53 = x$	Jessie and Roberto both collect baseball cards. Roberto has 53 cards and Jessie has 18 more cards than Roberto. How many baseball cards does Jessie have? $53 + 18 = x$ $x - 18 = 53$	Jessie and Roberto both collect baseball cards. Jessie has 71 cards and Roberto has 18 fewer cards than Jessie. How many baseball cards does Roberto have? $71 - 18 = x$ $x + 18 = 71$	

online resources ⤷ Available for download at **http://resources.corwin.com/problemsolving3-5**

Multiplication and Division Problem Situations

ASYMMETRICAL (NONMATCHING) FACTORS

	Product Unknown	Multiplier (Number of Groups) Unknown	Measure (Group Size) Unknown	
Equal Groups (Ratio/Rate)*	Mayim has 8 vases to decorate the tables at her party. She places 3 flowers in each vase. How many flowers does she need? $$8 \times 3 = x$$ $$x \div 8 = 3$$	Mayim has some vases to decorate the tables at her party. She places 3 flowers in each vase. If she uses 24 flowers, how many vases does she have? $$x \times 3 = 24$$ $$x = 24 \div 3$$	Mayim places 24 flowers in vases to decorate the tables at her party. If there are 8 vases, how many flowers will be in each vase? $$8 \times x = 24$$ $$24 \div 8 = x$$	
	Resulting Value Unknown	**Scale Factor (Times as Many) Unknown**	**Original Value Unknown**	
Multiplicative Comparison	Amelia's dog is 5 times older than Wanda's 3-year-old dog. How old is Amelia's dog? $$5 \times 3 = x$$ $$x \div 5 = 3$$	Sydney has \$15 to spend on dog treats. Her best friend has \$5. Sydney has how many times more dollars than her friend has? $$x \times 5 = 15$$ $$5 = 15 \div x$$	Devonte has 15 dog toys on the floor in his living room. That is 3 times the number of toys in the dog's toy basket. How many toys are in the toy basket? $$3 \times x = 15$$ $$15 \div 3 = x$$	

SYMMETRICAL (MATCHING) FACTORS

	Product Unknown	One Dimension Unknown	Both Dimensions Unknown
Area/Array	Mrs. Bradley bought a rubber mat to cover the floor under the balance beam. One side of the mat measured 5 feet and the other side measured 8 feet. How many square feet does the mat measure? $$5 \times 8 = x$$ $$x \div 8 = 5$$	The 40 members of the student council lined up on the stage in the gym to take yearbook pictures. The first row started with 8 students and the rest of the rows did the same. How many rows were there? $$8 \times x = 40$$ $$x = 40 \div 8$$	Mr. Donato is arranging student work on the wall for the art show. He started with 40 square entries and arranged them into a rectangular arrangement. How many entries long and wide could the arrangement be? $$x \times y = 40$$ $$40 \div x = y$$
	Sample Space (Total Outcomes) Unknown	**One Factor Unknown**	**Both Factors Unknown**
Combinations** (Fundamental Counting Principle)	Karen makes sandwiches at the diner. She offers 3 kinds of bread and 7 different lunch meats. How many unique sandwiches can she make? $$3 \times 7 = x$$ $$3 = x \div 7$$	Evelyn works at the ice cream counter. She says that she can make 21 unique and different ice cream sundaes using just ice cream flavors and toppings. If she has 3 flavors of ice cream, how many kinds of toppings does Evelyn offer? $$3 \times x = 21$$ $$21 \div 3 = x$$	Audrey can make 21 different fruit sodas using the machine at the diner. How many different flavorings and sodas could there be? $$x \times y = 21$$ $$x = 21 \div y$$

*Equal Groups problems, in many cases, are special cases of a category that includes all ratio and rate problem situations. Distinguishing between the two categories is often a matter of interpretation. The Ratio and Rates category, however, becomes a critically important piece of the middle school curriculum and beyond, so the category is referenced here. It will be developed more extensively in the grades 6–8 volume of this series.

**Combinations are a category addressed in middle school mathematics standards. They are introduced briefly in chapter 8 for illustration purposes only and will be developed more extensively in the grades 6–8 volume of this series.

References

Anghileri, J. (1989). An investigation of young children's understanding of multiplication. *Educational Studies in Mathematics, 20*, 367–385.

Bell, A., Fischbein, E., & Greer, B. (1984). Choice of operation in verbal arithmetic problems: The effects of number size, problem structure and context. *Educational Studies in Mathematics, 15*(2), 129–147.

Bell, A., Greer, B., Grimison, L., & Mangan, C. (1989). Children's performance on multiplicative word problems: Elements of a descriptive theory. *Journal for Research in Mathematics Education, 20*(5), 434–449.

Boaler, J. (2015). Fluency without fear: Research evidence on the best ways to learn math facts. Retrieved from youcubed.org.

Boucher, D. (2014, September 16). Are 6 x 5 and 5 x 6 the same? *Math Coaches Corner*. Retrieved from http://www.mathcoachscorner.com/2014/09/are-6-x-5-and-5-x-6-the-same/.

Bushart, B. (n.d.). Numberless word problems. *Teaching to the beat of a different drummer*. Retrieved from https://bstockus.wordpress.com/numberless-word-problems/.

Carpenter, T. P. (1985). Learning to add and subtract: An exercise in problem solving. In *Teaching and learning mathematical problem solving: Multiple research perspectives* (pp. 17–40). Hillsdale, NJ: Lawrence Erlbaum Associates.

Carpenter, T. P., Ansell, E., Franke, M. L., Fennema, E., & Weisbeck, L. (1993). Models of problem solving: A study of kindergarten children's problem-solving processes. *Journal for Research in Mathematics Education, 24*, 428–441.

Carpenter, T. P., Fennema, E., & Franke, M. L. (1996). Cognitively guided instruction: A knowledge base for reform in primary mathematics instruction. *The Elementary School Journal, 97*(1), 3–20.

Carpenter, T. P., Fennema, E., Franke, M. L., Levi, L., & Empson, S. B. (2014). *Children's mathematics: Cognitively guided instruction* (2nd ed.). Portsmouth, NH: Heinemann.

Carpenter, T. P., Hiebert, J., & Moser, J. M. (1981). Problem structure and first-grade children's initial solution processes for simple addition and subtraction problems. *Journal for Research in Mathematics Education, 12*, 27–39.

Confrey, J., & Smith, E. (1995). Splitting, covariation, and their role in the development of exponential functions. *Journal for Research in Mathematics Education, 26*, 66–86.

De Corte, E., & Verschaffel, L. (1987). The effect of semantic structure on first graders' strategies for solving addition and subtraction word problems. *Journal for Research in Mathematics Education, 18*, 363–381.

de Koning, B. B., Boonen, A. J. H., & van der Schoot, M. (2017). The consistency effect in word problem solving is effectively reduced through verbal instruction. *Contemporary Educational Psychology, 49*, 121–129.

Devlin, K. (2008, June). It ain't no repeated addition. Mathematical Association of America. Retrieved from http://www.maa.org/external_archive/devlin/devlin_06_08.html.

English, L. D. (1998). Children's problem posing within formal and informal contexts. *Journal for Research in Mathematics Education, 29*, 83–106.

Fischbein, E., Deri, M., Nello, M. S., & Marino, M. S. (1985). The role of implicit models in solving verbal problems in multiplication and division. *Journal for Research in Mathematics Education, 16*, 3–17.

Fosnot, C. T., & Dolk, M. (2001). *Young mathematicians at work: Constructing multiplication and division.* Portsmouth, NH: Heinemann.

Franke, M. L. (2018, April). *How and why attention to student thinking supports teacher and student learning: The case of Cognitively Guided Instruction (CGI).* Presented at the 2018 NCSM Annual Conference, Walter E. Washington Convention Center. Retrieved from https://www.mathedleadership.org/events/conferences/DC2/index.html.

Garfunkel, S., & Montgomery, M. (Eds). (2019). *GAIMME: Guidelines for assessment and instruction in mathematical modeling education* (2nd ed.). Philadelphia, PA: COMAP and SIAM. Retrieved from https://siam.org/publications/reports/detail/guidelines-for-assessment-and-instruction-in-mathematical-modeling-education.

Gravemeijer, K. (1999). How emergent models may foster the constitution of formal mathematics. *Mathematical Thinking and Learning, 1*, 155–177.

Gray, K. (2015, March 29). Commutativity in fraction multiplication. Retrieved from https://kgmathminds.com/2015/03/29/commutativity-in-fraction-multiplication/.

Gutstein, E., & Romberg, T. A. (1995). Teaching children to add and subtract. *The Journal of Mathematical Behavior, 14*, 283–324.

Heller, J. I., & Greeno, J. G. (1979). Information processing analyses of mathematical problem solving. In R. Lesh, M. Mierkiewicz, & M. Kantowski (Eds.), *Applied mathematical problem solving* (pp. 181–206). Columbus, OH: The Ohio State University. Retrieved from ERIC database (ED 180 816).

Hutchins, P. (1986). *The doorbell rang.* New York: Greenwillow Books.

Jenkins, S. (2011). *Actual size.* Boston, MA: HMH Books for Young Readers.

Karp, K. S., Bush, S. B., & Dougherty, B. J. (2014). 13 rules that expire. *Teaching Children Mathematics, 21*, 18–25.

Kelemanik, G., Lucenta, A., & Creighton, S. J. (2016). *Routines for reasoning: Fostering the mathematical practices in all students.* Portsmouth, NH: Heinemann.

Kieren, T. E. (1976). On the mathematical, cognitive and instructional foundations of rational numbers. In R. A. Lesh & D. A. Bradhart (Eds.), *Number and measurement: Papers from a research workshop* (pp. 108–151). Retrieved from https://files.eric.ed.gov/fulltext/ED120027.pdf.

Kouba, V. L., & Franklin, K. (1993). Multiplication and division: Sense making and meaning. In R. J. Jensen (Ed.), *Research Ideas for the Classroom: Early Childhood Mathematics* (pp. 103–126). Reston, VA: National Council of Teachers of Mathematics.

Lamon, S. J. (2012). *Teaching fractions and ratios for understanding: Essential content knowledge and instructional strategies for teachers.* Mahwah, NJ: Routledge.

Leinwand, S., Brahier, D. J., Huinker, D., Berry, R. Q., Dillon, F. L., Larson, M. R.,… Smith, M. S. (Eds.). (2014). *Principles to actions: Ensuring mathematical success for all.* Reston, VA: National Council of Teachers of Mathematics.

Lesh, R. A., Post, T., & Behr, M. (1987). Representations and translations among representations in mathematics learning and problem solving. In C. Janvier (Ed.), *Problems of representations in the teaching and learning of mathematics* (pp. 33–40). Hillsdale, NJ: Lawrence Erlbaum Associates. Retrieved from http://www.cehd.umn.edu/ci/rationalnumberproject/87_5.html.

McCallum, W., Daro, P., & Zimba, J. (n.d.). Progressions documents for the Common Core math standards. *The University of Arizona Institute for Mathematics and Education.* Retrieved from http://ime.math.arizona.edu/progressions/.

Mulligan, J. T., & Mitchelmore, M. C. (1997). Young children's intuitive models of multiplication and Division. *Journal for Research in Mathematics Education, 28,* 309–330.

Murphy, S. J. (1997). *Divide and ride.* New York: Harper Collins.

Murphy, S. J. (2003). *The sundae scoop.* New York: Harper Collins.

National Council of Teachers of Mathematics. (2000). *Principles and standards for school mathematics.* Reston, VA: Author.

National Governors Association Center for Best Practices and Council of Chief State School Officers. (2010). *Common Core State Standards for Mathematics.* Washington, DC: Author.

Petitto, A. L., & Ginsburg, H. P. (1982). Mental arithmetic in Africa and America: Strategies, principles, and explanations. *International Journal of Psychology, 17*(1–4), 81–102.

Philipp, R. A., & Hawthorne, C. (2015). Unpacking referent units in fraction operations. *Teaching Children Mathematics, 22*(4), 240–247. Retrieved from https://doi.org/10.5951/teacchilmath.22.4.0240.

Piaget, J., & Inhelder, B. (1973). *The psychology of the child.* New York: Basic Books.

Pólya, G. (1945). *How to solve it: A new aspect of mathematical method.* Princeton, NJ: Princeton University Press.

Riley, M. S., Greeno, J. G., & Heller, J. I. (1984). Development of children's ability in arithmetic. In *Development of Children's Problem-Solving Ability in Arithmetic. No. LRDC-1984/37.* (pp. 153–196). Pittsburgh University, PA: Learning Research and Development Center, National Institute of Education.

Rosenthal, A. K. (2011). *This plus that: Life's little equations.* New York: Harper Collins.

Rudnitsky, A., Etheredge, S., Freeman, S. J. M., & Gilbert, T. (1995). Learning to solve addition and subtraction word problems through a structure-plus-writing approach. *Journal for Research in Mathematics Education, 26,* 467–486.

SanGiovanni, J. J., & Milou, E. (2018). *Daily routines to jump-start math class, middle school: Engage students, improve number sense, and practice reasoning.* Thousand Oaks, CA: Corwin.

Sayre, A. P., & Sayre, J. (2003). *One is a snail, ten is a crab.* London: Walker.

Schliemann, A. D., Araujo, C., Cassundé, M. A., Macedo, S., & Nicéas, L. (1998). Use of multiplicative commutativity by school children and street sellers. *Journal for Research in Mathematics Education, 29,* 422–435.

Scieszka, J., & Smith, L. (1995). *Math curse.* New York: Viking.

Sowder, L. (2002). Story problems & students' strategies. In D. Chambers (Ed.), *Putting research into practice in the elementary grades* (pp. 21–23). Reston, VA: National Council of Teachers of Mathematics.

Tang, G. (n.d.). Word problems. Retrieved from https://gregtangmath.com/wordproblems.

Thompson, P. W. (2010). Quantitative reasoning and mathematical modeling. In L. L. Hatfield, S. Chamberlain & S. Belbase (Eds.), *New perspectives and directions for collaborative research in mathematics education* (Vol. 1, pp. 33–57). Laramie, WY: University of Wyoming.

Usiskin, Z. (2012, April). *Unpacking mathematical understanding in the Common Core State Standards.* Presented at the National Council of Supervisors of Mathematics (NCSM), Philadelphia, PA. Retrieved from https://www.mathedleadership.org/events/conferences/PA/allsessions.html.

Watanabe, T. (2003). Teaching multiplication: An analysis of elementary school mathematics teachers' manuals from Japan and the United States. *The Elementary School Journal, 104,* 111–125.

Index

Figures and notes are indicated by f or n following the page number.

Mathematics

Supporting TEACHERS | Empowering STUDENTS

**BETH MCCORD KOBETT,
RUTH HARBIN MILES,
LOIS A. WILLIAMS**

Plan math lessons that enhance the purpose, rigor, and coherence of state standards and address the unique learning needs of your individual students.
Grades K–2, 3–5, and 6–8

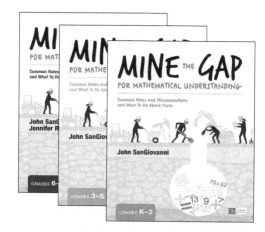

**JOHN SANGIOVANNI,
JENNIFER ROSE NOVAK**

Discover the "why" behind students' math mistakes with this bank of downloadable, standards-aligned math tasks, common misunderstandings, and next instructional steps.
Grades K–2, 3–5, and 6–8

**FRANCIS (SKIP) FENNELL,
BETH MCCORD KOBETT,
JONATHAN A. WRAY**

Mathematics education experts Fennell, Kobett, and Wray offer five of the most doable, impactful, and proven formative assessment techniques you can implement every day. Includes companion website.
Grades K–8

SARAH B. BUSH, KRISTIN L. COOK

Build cohesive and sustainable STEAM infrastructures—grounded in grade-level standards and purposeful assessment—to deepen the mathematics and science learning of each and every student.
Grades K–5

To order your copies, visit **corwin.com**

ALL students should have the opportunity to be successful in math!

Trusted experts in math education offer clear and practical guidance to help students move from surface to deep mathematical understanding, from procedural to conceptual learning, and from rote memorization to true comprehension.

Through books, videos, consulting, and online tools, we offer a truly blended learning experience that helps you demystify math for students.

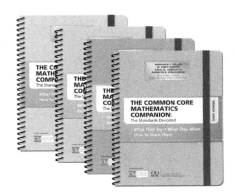

A SAGE Publishing Company

CORWIN HAS ONE MISSION: to enhance education through intentional professional learning.

We build long-term relationships with our authors, educators, clients, and associations who partner with us to develop and continuously improve the best evidence-based practices that establish and support lifelong learning.

CPSIA information can be obtained
at www.ICGtesting.com
Printed in the USA
JSHW051909110622
26964JS00003B/24